PIERS PLOWMAN: THE A VERSION

PIERS PLOWMAN

The A Version

Edited by Míceál F. Vaughan

The Johns Hopkins University Press
Baltimore

The Johns Hopkins University Press
2715 North Charles Street
Baltimore, Maryland 21218-4363
www.press.jhu.edu

Library of Congress Cataloging-in-Publication Data

Langland, William, 1330?–1400?
  [Piers Plowman]
  Piers Plowman : the A version / edited by Míċeál F. Vaughan.
     p. cm.
  Includes bibliographical references.
  "One text of the Piers Plowman poems is found in the Bodleian Library's Rawlinson Poetry MS 137. This manuscript presents an important witness to the A version, and it is on that text that the present edition is based"—Text.
  ISBN-13: 978-1-4214-0139-3 (hardcover : alk. paper)
  ISBN-13: 978-1-4214-0140-9 (pbk. : alk. paper)
  ISBN-10: 1-4214-0139-8 (hardcover : alk. paper)
  ISBN-10: 1-4214-0140-1 (pbk. : alk. paper)
  1. Christian pilgrims and pilgrimages—Poetry. 2. Christian poetry, English (Middle) I. Vaughan, Míċeál F. II. Bodleian Library. Manuscript. Rawlinson Poetry 137. III. Title.
  PR2013.V38 2011
  821'.1—dc22

                                                                    2010050255

A catalog record for this book is available from the British Library.

Special discounts are available for bulk purchases of this book. For more information, please contact Special Sales at 410-516-6936 or specialsales@press.jhu.edu.

The Johns Hopkins University Press uses environmentally friendly book materials, including recycled text paper that is composed of at least 30 percent post-consumer waste, whenever possible.

Contents

Preface

My deepest scholarly and personal debts are to my late colleague David C. Fowler (to whom I dedicate this edition) and to my former doctoral student Gerald Barnett, who have each provided me with stimulating commentary and conversation about editing *Piers Plowman* for decades. Without their encouragement and critical engagement, I would never have undertaken the editing of this (or any) version of the poem. When he learned of the project, Professor Andrew Galloway (Cornell University) encouraged me to shift my base manuscript from that used by Knott-Fowler (and Kane and Schmidt), and I was happy to acknowledge the insight of his suggestion, and to adopt it, even when this caused some delay in my completing the edition.

My interest in *Piers Plowman* (the B version, needless to say) was fostered by another Cornell scholar-teacher, the late Robert Kaske, whose wit and insight into the poem set a high standard for me and all his graduate disciples, and indeed for all readers of *Piers*. I owe Hoyt Duggan, and all our colleagues in the *Piers Plowman* Electronic Archive, an immense debt for their critical attention to transparent editorial principles *and* their respect for the minutiae of the extant texts of *Piers*. Their commitment to sustaining lively debate about what some have called an uneditable poem is a witness to the importance of this fourteenth-century work and a promise of its continuing influence on our understanding of the later Middle Ages in England.

I am particularly grateful to my University of Washington colleague Terry Brooks for his many hours assisting me with producing a well-structured and marked-up XML text from which the many presentations of this text and its notes have been derived. I also owe much to students in my Spring 2008 seminar and to participants at an Information School session organized by Professor Brooks in May 2008: they helped me sharpen my thinking about the practical requirements for a modern printed, and electronic, edition of a medieval poem.

An anonymous reader for the Johns Hopkins University Press provided careful and helpfully detailed comments on a wide range of matters involving both the substance and the form of this edition. Without all of them, and the active encouragement of Associate Editor Michael Lonegro and Editor-in-Chief Trevor Lipscombe, this edition would not be in your hands in anything approximating the form it now takes. Other editorial staff at Johns Hopkins, in particular Humanities Editor Matthew McAdam, as well as Brian MacDonald, took exceptional care in the final production of this book.

I especially acknowledge the permission granted me by the Bodleian Library, University of Oxford, for use of the text of its MS. Rawl. poet. 137 as the basis for this edition. My thanks go to the Bodleian Library's keeper of special collections and associate director, Mr. Richard Ovenden, and to Dr. Bruce Barker-Benfield, senior assistant librarian,

Finally, although she has always been baffled by my abiding interest in *Piers Plowman*, my wife, Sheila Dietrich, has provided me with immeasurable encouragement and support over the protracted years of my evolving engagement with what long ago began on a May morning in the Malvern Hills.

The Poems Called *Piers Plowman*

The Middle English poems collectively titled *Piers Plowman* (or *Piers the Plowman*) come down to modern readers in distinct versions, dating from the second half of the fourteenth century. Since the mid-nineteenth century, when *Piers* was being seriously studied for the first time, most who have studied the poem have agreed with its great early editor, W. W. Skeat, that the surviving manuscripts attest to the existence of three distinct authorial versions, which he titled A, B, and C, indicating his view of the poem's chronological development by that alphabetic order (Kane, "The Text"). Each of these versions of *Piers* is witnessed by a dozen or more manuscripts (seventeen for A, thirteen for B, eighteen for C). In addition, there are fragments of A and C, and hybrid or composite versions.

Until the work of Skeat and his contemporaries and successors, no one had advanced the view, at least in print, that there were indeed distinct poems, each claiming to be *Piers Plowman*. But the clarity of these groupings, and their status as representing discrete sequential stages in the development of a single work, may be more apparent than real, and a complete inventory of manuscript and early printed witnesses to *a* poem *Piers Plowman* reveals (unsurprisingly for a vernacular text transmitted over the course of more than a century by hand copying in separate locales in the British Isles) not an altogether controlled process of authorial revision and publication but rather a less centralized transmission of a popular and influential text, one that many writers (and no doubt readers) made their own in both smaller and larger ways.

Among the surviving manuscripts there are, of course, the inevitable variations in spelling and word choice that attend hand copying of any but the most canonical and official texts in the period before printing. Because copying by hand is seldom if ever exact, each of these manuscripts offers its readers a literally unique *Piers Plowman*. Words, phrases, and whole lines are misread, miscopied, or left out; passages are actively revised; and substantive corrections, continuations, and additions alter the effect and emphases of the surviving witnesses to all versions of the poem. In the more open-text culture of premodern textual production, these may count as unsurprising variations. The addition of a twelfth *passus* (pl. *passūs*; Latin for "step") in three manuscripts of the A version may indicate that the original

author, or some early reviser, considered the conclusion of A weak or un-
finished or unsatisfactory and chose to continue the dream (which in A's
Passus 11 is not explicitly ended). And a similar response to A can be inferred from the lengthy B continuation that nearly triples the size of the
A version. In the one manuscript (Bodleian Library, University of Oxford,
MS. Rawl. poet. 137) that contains "all"—or, more properly, the most we
have—of the additional Passus 12 of A, the final lines (internally attributed to
one Johan But) refer apparently to the death of the author ("Wille") of what
"here is wryten, and other werkes bothe, / Of Peres the plowman . . ." (12.
98–99).

In addition to complete (or fragmentary) manuscripts of the various
versions, there are composite or conjoint manuscripts, which bring together
parts of the texts of two or three of the versions: for example, seven A
manuscripts are "completed" by lengthy passages from the C version; another conjoins a B beginning [Prologue to 5.127] with an A conclusion
[5.106–11]; three manuscripts precede a text of B Passus 3–20 with three
passūs of C along with an expanded version of about a hundred lines of A;
and yet one other conflates in a complex pastiche lines and passages from A,
B, and C (Kane, "The Text"). If one includes surviving fragments, we have in
total about fifty-six surviving manuscript witnesses to variously shaped, dis-
tinctively constituted poems we call Piers Plowman. While the three versions
of Piers are usually dated from about 1370–85, their manuscripts can be
dated, with more or less precision in individual cases, from the last two
decades of the fourteenth century to about the middle of the sixteenth.
Despite the obvious variety among the manuscripts and versions of the
poem, even well-informed modern scholars and critics continue to refer to
all of these variant texts by the single title Piers Plowman. This tendency
poses difficulties in critical discussion of Piers: disagreements in interpretation are bound to be aggravated when debates involve not merely differing
critical readings of the text but refer to texts that literally differ from each
other and, more importantly, differ quite substantively.

As if the three versions in multiple manuscript configurations were not
enough to challenge critical interpretation, to Skeat's three versions there
has recently been added a fourth claimant (called Z), evidenced in a single
manuscript (MS. Bodley 851), which has been accepted by some specialists
as another early "authorial" version of Piers. Other Piers scholars, however,
remain skeptical about Z's autonomous versional status and continue to
consider it a distinctive scribal (and not authorial) variant of the first two
dreams in A, whose scribe (like others of A MSS) follows his unique version
with a C "conclusion." Those who accept Z as a distinct version place it
before A in the evolution of the poem's text; those who reject its authorial

status would relegate it to an interesting but tangential (and post-C) twig on the poem's genealogical tree.

There are also two manuscripts of the B version (designated R and F) that contain differences that are significant enough to be considered a distinct branch in the B tradition, and some scholars hold that the changes in these manuscripts warrant our categorizing them as an identifiable intermediate stage in the substantial revision from B to C. Whether they warrant separate status as a distinct *version* of the poem, however, has not been seriously proposed. The already-mentioned existence of three manuscripts of the A version with an additional concluding passus may likewise warrant our referring to it as an "A-plus" version. Together, all these unique manuscripts cumulatively indicate that *Piers Plowman* is a title readers and critics now routinely accord to a constellation of Middle English poems constituted by complexly interrelated texts that do not reveal in any clearly obvious fashion a lineal evolution or development of a single work. Of course, one *could* argue that the poem is a single evolving work of a poet called William Langland: indeed, that has been the consensus among most critics and scholars of *Piers Plowman* for more than five decades.

While no one has expressed any substantial reservations about the C version's being a later revision of B, the same cannot be unproblematically asserted about the temporal relations of A and B. Important voices (Hudson, Mann, Bowers) have questioned the chronological sequence of A and B and have argued that A is not indeed a briefer, earlier version extended and considerably revised in B but rather is a stripped down version of B's more elaborate and "academic" account. Other scholars (e.g., Kane and Lawler) have rejected this hypothesis, and the view that B follows A remains the general consensus, even if most critics and scholars of the poems have relegated the matter to the margins of their attention.

Such questions have exercised, and will properly continue to exercise, the skills of textual scholars and literary and cultural critics. But the questions also have an identifiable effect on basic matters that should engage even the beginning reader. For example, *if* we hold (as most do) that the three (or four) versions of *Piers Plowman* constitute stages in the evolving form of a single work of literary art, then we must also decide whether the stages in that evolution were determined by a single "author" or were produced by revisions carried out by others—and if by a single author, then whether from a continuing sense of singular purpose until reaching a state of intended completion, or arising from one or more realizations or shifts in position requiring revision and reclamation of arguments from earlier attempts. From a modern perspective, the "text" of a poem requires a single "author" for its production—or at least some individual or corporate "authority" responsible for its "publication." Modern book publishers and moviemakers involve numerous individuals in the production of their texts. Such institutions did not exist in the Middle Ages, and such institutions involved in book production that did exist (e.g., monasteries, or commercial houses in London or near European universities) were less controlling, particularly as access to the skills and materials for producing manuscript texts moved outside the confines of the monastic and clerical communities, which had held a virtual monopoly in earlier times.

Faced with the more dynamic, open-textual world of later medieval manuscripts—handwritten products of individual scribes, not always overseen by any identifiable (much less originary) controlling "authority"—we may well need to reexamine our modern, post-Gutenbergian (or xerographic) concepts about texts and authors. Indeed, in the contemporary cyber world of Internet "publishing," we may even find ourselves more familiar with the kind of fragmented universe that defined medieval textual production, and we may search in vain for any trustworthy "authority" or even stable texts that come onto our screens from the digital streams in cyberspace. Do we in fact need to determine the *exact* status of these texts we read and reproduce any more than a medieval scribe or reader? If the text satisfies or entertains us, does it finally matter who produced it, or whether it corresponds to an author's original? How can you *know*, without laborious comparison of archived data, that the text you looked at on an Internet page today is the same as the one you looked at yesterday? While we struggle with establishing the appropriate conventions for citing texts in cyberspace, we remain (most of us, anyway) unable to verify that the cited text is in fact the one that existed at that URL at the specified time. Because we are unable to reproduce that moment in cyberspace, we are largely asked to trust the writer or reporter of the text—or, finally, to decide for ourselves whether the text before us is plausible, or true.

Without the centralized industry of printing-press publishing and the kinds of exact duplication possible in modern photo-offset and xerographic printing, we are faced with encouragement to redefine—or abandon—terms such as *text, poem, author, work, edition,* and *version.* Indeed, we have already begun to respond to those pressures and entertain as a probability that such textual and literary phenomena may have been substantially different in the less author-centered world of premodern texts. But theorizing the "text" in "cyberspace" will continue to run well behind its practical production and its repeated versioning. Even the idea that "author" is a single, personal noun (much less a "person") is increasingly under pressure. We have only to look at the entries in Wikipedia, or at the proliferation of jointly authored texts marked up in cyberspace with special colors and codes that identify (under, e.g., Microsoft Word's "Track Changes") distinct authors and separable temporal interventions in the production of the finished, clean, final text. The texts and versions of *Piers Plowman* in their manuscripts raise many of those same questions from a time when "digital text" would have referred to the letters being inscribed on parchment and paper by quills or pens held in the fingers (*digits*) of amateur and professional scribes of varying competence as readers and copiers of their exemplars.

Scholars and advanced students of *Piers Plowman* have in the Athlone editions of *Piers* what will remain for the next generation at least *the* edition of the A, B, and C versions. In the edition by Rigg and Brewer, the Z version has its text established and its claims for versional status presented. With Schmidt's parallel, four-text edition, we can usefully advance comparative analysis of the versions in texts that supersede those presented in Skeat's earlier and widely used parallel, three-text edition (2 vols., Oxford 1886), and now that the second volume containing Schmidt's notes has appeared, we are in a position to move to a new stage in comparative study of the work(s) these texts enunciate. The beginning, or early, student of *Piers* also has access to readable and useful translations of all three versions into modern English (e.g., Covella for A; Goodridge and Donaldson for B; Economou for C).

Yet between these translations and the comprehensive critical editions in Kane's Athlone Press series and Schmidt's parallel-text edition, the student of *Piers* has little to choose: all are aiming at establishing texts that come as close as possible to what they conceive as the originals of the various works of a single author, William Langland. The *Piers Plowman* Electronic Archive (PPEA) and its SEENET (Society for Early English and Norse Electronic Texts) editions will continue this process, by producing critically edited individual documentary editions of all the manuscripts of *Piers Plowman*. The slow process of marking up all these texts and obtaining digital facsimiles of their source manuscripts will pay considerable dividends for scholars in the future, and a team of PPEA editors is at present on the verge of publishing a new critical edition of the B version archetype. This will offer a textual alternative to both the Athlone edition of Kane and Donaldson's B version and that produced by Schmidt. In the future, similar editions of the A and C archetypes are planned.

Derek Pearsall's (recently revised) edition of the C version and Schmidt's *Critical Edition* of B offer excellently edited and accessible texts for those versions of *Piers*; both provide ample introductory materials, notes, and glossaries that will permit the relative beginner to become familiar with *Piers* in Middle English. But the A version has remained the neglected version in students' editions. Knott and Fowler's 1952 edition of A, now long out of print, offered the only previous edition of the A version intended for beginning students, and this present edition is in many important respects a child of that edition and seeks to introduce the world of *Piers Plowman* to a new generation of undergraduate students and general readers of late Middle English literature and history. The A version is interesting in its own right and not only as a stage in the complex and extended history of *Piers Plowman*. At a practical level, too, this more compact text of A may fit more easily into a course syllabus introducing Middle English literature.

The Date(s) of *Piers Plowman*

Establishing the dates for medieval texts is seldom straightforward. The tradition of formally dating the publication of a book is largely alien to the world of handwritten (and many early printed) copies. Even if we could certainly determine the date of the earliest surviving manuscript copy, by doing so we would have shown only the latest date at which that text of the poem could have been composed. On the other side of the matter, if we can identify in the text a reference (or allusion) to an event whose date we can determine, what we have settled is the earliest date at which this reference could have been made, the date *after* which this text (or at least the passage containing the reference) was created. Between these two dates often lies a considerable extent of time, within which we can reasonably expect the original text was composed.

Before 1500, it was unusual for a book to be formally marked with the date at which it was "published," much less when it was originally written. Some scribes and printers did note the date of their productions, but more often than not we are left only with vaguer, indirect indications of the date of textual production and must negotiate the thickets of scholarly disputation over historical allusions and the comparative dating of an individual scribe's handwriting. Although dating medieval texts on the basis of allusive, or even explicit, references within them is not exact, scholarly consensus may agree on what the earliest date of the poem's creation must be; similar agreement about its text's latest date, however, is altogether less likely. References to historical events or previous texts can indicate only that the text must have been composed *after* the historical events mentioned in it; they cannot, in most cases, indicate exactly how long after—or when that reference might have been inserted into an earlier original. To date a work, then, we need to look outside the text itself, to evidence of dates at which it was copied, published, or read and referred to by others. Here, the study of paleography (scribal handwriting) and of watermarks (for paper) can offer some assistance, but these can seldom provide precise dates, only relative ones.

On the basis of historical references in its text, the A version of *Piers Plowman* can probably be dated about 1370, give or take a couple of years. The reference to the Saturday evening southwest wind (5.14) apparently refers to a particularly destructive storm that occurred on 15 January 1362. Bennett ("Date of the B-Text") argued that the reference to "Rome-renneres" (4.109) would be appropriate only while the pope at this time (in this case Urban V) was actually residing in Rome, and because Avignon was the regular residence of the popes for most of the fourteenth century, this usage could therefore be accurate only between October 1367 and September 1370. Alternatively, one might argue that, given Rome's identity as the traditional "home" of ecclesiastical bureaucracy, the reference may not strictly require the actual current residence of a pope in Rome.

We may confidently take the reference to the 1362 storm as marking that as the earliest date at which the A version (or, more specifically, this beginning to its second dream) could have been written, what editors refer to as the *terminus a quo* or *post quem*, the "end point from which" or "after which" the text originated. Although Fowler earlier (Knott-Fowler) was open to dating the A version later in the 1360s, in his most recent work he has moved the poem's origin back to the earlier date, declaring unambiguously (in his introduction to Covella's translation and in *"Piers the Plowman* as History") that the A version's date is 1362. Kane ("The Text"), on the other hand, is convinced by Bennett's argument and would place the origin of the textual tradition of the A version in the period 1368–74.

If, with most critics, we held with the sequence (Z)ABC for the versions of *Piers*, and likewise assumed the versions are by a single author, we might logically conclude that the latest date for A would necessarily provide us with the earliest date for the B version, which revises and expands A. The reference to an outbreak of plague and a consequent papal "pardoun" (in B 13.246–49) may point to events of 1375–76, and it is from this, for example, that Kane ("The Text") concludes 1374 as the *terminus ad quem* (i.e., the "date before which") for A. But as we noted, serious questions have been raised about the sequential order of the A and B versions; and continuing uncertainties about the common authorship of the two versions could further impact the logic of such an argument for the latest date of A. The ending of *Piers* we print here, and which we may call the A-plus version (with the additional Passus 12), must of course be later than this, because its concluding lines refer to "Richard, kyng of this rewme" (12.110) and can refer only to Richard II, who ascended to the throne on the death of his grandfather Edward III, in 1377, and reigned until he was deposed by his cousin Henry of Lancaster (Shakespeare's Bolingbroke, later King Henry IV) in late 1399. Although these lines certainly (and perhaps even more of Passus 12) may be a substantially later addition to the A version that concludes in other manuscripts at the end of Passus 11, we are not bound to date the entire text to the reign of Richard II.

For the purposes of this edition, we assume as little as we can about authorship and versions, focusing, to the extent allowed, on this text of the A version alone and the textual and literary issues raised by it. Of course, because the text in surviving A manuscripts (many of which can be confidently dated *later* than those containing copies of B and C) may have been contaminated by their scribe's awareness of "other" versions of the poem, it will not always be possible to maintain the fiction of the A version's distinct autonomy. A striking instance of this occurs in the second half of the poem's opening line.

The Authorship Question

We have already touched on the contested issue of the author(s) of *Piers Plowman*. It is possible, of course, to read a text without needing to attach it to a named and identifiable author; however, even if we do not require the "idea" of a single author (or even of any author) to make sense of a text, in the case of a poem that exists in multiple versions, hypotheses about the author(s) will have substantial influence on how we relate the versions to one another, especially when we may wish to use one to interpret (or even establish the text of) another. If we are confident about the existence of a single author, engaged in ongoing revision of his single "work," then we may more easily invoke some changes in a later text as an effort to clarify something that was less clear in the earlier one. Or we may hypothesize that certain textual changes were the result of the author's change of mind or circumstance. Distinguishing authorial texts of *Piers* from scribal alterations is the foundational principle supporting Kane's Athlone editions, and while specialists may disagree with individual judgments regarding those readings, the distinction is a crucial, and critical, one for scholarship in texts like *Piers Plowman*. Manuscripts are, most literally, the result of manual labor and so will inevitably differ from each other, sometimes in quite substantial ways. By understanding the craft and common errors that accompany the laborious copying of medieval manuscripts, we can at least begin to distinguish authorial revision from scribal alteration of the text before us.[*]

If, however, we are less than completely certain that the versions are the work of a single author who exerts continuing supervision over the poem's evolving text, then more radical disagreements between those texts and versions can be accepted without any need for us to find a unified (psycho)-logical explanation that persuasively harmonizes the many variants. Different authors can have substantially different, even incompatible, views on any number of topics. When such differences appear in the opinions of a single author, we may feel that he or she is being inconsistent or has under-

---

[*]The variants, and the editors' decisions about which are scribal and which are authorial, can be found in the editions by Knott-Fowler, Kane, and Schmidt, Kane's being the most complete and detailed. The forthcoming editions by the *Piers Plowman* Electronic Archive (PPEA) promise to provide (when complete) the fullest detail.

gone some conversion in attitude, so we set about to explain or justify the changes. If we accept multiple authorship, however, or simply admit the vagaries in the transmission of a text unsupervised (by its single author) in an open-text culture, then these changes may require fewer inferences and can be recorded as distinctive features of (semi-)independent witnesses to the text's reception and transmission by later readers and scribes.

The preponderance of scholarly opinion at the beginning of the twenty-first century holds that *Piers Plowman*, in its three versions, is the work of a single man, William Langland. This consensus dominated scholarly opinion in the second half of the twentieth century, after earlier heated debates over single- versus multiple-authorship. These debates brought to a more or less settled state centuries of uncertainty about the authorship of *Piers Plowman*, including questions about which *name* to give the author: Robert Langland, William Langland (or Langley), John Malverne, Willelmus W, and others. But in the last decades of the twentieth century doubts were again surfacing in certain quarters about the hypothesis of single authorship, what has been called "the Langland myth" (Benson). The "evidence" for a single author with the name William Langland is relatively small, but its masterful discussion by George Kane (*Evidence*) established it as the ordinary view among specialists who study and teach *Piers Plowman*. It might not be entirely cynical to say, however, that the real attraction of this hypothesis (aside from articulating the foundational principle behind the editing decisions of the Athlone editors) is that it has enabled most critics to continue to think and talk about *Piers Plowman* as a single, coherent work: even when it evolves considerably through various stages, they can continue to treat it as a single, if textually complex, work. The single-author hypothesis, then, has underwritten editorial interventions to harmonize the readings across the versions and has allowed critics to speak of all the texts of *Piers Plowman* as if they were a single poem. Putting aside the "authorship problem" as having been settled has allowed readers and scholars to turn their attention to other interesting matters raised by the unitary "poem." If identifying an author proves to be of relatively minor importance with regard to any given manuscript of a work, when readers seek to reconcile multiple texts from different manuscripts, the matter of authorship, or unity of authorship, becomes crucial.

Despite the general consensus, a few voices have continued to argue for multiple authorship, but none espoused the extreme view produced during the authorship debates in the earlier twentieth century, when Manly argued at length for the poem's being the work of at least five separate authors, including one for each of the two parts of A (*Visio* and *Vita*), the B continuation, and the C revision. In the later twentieth century, David Fowler was the best-known proponent of multiple authorship, arguing in *Literary Relations*

that the B continuation was the work of the Oxford scholar John Trevisa (ca.
1342–1402), who extended and revised the existing A version in the 1380s.
While few have accepted his arguments, some have responded to this recent, rather understated, stage of the authorship controversy with a more
skeptical view, one that acknowledges that the evidence, internal or external
to the surviving texts of the poem, is capable of supporting claims on either
side: we cannot, in other words, conclude that there was one author *or* that
there were demonstrably many. In the face of these uncertainties, a considered choice is, preliminarily at least, to accord the various "versions" textual
autonomy from one another and to treat each as a distinct poem whose
sense and meaning do not require that it be placed in any sequence with
others or that it be attributed to the same author (or the same mental state of
an author) as one or more of the other distinct versions. The *texts*, after all, of
these various poems are distinct(ive) enough to warrant attention being paid
to them on their own account and not merely in the context of the intellectual and poetic life of a supposed single fourteenth-century author, whatever
his name. According individual status and literary importance to the various
texts we title *Piers Plowman* acknowledges their places in their own time and
avoids imposing more modern literary conventions and expectations on the
more fluid textual world they arose from and constituted.

One text of the *Piers Plowman* poems is found in the Bodleian Library's
MS. Rawl. poet. 137. This manuscript presents an important witness to the A
version, and it is on that text that the present edition is based. The sole
manuscript witness to what appears to be the "complete" thirteenth passus
addition to A, this Rawlinson MS might well qualify for being titled the
A-*plus* version of *Piers*. This edition based on MS. Rawl. poet. 137 presents a
lightly edited text of *Piers* A in a readable and coherent fashion, which stays
close to its manuscript source except in cases where it appears to be defec-
tive or seems not to make any clear or good sense. On occasion, the notes
will alert the reader to alternative (or additional) readings found in other
manuscripts of the A version—or to B and C. However, the purpose of this
edition is to present the poem in a form that has not been published before,
not to attempt a new critical edition of the A version of *Piers Plowman* that
seeks to recover an authorial or even archetypal original of that poem. Having become familiar with this text of *Piers*, the interested reader will be well
prepared to investigate other instances of the poems, including those that
other editors reconstruct as authorial texts of the various versions of *Piers
Plowman*.

The Structure of *Piers* A

Distinct structuring principles become evident to a reader of what MS. Rawl.
poet. 137 titles *liber qui vocatur Pers Plowman* (the book called Piers Plow-

man). The work is composite in the sense that it comprises distinct parts and layers of narrated action, and it will be useful to identify and discuss these in some detail here. The poem is arranged in thirteen sections of varying length, labeled in the manuscripts as *prologus* and twelve *passūs*. It is not clear what principle (if any) determines the length of the sections, which vary from III lines (the Prologue) to 316 lines (Passus II) of unrhymed alliterative verse. An oral reading or performance of the poem's nearly 2,700 lines would last somewhere between three and four hours.

In addition to the chapter-like passūs, other divisions shape the presentation of the entire poem and might allow the poem to be heard or read in sensible, distinct parts. *Piers* A is made up of events recounted by the narrator in three separate dreams: Prologue through Passus 4; Passus 5 through 8; and Passus 9 through 12. The first two of these constitute a section usually titled in manuscripts and editions as the *Visio*, and the concluding dream is called the *Vita* (Latin for "Life"). The conclusion of Passus 8 in MS. Rawl. poet. 137 offers a fairly representative colophon:

> *Explicit hic Visio Willelmi de Petro . ҩ cetera.*
> *Et hic incipit Vita de Dowel . Dobet . ҩ Dobest secundum wit ҩ resoun.*
>
> (fol. 29r)

The dream vision is a well-established literary form, going back (at least) as far as biblical and classical literary sources. But *Piers* is exceptional in combining a sequence of separate dreams in a single poem involving (ostensibly at least) the same dreamer/protagonist (Burrow, *Langland's Fictions*). Some understanding of a possible rationale for this combination of dreams and for their particular sequence may be gained from examining the key terms used in titling the parts of the work's structure: *passus*, *visio*, and *vita*.

Passus

The root meaning for the term *passus* (pl. *passūs*) is "step," or "pace." As a literary term, it is not widely used outside *Piers* (and the *Piers* tradition), but it is regularly used in the headings and rubrics of virtually all manuscripts of this poem and has been retained as the distinctive way of referring to the "chapters" of *Piers Plowman*. The word suggests that these segments of the poem constitute separately identifiable episodes in the work's progress, steps on a journey that begins as a search for "wondrys to hure" (Pr.4) and (after becoming a search for Charity and Truth) concludes as a journey to find "Do-well."

Visio

In the scribal colophon that closes the second dream (at the end of Passus 8 and quoted above), we are told that here ends ("Explicit hic") the "Visio

Willelmi de Petro" (William's Vision [or Dream] of Piers). What follows is called "Vita de Dowel, Dobet, & Dobest secundum wit & resoun" (the Life of Do-Well, Do-Better, and Do-Best according to wit and reason). It has become commonplace for scholars to use the short forms of these two "titles"— *Visio* and *Vita*—to name these two distinct stages of the poem's action. Although Piers plays a significant role only in the second dream, *Visio* is generally used to refer to the first two dreams as a composite unit (the first dream involving Holy Church, Mede, Conscience, and Reason; and the second Piers, Hunger, and the Confession of the Deadly Sins).

Vita

The *Vita* (Passus 9–12) takes up the search for Dowel, which quickly evolves into one for the triad of Dowel, Dobet, and Dobest. The *Vita* also is presented as a dream (one meaning of *visio*), but like the first dream of the poem, it does not explicitly include reference to (or an appearance by) Piers. The ordinary meaning of Latin *vita* is "life," and it is frequently used as the title for biographical narratives, especially for those of saints (e.g., the *Vita Sanctæ Margaretæ*) or important historical figures (e.g., the *Vita Caroli Magni*). Given the emphasis on various forms of Do-ing in this section of the poem, the concept of "life" implies a life of "action," of practicing (for instance) what one has contemplated in vision. In the moral universe of this poem, and of medieval Christian theology, knowledge and intentions are important; however, it is only when they are enacted in real life that they can become the decisive expression of a moral life and be deserving of the kinds of reward that the Dreamer seeks when he asks Lady Holy Church to tell him "Hou I may save my soule . . ." (1.82).

Dreams

While it is common in criticism for readers to refer to the Dreamer-Narrator, the "I" of *Piers Plowman*, as "Will," that name is not explicitly, or unambiguously, attributed to the narratorial first person of A, as it is in the oft-cited line from the B version (15.152):

"I have lyve in londe," quod I, "my name is Longe Wille."

There is nothing like this in the text of A—apart from the *explicit* to the *Visio* ("visio Willelmi"), which may be a scribal addition—until later in Passus 12, where the name may be associated with the Dreamer-Narrator. At line 53, Scripture there tells the "clerioun . . . hyght *Omnia-probate*":

"Thou shalt wende with wil," quod she, "whiles that him lykyth."

A few lines later, the name is used again, by Fevere-on-the-ferthe-day, in direct address to the Dreamer (12.86–87):

"Nay, Wil," quod that wyghth, "wend thou no ferther,
But lyve as this lyf is ordeyned for the . . ."

Finally, we find in the lines, perhaps added even later by "Johan But" at the conclusion to A 12, the name Wille is connected with the author (12.96–102):

Wille thurgh inwit tho wot wel the sothe—
That this speche was spedelich, and sped him wel faste,
And wroughthe that here is wryten, and other werkes bothe—
Of Peres the plowman and mechel puple also—
And whan this werk was wrought, ere Wille myghte aspie,
Deth delt him a dent, and drof him to the erthe,
And is closed under clour—Crist have his soule!

Because most editors previously have excluded Passus 12 from the authorial text of the A version, however, we may take A's other references to a "character" named Will as suggesting someone other than the speaker addressed in these lines. This is reasonable because all the earlier references are to a *third* person, not to the *first* person, that is, the poem's Dreamer-Narrator.

Than Repentauns rehersed his teme,
And made Wille to wepe water with his eye.

(5.43–44)

Than were marchauntes merie and some wepe for joye,
And gaf Wille for his wrytyng wollene clothes;
For he copiede thus hire clause, hy konne him gret mede.

(8.42–44)

In these instances, it is possible to take "Wille" as something less than a fully personified allegorical character, as in a case like the following:

Than shalt thou come to a court, as clere as the sunne;
The mot is of Mercy, the maner al aboute,
And alle the walles beth of Wit, to holde Wil theroute . . .

(6:71–73)

Compare these instances to those where the Dreamer-Narrator does speak about himself and invariably employs the first person. This is the case in the waking moments that precede and follow the dreams. The Prologue opens (1–4):

In a somyr sesoun, whenne I south wente,
I schop me a schroude, as I a schep were.

In abyte as an ermyte unholy of werkys,
Y wente wyde in this worlde, wondrys to hure.

And the *Visio* concludes (8.126–30):

The prest and Perkyn aposed here eyther other,
And thorw here wordes I awok, and wayted aboute,
And saw the sonne evere south sytte that tyme.
Meteles and moneyles upon Malverne hullys,
Mamelyng on this metelys made me to studie . . .

The first person pronoun also appears in the few instances when the dreaming "I" participates directly in the action within his dreams, as in 8.90–95:

And Peres, at his prayer, his pardoun unfoldeth,
And I, byhynde hem bothe, behelde al the bulle.
In two lynys hit lay, and not a lettere more;
Hit was wryten ryght thus, in witnesse of Truthe:
Et qui bona egerunt, ibunt in vitam eternam;
Qui vero mala, in ignem eternum.

Only a single instance remains in A, where the reference to a character
named Will *may* logically point to the Dreamer-Narrator. Variant readings of
the last line of Passus 9 have provided a basis for editors (from Skeat to
Schmidt) to present it in a form that personifies the "wil" and associates that
name with the Dreamer-Narrator:

1. "Oure Wille wolde I-witen · ʒif Wit couthe him techen" (Skeat 9.118)
2. "Here is Wil wolde wyte, yif Wit couthe hym teche"
                                                            (Knott-Fowler 9.118)
3. "Here is wil wolde wyte ʒif wit couþe hym teche" (Kane 9.118)
4. "Here is Wil wolde wyte ʒif Wit couþe teche" (Schmidt 9.118)

Turning "wil" into "Will" here has proved an attractive editorial choice, but
on the basis of the practice elsewhere in A (as we have seen), we can with
reason hesitate from concluding that we may call the Dreamer-Narrator of A
by the name Will. As a result, I adopt without emendation the closing lines
in the Rawlinson MS, which read as follows:

Thanne Thoughth in that tyme sayde these wordes:
"Where that Dowel and Dobet and Dobest were in londe,
Here his wil wolde I wite, yif wit coude teche."
                                    (9.117–19; all capitals here are editorial)

Ending(s)

Critics are in substantial disagreement about whether (and how) the A
version of *Piers* ends. The so-called John But passus (Passus 12), though it

appears in three manuscripts (and possibly was part of a fourth: see Vaughan, "Filling the Gap"), is generally considered not to be, in whole or part, the work of the putative author (or authors) of the preceding *Visio* and *Vita*. But, even setting aside consideration of this appendicular passus, with its final lines added later by John But, there is considerable disagreement about the ending of the *Vita* represented by the conclusion of Passus 11. And this disagreement remains even though the scribes of those A manuscripts that omit Passus 12 give little indication that the work seemed to them incomplete or unconcluded (see Vaughan, "Ending(s)"). We can, of course, exclude here those six scribes who continue their A versions with text from C: for them A's Passus 11 is obviously not a conclusion to their *Piers Plowman*.

Crucial to the debate over whether A in fact concludes is the absence of any explicit mention of the Dreamer-Narrator's waking from the third dream. Nevertheless, many infer from the final fifty-four lines of Passus 11 that the dream has indeed ended and the voice is that of the awakened Dreamer reflecting on his just-concluded dream. Previous editors of *Piers* A make this clear in the way they lay out their texts: the Knott-Fowler edition inserts two blank lines between its lines 249 and 250 (= 259 and 260 in this edition); and Kane introduces an initial em-dash at the beginning of his line 258 (= 260). But while both of these are defensible presentations of the surviving texts and arise from arguable interpretations of the passage—and some of the scribal variants support the view that these would be consistent with inferences based on their texts—it is also the case that other scribes clearly did not take the dream (or the poem) as ended here. And while Schmidt, the most recent editor of A, also inserts a blank line at this same point, he significantly does not imply by it that the dream ends here: he indents (and opens a new quoted passage) with his line 258 (= 260) and goes on to include (all but the final lines of) Passus 12 as a constituent part of his text of the A version. In this, he follows the three manuscripts that continue with Passus 12 and narrate actions and discussions continuous with those in Passus 11.

Summary of the Poem
Prologue

The Narrator, dressed as a hermit and resting from his wandering in the Malvern Hills, falls asleep on a May morning. He dreams he is in a wilderness and sees a tower on a hilltop to the east and a stronghold in a deep valley below it. In a field between them are all sorts of people: some work, while others strut about in fine clothes; some pray, do business, entertain; some are beggars, and others are pilgrims. Churchmen (friars, parish priests, bishops, archdeacons, a pardoner, etc.) and lawyers in their silk hoods the Narrator criticizes for being more interested in money than in the "love of our Lord." The assembly is filled with nobles and townspeople, workers, and practitioners of various crafts, and the passus ends with singing and cries for food and drink.

Passus One

A lady appears in the dream and the Dreamer asks her what is the meaning of the scene before him. The tower is where Truth lives, she says, the Creator and "Father of Faith," who has provided us with all our necessities: clothing, food, drink. Her advice is to avoid excess: moderation is best. Avoid the temptations of the world, the flesh, and the devil. Thanking her for these words, the Dreamer asks to whom money belongs. She says that the Gospel says it is Caesar's. What is the dungeon in the dale? the Dreamer asks. It is the castle of Care, she answers, in which the Father of Falsehood lives.

All this makes the Dreamer wonder who the lady is, and so he asks her. "I am Holy Church," she answers; "you should recognize me!" The Dreamer asks her to pray for him and requests her instruction how he might save his soul. "Truth is the best," she answers; even Lucifer and his followers know this! "But where does it come from," he asks. "You know what it is by nature," she replies; "it is in your heart!" After telling him to love God better than himself and to avoid evil, and asserting that Love is the greatest thing, that he should love his neighbor, and that the rich should be charitable to the poor, she prepares to leave.

Passus Two

The Dreamer begs Lady Holy Church to stay and teach him how to recognize the False. "Look on your left side," she says. He sees a richly dressed woman wearing a crown, whom Holy Church identifies as Mede, the daughter of Wrong. She has annoyed Holy Church for a long time and is as influential with the pope as Holy Church is. Holy Church says that Mede and False will marry the next day, and all False's retinue will be there. They fill the mountainside with ten thousand tents and pavilions. The marriage contract is read out and formally witnessed.

Theology objects to Mede's marriage to False: she is nobly born, he says, a cousin of the king, and has been given by God to Truth. He tells them to take her to London so that the king can determine who should marry her. The supporters of Wrong distribute bribes and express confidence that they can win the case for Wrong in London. The company mounts horses and carts for the journey, but the news first reaches Conscience, at the king's court, and he informs the king, who sends constables to arrest the various malefactors. Falseness and the others scatter: hiding out with friars and merchants, pardoners and doctors, minstrels and messengers. They abandon Mede who, alone and trembling and weeping for fear, is arrested.

Passus Three

Mede is taken to the king, and she is courteously received by the lords and clerks of court, who are rewarded well by her. A friar confessor promises to absolve her of all her sins and destroy Conscience. When she promises to pay for a new church window, the Narrator points out that God forbids such self-promoting charity, and goes on to criticize the misdoings of civil officers and businessmen, asserting that the Bible predicts their impending punishment.

The king summons Mede and asks her if she will marry his knight Conscience. She quickly agrees. Conscience, however, forcefully refuses, when the king asks him: she is weak and fickle, and she corrupts people, secular and religious. When she is allied to the king, he says, the kingdom is in trouble; she perverts the law and society.

Mede complains to the king, who gives her a chance to defend herself. Mede, she says, can help when misfortune hits, and tells Conscience that he has himself benefited from distributing her gifts. Unlike you, she says, I never killed any king, nor did I cause him difficulties in Normandy or sneak away with money taken from poor men to distribute in Calais. I stayed at home with the king and raised his spirits. And, besides, she goes on, a king needs to distribute money and rewards to those who serve him faithfully and to gain him supporters abroad. Beggars and minstrels ask for donations, and priests and merchants require payment for what they provide. These are what she stands for.

The king tells Conscience that Mede seems to be winning the debate. Conscience replies that there are *two* kinds of mede: God's and "mede mesureles." He then insists that payment for labor or merchandise is not "mede" at all but "mesurable hyre." He concludes that a time is coming when ideals of justice and reason, not Mede, will reign.

Passus Four

The king commands an end to the dispute and orders Conscience to kiss Mede. He refuses, saying he will do it only if Reason advises it. The king tells Conscience to go get Reason and bring him to court, where he will rule the kingdom and direct Conscience's teaching. Conscience rides to Reason, and they quickly ride back to court, where the king puts Reason between himself and his son on the judges' bench.

A character named Peace comes into the Parliament to complain in detail about the actions of Wrong (i.e., Mede's father). Because the king knows the complaint is well grounded, Wrong asks Wary Wisdom to gain supporters by spreading money around. Wisdom (and Witty) take Mede in hand, by which time Wrong has already been put in chains at the king's command. While Wisdom and Witty make the case to the king, Mede approaches Peace directly to settle matters. Peace is satisfied by what Mede offers, but the king is not and awaits Reason's judgment on whether Wrong should be set free. His decision is that, until an age of ideal justice returns, he will have no pity on Wrong. His argument wins the day, and Mede is laughed at by everyone. Wisdom cannot defeat Reason's case, and the king takes Reason's advice, asking him to stay in his court. Reason agrees, as long as Conscience is another member of his council. The king agrees.

Passus Five

When the king and his knights go to church, the Dreamer awakes, sorry that he had not seen more. After a short walk he sits down to mumble his prayers and falls asleep. In this second dream, Conscience enters as a bishop and preaches to the "field full of folk" that the recent plague and storm were a warning of the coming Day of Doom. He calls on personified abstractions (such as Wastour), representative individuals (such as Peronel and Watte), and groups (prelates, priests, religious) to reform their lives.

This inspires Repentance to come in and he causes Will to weep. Then follows the contrition and confession of six of the Seven Deadly (or Mortal) Sins: Pride (Peronel), Lust (Lecchour), Envy, Covetousness, Gluttony, and Sloth. (Wrath is the only one of the traditional seven who is omitted.)

Robert the Robber prays to Christ for mercy, even though he cannot pay back what he has stolen. The Narrator, though convinced of this felon's penitence, is not sure what happened to him. The passus ends with a crowd of a thousand and more crying out for the grace to seek Truth.

Passus Six

The crowd does not, however, know where to look and asks a wide-traveled pilgrim they meet where Truth dwells. But he has never even heard of him before. A plowman (Piers) intervenes and says he knows Truth well: he's been his servant for forty years. Piers angrily rejects the pilgrims' offer to pay him for the information they seek, but he does provide a detailed set of directions to Truth's tower. The metaphorical landscape of this journey includes the Ten Commandments and other moral virtues. The password for entering the castle of Truth is "I have performed the penance the priest gave me and am sorry for my sins, and will always remain so."

A cutpurse, a thief, and a waferer doubt they can meet these requirements, but Piers assures them they can, through the help of Mercy and her maiden (Mary) and her son.

Passus Seven

Piers offers to guide the people to Truth, if they help him plow his half acre. He arranges various jobs for the group, because not all can plow.

Ladies can sew sacks and clothes; the knight can protect the church and hunt animals that damage Piers's crops. Piers prepares to sow his corn and promises to feed any who help him; but some he will not feed: Jack the juggler, Jonet from the stews, and Robin the ribald.

In anticipation of his pilgrimage, Piers makes his will. Then he and the pilgrims set about working the half acre. Many work hard, digging and pulling weeds, and at midmorning, Piers takes a break from plowing to see how things are going. He finds some sitting around, drinking ale, and singing, and he threatens them with starvation. They respond by faking various disabilities, and offering to pray for Piers. He responds that he will give alms to those genuinely disabled or sick, or faithful religious, but not to wasters.

A Breton braggart challenges Piers and threatens him. The knight is asked to step in, and he courteously warns the wasters, who continue to threaten Piers. Piers calls for Hunger to take vengeance on the wasters, and he grabs the Breton and others by the stomach. Then many of them get to work to try to drive Hunger away. All their efforts inspire Piers to ask Hunger to leave, first inquiring what he should do about beggars and panhandlers. Hunger tells him that he should feed them but only with basic foods. Hunger supports his advice by quoting Scripture and recommends a simple diet to cure sickness. Piers thanks him for his advice and asks him to leave. Hunger says he will not depart till he has eaten and drunk, to which Piers replies that he has little to offer because the harvest is far off. All the poor people bring their food to feed Hunger, who keeps asking for more. When the harvest arrives, the food they offer him improves in quality and quantity, but by then even beggars are rejecting the simpler foods, and laborers will not settle for day-old leftovers.

The Narrator discourses against such attitudes and warns that Hunger will come back, and there will be famine within five years as a result of bad weather.

Passus Eight

Truth sends a pardon to Piers and to all who help him till his land, including knights and bishops who perform their duties. Merchants are given a private communication, indicating that they too will qualify for salvation if they put their ill-gotten profits to good service. Lawyers, likewise, will be saved, if they use their skills on behalf of the poor and innocent. Beggars are not included in the pardon—unless their needs are genuine; too many of them are frauds and perverts.

A priest asks to examine Piers's pardon and declares that he does not find any pardon in it; it is only two clauses from the Athanasian Creed: "Those who do good will be saved; but those who do evil will proceed into eternal fire." Piers angrily tears the pardon and declares he will give up his field work and devote himself to prayers and penance. The priest and Piers sarcastically comment on each other, and at this point the Dreamer awakes back in the Malvern Hills. He reflects on the content of his dreams and on the various opinions about the value and truth of dreams. His commentary concludes that indeed the pope has the power to grant pardon, but that doing well in one's life is a better means to gaining salvation.

Passus Nine (Prologue to *Vita*)

The Narrator undertakes a search for Dowel and meets two friars who say Dowel lives with them. Disputing with them, the Dreamer says because everyone sins, Dowel cannot be always with them. The friars distinguish between kinds of sins, and the Dreamer says he does not have the natural understanding to grasp this distinction. He leaves to look further for Dowel. He hears birds singing and falls asleep.

In his dream, he meets a character who looks like himself, named Thought. Thought says that Dowel, Dobet, and Dobest are not too far away and describes the characteristics of the three. The Dreamer is not satisfied and desires more learning about what the three do. If Wit cannot teach you, says Thought, you will never learn. After three days of disputation, they meet Wit.

Passus Ten (Passus One of Dowel)

Wit says Dowel lives in a castle made up of the four elements, in which its creator, Kynde (identified as God later), has installed his lady love, Anima (Soul). The castle is called Caro (Flesh) and is entrusted to Dowel. Dobet, his daughter, serves Anima as her damsel, and the constable of the castle is Sir Inwit, who is assisted by his five sons.

Wit's lengthy monologue provides a detailed account of Inwit (which is the faculty of [natural or intuitive] human understanding aligned with Divine Reason) and its relations to moral responsibility (i.e., doing well). Wit then turns to narrate and comment on much of the Creation story from Genesis, including the cursed marriages among the descendants of Cain and Seth and story of Noah and the ark. He discusses the inheritance of virtue (and vice) in human generation and criticizes marriages that are motivated by economic reasons, which he singles out as particularly prominent since the Pestilence (Black Death).

Passus Eleven (Passus Two of Dowel)

Dame Study, Wit's wife, berates him for wasting her wisdom on fools and flatterers like this Dreamer—that is, casting pearls before swine. She berates her husband at length, criticizing those who are more interested in appearing learned than truly being so, and who abuse the truths of religion to gain points at dinner parties.

Wit is reduced to stunned silence and signals to the Dreamer that he should seek Study's assistance. He kneels to her and promises to be her lifelong servant, and she, because of his meekness, directs him to her cousin Clergy and his wife Scripture, who will be able to guide him to Dowel. Study gives detailed directions for his journey to where Clergy lives. In the course of this, Study comments at some length about the various branches of learning and especially about the difficulties with theology. She ends by warning the Dreamer away from sciences (such as astronomy and alchemy), which she invented in the first place to deceive people.

Thanking Dame Study, the Dreamer sets off and quickly arrives at Clergy, whose wife Scripture welcomes him warmly and describes Dowel, Dobet, and Dobest, primarily in terms of religious behavior. But she singles out for criticism those who profess the religious life but do not live it faithfully. The Dreamer admits he thought the three Do's were military and political leaders: knights, kings, and kaisers. Scripture says that they are no help in gaining salvation, and the same is true of earthly wealth: only the poor are saved. The Dreamer objects, saying that St. Peter says that anyone who believes and is baptized will be saved. But Scripture says that is true only *in extremis*—that Christians have to meet higher standards to achieve salvation.

These requirements move the Dreamer to fall back on the idea that he is predestined either to salvation or to damnation and that learning ultimately provides no help toward salvation.

Passus Twelve (Passus Three of Dowel)

Clergy dismisses the Dreamer as one who wants to learn but not to study, to be able to sound learned but not to act on the basis of what he learns. Scripture tells Clergy to teach him no more, and Clergy goes into his cabin and shuts the door, telling the Dreamer to go do well, or wickedly—whichever he wanted.

The Dreamer offers to become Scripture's servant if she will direct him to her cousin Kind Wit, her confessor. She embraces him and gives him directions and a guide to lead him to where Kind Wit lodges with Life. The journey takes some years, and along the way they meet with Hunger (who dwells with Death). The Dreamer feels faint, but Hunger offers him bits of bread and they meet with another confessor (called Fever on the Fourth Day), another companion of Death's, and his messenger. The Dreamer says he would travel with him and his servants, but Fever says that he should not go with him but live his own life, doing well, praying, and performing good works as long as his life lasts.

Appendix: Will did as he was told and wrote about Piers Plowman, and Death took him, and he is now buried: may Christ have his soul! So prayed John But, who added this conclusion. The Narrator closes with a prayer that God keep King Richard sound, and all lords who loyally love him, and bring us all to bliss.

Literary Backgrounds

For all its originality and individuality, *Piers Plowman* is not of course unique. It shares with other works of its time and cultural place features that were, or became, conventional. A brief account of some of these help place the poem in its literary environment.

Alliterative Poetry

The features that distinguish certain sorts of expressions as "poetry" vary from language to language, time to time. For some, strict meter is required; for others, a more or less rhythmic style is enough. For some, rhyme is essential; for others, it is unnecessary or even excluded. The verse forms favored in late Latin and early French literature, including the Anglo-Norman of post-conquest England, tended to be rhyming couplets of iambic tetrameter. These lines from the opening of Marie de France's *lai* "Le Fresne" (from the edition of A. Ewert) are followed by their Middle English translation in the Auchinleck MS (National Library of Scotland, Advocates MS 19.2.1 [fol. 261]):

Le lai del Freisne vus dirai
Sulunc le cunte que jeo sai.
[Ac herkneth, lordinges, sothe to sain,
Ichil you telle Lay le Frayn.]

In much of the surviving poetry of Middle English we can see the distinct influence of these forms. In the verse of Chaucer, whose work was contemporary with *Piers*, we see a mature English verse style that derives from these Norman models, influenced perhaps by similar verse forms in later French and Italian, of which Chaucer was aware and by which he was influenced. He uses iambic tetrameter couplets in *Book of the Duchess* and *House of Fame*, but favors iambic pentameter in most of his other poetry, in either couplets (*Legend of Good Women*, and many of the *Canterbury Tales*) or stanzas (*Parliament of Fowls, Troilus*, and some *Canterbury Tales*).

A brief glance at the text of *Piers Plowman* quickly shows that the syllabic meter and rhyme of Chaucer and his earlier English and Romance models do not define the formal features of its verse. We find here, instead, an alliterative poetry that has similarities to earlier forms of Germanic English poetry, like that found in Anglo-Saxon (Old English) poems such as *Beowulf* or *The Dream of the Rood*. The form of this alliterative verse line is defined not by the sounds that end it (i.e., rhymes) but rather by the *initial* sounds of stressed syllables in the line. The standard form of English alliterative verse in Old and Middle English consists of a four-stress line with a central break (the *caesura*). The two halves of the line are linked by stressed syllables with the same initial sound: the first and/or second stressed syllable alliterates with the third (i.e., the first in the second half-line), while the fourth stress alliterates only in exceptional circumstances. An analysis of features of the first four lines of *Piers* provides some further details about the regular practices of alliterative verse:

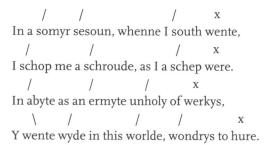

In a somyr sesoun, whenne I south wente,

I schop me a schroude, as I a schep were.

In abyte as an ermyte unholy of werkys,

Y wente wyde in this worlde, wondrys to hure.

Consonants (and consonant clusters, e.g., *sch*) generally alliterate with themselves. Vowels alliterate with other vowels (and with unvoiced *h*). As the fourth line above shows, other (nonstressed) syllables may also alliterate, and this may provide the poet with a way of establishing particular emphasis or indulging in stylistic display:

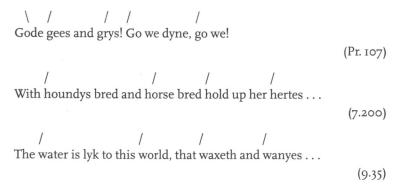

A fayr felde ful of folke fonde I bytwene . . .

(Pr.17)

Another way of providing variety or emphasis is to include the fourth stress in the alliteration:

Gode gees and grys! Go we dyne, go we!

(Pr. 107)

With houndys bred and horse bred hold up her hertes . . .

(7.200)

The water is lyk to this world, that waxeth and wanyes . . .

(9.35)

While it is usual to vary alliteration from line to line, sometimes an alliterative sound will be continued for a second line:

> For he is fader of feyth, and formed us alle
> With fel and whyt face, and a fyn wyt

$$(\text{I}.14-15)$$

Or it can continue for even three (*c* and *k* here represent the same sound):

> Clerkes that hit knoweth schulde kenne hit aboute,
> For crystene and uncrystene cleymeth echone.
> Kynges and knyghthes schulde kepe hit by resoun . . .

$$(\text{I}.90-92)$$

While it is regular (in *Piers*) for both stressed syllables in the first half-line to alliterate, in some cases one or the other varies from the alliterating sound:

>   x   /   /   x
> Ther gan I to mete a merwelous swovene . . .

$$(\text{Pr.}11)$$

These features define the standard, but not all lines alliterate regularly (or even at all). Some editors (e.g., Kane) will justify emendations on the grounds that fully regular alliteration is required by the verse form used by the author. Others (including myself) may be less confident of this "law," and there is sufficient evidence of variation across the entire corpus of Middle English alliterative verse to challenge an unreflective assertion of complete regularity as the underlying model. Indeed, Skeat (and others) noted early on that "[Langland] frequently neglects to observe the strict rules" found in other ME alliterative verse (Skeat, *Parallel Texts*, 2.lxi), and recent students of Middle English metrics have become distinctly less certain about the application of such "categorical metrical rules" to *Piers Plowman*.* When one factors in the variability of scribal understanding and differing metrical tastes, the issue becomes further complicated. As a result, there have been no emendations made in this edition in response to the application of solely metrical "rules."

In addition to general principles guiding the alliteration of stressed syllables, there seem to be some constraints on the number and arrangement of stressed and unstressed syllables in the verse lines, with possibly significant differences between the principles governing the first half-line and those governing the second. In general, then, there is at least one unstressed syllable between stressed syllables and usually no more than three such; and the final stress in a line is followed by a single unstressed syllable. Variations occur, of course, but unless sense demands it, this edition avoids emending, even on the basis of these general metrical principles.

While elements of alliteration continue to appear in English poetry after

---

*Duggan, "Notes"; quotation is from p. 185.

the Norman Conquest introduces influential new cultural forces into the linguistic and literary forms of "received" English, much of the English verse that survives from this period follows the metrical and rhyming forms from medieval Latin and Romance verse. In the middle of the fourteenth century, however, the literary record shows increasing evidence of a growing body of English verse with features strongly reminiscent of the Old English four-stress alliterative line. Of course, the evolution of the language in the three hundred years after the Norman Conquest not only profoundly altered the word hoard, the vocabulary of English, but also affected basic principles of English syntax, transforming a group of Western Germanic dialects so that there was a steady decline in the inflected forms of words that made clear the syntactic relations among them. English increasingly grew toward its modern form, in which word order (and the use of prepositional phrases) did more to make clear the meaning and relations of phrases, clauses, and sentences. What we find in fourteenth-century alliterative verse is a much longer, metrically looser line than in Old English, though it remained one that favored the principle of four stresses and two (or three) alliterating sounds.

Because highly accomplished alliterative poems survive in manuscripts beginning in the middle of the fourteenth century, it has become usual to refer to an "alliterative revival" in this period (Lawton). Although there may be fewer attempts to explain this revival by recourse to claims of some sort of self-conscious, or nationalistic, intent, that is not completely anachronistic for the period (Turville-Petre). Even without adopting that (or any) explanation for its occurrence, we may still use the term to describe the historical evidence for a marked increase in surviving written poetry in this "older" form by the middle of the fourteenth century. Whether it was fostered by an English nationalism prompted by the beginning of the Hundred Years' War with France, or whether it was merely the result of the economic improvements in a class of people for whom English rather than (Anglo-Norman) French had cultural prestige, nevertheless the manuscripts of the second half of the fourteenth century contain some strikingly accomplished masterpieces written in alliterative verse. *Piers Plowman* is among the most widely copied poem in that form, but it is by no means the only example.

The Dream Vision Genre

For readers of the twenty-first century, dreams are usually interpreted as guides to the dreamer's own situations and concerns. They may present reimagined constructs of our thoughts and experiences; or they may provide gateways to understanding deep (even repressed) drives and desires of our subconscious selves. For the premoderns, dreams could provide access to transcendent and spiritual realities, alternative or parallel modes of being that only mystics and dreamers could see. (They could also be the work of the devil or of their own desires.) The inventory of literary texts that present dreams and dreamers and the interpretation of dreams as crucial to human culture is extensive and includes examples from most societies whose records and traditions we can examine (Barney).

The sacred books of Judaism, Christianity, and Islam provide examples (e.g., Joseph [in Exodus], the book of Daniel; John's Revelation, *Shepherd of Hermas*; Mohammed), as do the writings of ancient Greece (end of Plato's *Republic*) and Rome (Cicero's *Dream of Scipio*; Boethius's *Consolation of Philosophy*). In the European Middle Ages, we find a particularly rich collection of works that use the dream vision as the essential frame for their narratives. Whether as sleeping dreams or waking visions, many of them introduce visitors from, or journeys to, other worlds, that provide lessons and insights to the narrator-dreamer. These may articulate metaphysical or spiritual truths, conventionally professed but not as often observed in practice (as in Boethius); or they may address contemporary political and social realities, using the visionary form to displace the criticisms to a safe distance from the narrator, and the author (Dante's *Commedia*).

Fourteenth-century England offers striking examples of the variety of topics that could be treated by means of dream-vision poems: satire of socioeconomic and political or moral values (the alliterative *Wynnere and Wastoure, Piers Plowman*); meditations on death (*Pearl*, Chaucer's *Book of the Duchess*), on love (Chaucer's *Parliament of Fowls*), and on fame (Chaucer's *House of Fame*); and debate over the contested status of women (Chaucer's *Legend of Good Women*). Many of these are consistent with, and sometimes consciously derived from, a body of influential dream visions that circulated in medieval Europe: in Latin (Boethius; Alan of Lille's *The Complaint of Nature*; Bernard Silvestris's *Cosmographia*); in French (the *Roman de la Rose* of Guillaume de Lorris [continued by Jean de Meun]; Guillaume Deguilleville's three *Pelerinages*; Guillaume de Machaut's *Remede de Fortune*); in Italian (Dante); in Welsh (the *Dream of Rhonabwy*); and in English (*Dream of the Rood*; *Owl and the Nightingale*).

Many of these visionary poems are intended as satires, calling for reform, and *Piers* shows, as the first part of A reveals, a focused critical attention on and familiarity with the workings of London and Westminster officialdom. Though it opens in the Malvern Hills in the West Country and is concerned in the second dream with the rural and agricultural economy (Piers and the plowing of his half acre; Hunger), the poem's first dream moves (in the Lady Mede episode) from the countryside to the urban and courtly environment of London and Westminster. The juxtaposition of urban and rural societies, of royal administration and plowing the half acre reveals an author exercised by the interdependencies of late medieval English society, both secular and religious. The prolonged search (begun in A and continued in B) for a persuasive definition of what it means to Do Well (Better, and Best) engages the Dreamer-Narrator, and the reader, in challenging reflections on both the practical and the ethical parameters of any of the suggested referents for those combinations of verb and adverb.

Personification

Because they frequently deal with characters that inhabit a supernatural, or extraterrestrial, world, the characters in dream visions embody abstract ideas or impersonal institutions, such as Philosophy, Nature, Love, Conscience, or Holy Church. Personification is a literary technique that assigns the characteristics of human personality to abstract ideas or nonhuman beings (such as animals). We find this technique in ancient literature (think of Aesop's *Fables*) and in modern comics and cartoons (e.g., Snoopy in *Peanuts*, or Bugs Bunny). In *Piers Plowman*, personification is a dominant feature of the dreams, which are inhabited by characters, situations, and actions that recall human individuals and their lives but are in fact fictional constructs to illuminate moral (and other) abstractions. Thus, a figure like Holy Church in the first dream appears as an aristocratic lady who addresses the Dreamer with authority. That she also evidences a sharp, even catty, attitude toward Lady Mede attests to the poet's sensitivity to tonal nuances in her language and also to his recognition of very real features of human psychology and behavior. If the underlying ideas help define characteristics of the personification, it is also the case that treating such ideas as individuals, subject to the human limitations and foibles of real people, can also affect how a poet perceives and presents those ideas. The character of Envy (in the Confession of the Deadly Sins in Passus 5) is more than simply envious: he exposes characteristics that, abstractly at least, would belong to other "sins" (such as anger). He becomes, in other words, a character whose defining vice may be envy, but he is not limited to being *only* envious. And a character like Glutton takes on a rich three-dimensionality and his own complex life story. Should this complex mingling of the ideal abstract and the all-too-human real lead us to reexamine the richer implications in the disagreements between Mede and Conscience (in the first dream), and between Lady Holy Church and Theology over Mede's parentage (in Passus 2)?

Allegorical Interpretation

A recurrent feature of medieval commentaries on the Bible is the effort to get below the surface of the literal text to the fundamental truths that it was believed to contain. Because human language was quite obviously varied and not limited to its literal meanings only, so too the language of the Bible was amenable to rhetorical analysis, and the truths it taught were subject to interpretation. The *allegorical* method opened the way to discovering the truths expressed beneath the surface, by empowering readers to see that the words could say one thing and mean another. And that *other* could itself be subject to a number of (even incompatible) meanings. One of the powerful tools of allegorical exegesis (interpretation) is the categorization of interpretative moves as either *in bono* (in a good sense) or *in malo* (in a bad sense). So, for example, a single figure, such as a lion, might be interpreted in one instance as Jesus and in another as the Devil (Augustine, *On Christian Doctrine* 3.25).

If such binaries are available to readers of texts, they are presumably also available to their creators. As we have seen, the contention over the meaning of Mede in the first dream is not easily resolved. If there are, as Conscience says, two kinds of meed, then at the basic etymological or grammatical level, the identity of a character whose name *is* Mede must itself be ambiguous. If such ambiguity exists even at the level of a word's basic denotation, its meaning, then it must also attach itself to events and situations that are described by that word. So, to choose a particularly vexing example, what meaning should we, *can* we, give to Piers's action of tearing Truth's pardon at the end of Passus 8 (see 8.100ff.)? Once we have identified reasonable possibilities, how are we then to *choose* between them? Should his action be seen *in bono* or *in malo*? And who has the final authority to adjudicate between the two?

In one sense, the *Vita* that follows this dramatic event examines that very issue: by involving his Dreamer in the methods of logical disputation and the art of dialectic, the *Vita* engages the *sic et non* (yes and no) of medieval scholastic debate over philosophical and theological truths. Truth no doubt exists: that is a certainty for the European Middle Ages. But discovering it and recognizing its constituent parts are the result of an academic enterprise that values postponing certainty in the interest of continued fruitful reflection and discourse. Practically engaging with the personal, moral implications cannot, however, be indefinitely postponed. Doing *well* is required, even if knowing what is *best* may be beyond what we can determine at any given instance.

Voices: Author, Narrator, and Dreamer

Because the voice speaking in a text is always to some extent a performance by its author, readers are well advised to distinguish the historical author from the fictive speaker who narrates the action. This is the case even when the Narrator adopts the first-person pronoun and speaks with what appears to be the creator's omniscience. The presumption of an exact correspondence between author and speaker is always dangerous in works of fiction; it is wise for a reader to hesitate in giving total credence even when a writer purports to be recounting fact.

Dream visions complicate matters further by establishing formal distinctions between the waking and dreaming actions in their narratives. The distinctions are at least temporal, because the Narrator usually recounts the dream as a recollection, from the vantage point of having awakened from the dreaming state. Consequently, a reader should distinguish not only between the Author's reality and the Narrator's fictional world but also between the latter's waking events and those within the dream. Because dream visions may recount some advance in knowledge and understanding on the part of the "I" of the poem, they are normally narrated in the past tense. As a result, the reader should maintain a clear distinction between the present-tense speaking voice of the poem's Narrator and the experiences, thoughts, words, and actions that he narrates as having occurred (to himself or others) in the past tense. Furthermore, there are frequently marked differences between this (doubled) Narrator and the main actor/speaker within his dreams, and we can best conceive of this "I" as a distinct character, the Dreamer. If it is proper to distinguish between Author and Narrator, it is likewise wiser to maintain a clear distinction between Narrator and Dreamer. The formal divisions between dream and waking "reality" are at least as strong as those between the world of the living Author and the fiction of a literary work's Narrator.

England circa 1370: Church and State in Later Medieval England

King Edward III's fifty-year reign (1327–77) is usefully divided into three stages (Ormrod, Waugh), with the first (1327–38) marked by his rise to power and wars against Scotland. The second includes the initial successes of the Hundred Years' War with France (1338–60), while the third covers a period of truce (1360–69) followed by a decline in England's fortunes abroad and dissatisfactions with the court and government as a result of military losses abroad and taxation at home. The economic, social, and political difficulties did not stop when Edward died in 1377 and was succeeded by his ten-year-old grandson, Richard II (1377–99).

Edward of Windsor, Earl of Chester, was himself fourteen when he was crowned king (1 February 1327) after the deposition (and subsequent murder) of his father Edward II, who had succeeded his father Edward I in 1307. During the first few years of the young Edward III's reign, the kingdom was essentially ruled by his mother, Queen Isabella, and her lover Roger Mortimer, who had led the insurrection against Edward II. This inauspicious beginning to the young king's reign lasted only a short time, however, and Edward asserted his power with the abrupt arrest (19 October 1330) of Mor-

timer and the queen. Mortimer was soon after condemned to death as a
traitor by Parliament and executed, while the queen retired to Castle Rising
in Norfolk. Having now established his rule in fact as well as in name,
Edward reopened conflict with Scotland, repudiating the Treaty of North-
ampton that had been forced on him in 1328. Despite some military successes, he failed in his aims and meanwhile was being increasingly dis-
tracted to the south by the French allies of the Scots. They were repeatedly
attacking English coastal towns, and threats of invasion were in the air. In
1337 the French king Philip VI confiscated Edward's duchy of Gascony, and
war with France was on the horizon.

The second part of his reign (1338–60) began with Edward's asserting a
claim (as the heir of his maternal grandfather, Philip IV) to be the rightful
king of France. This initiated a century-long conflict between England and
France, which concluded only in 1453 when the resurgent French (under
Charles VII) reduced England's once-extensive continental holdings to a
single town, Calais. The beginnings of the Hundred Years' War, however,
were marked by English victories at sea (near Sluys in 1340, which gave
England control of the Channel) and more importantly on land—for example, the battle of Crecy in 1346 and the siege of Calais the following year. The
pinnacle of English success in these first campaigns came toward the end of
the 1350s, with the extension of English territory in northern and western
France and with the capture of the French king, John II, by Prince Edward's
victorious (though outnumbered) forces at Poitiers in September 1356. He
(Edward, the Black Prince, heir to the throne of England) went on to encircle
Paris in 1359, inducing the French to sue for peace. In the resulting Treaty of
Bretigny in 1360, while King Edward gave up (at least nominally) his claim
to the throne of France, he effectively reinforced English sovereignty over
considerable territories of France.

A decade of relative peace followed Bretigny. King John died in captivity
in England in 1364 and was succeeded by Charles V. The formidable general
of the English, Prince Edward, retired from active campaigning as a result of
illness contracted in wars in France and Spain as Duke of Gascony. His
brother John of Gaunt, by marriage Duke of Lancaster, had less success in
the field when hostilities started up again following the confiscation and
invasion of Gascony by King Charles in 1369. King Edward no longer played
a very active role in military actions after 1360 and, indeed, seems to have
reduced his participation in domestic politics also during this third period of
his reign. He was content to leave the government in the hands of trusted
officers such as William Wykeham (keeper of the Privy Seal, later, bishop of
Winchester and chancellor), or (during the last decade, at least, of his life) to
the machinations of his accomplished mistress, Alice Perrers.

As we enter the last decade of the reign of Edward III, England was experiencing something of a decline. The heir, Edward, was seriously ill and his brother John was in considerable disfavor. It is not altogether clear whether the king was senile, or in the power of Alice and others, or simply uninterested in ruling. In any case, the last years of Edward's reign were neither hopeful nor particularly glorious. The English fleet was badly defeated by the French and Castilians off La Rochelle (1372), and English power in France was reduced to Calais and a strip of the coast of Bordeaux. Prince Edward died in 1376, the year before his father, and his place on the throne was taken by the ten-year-old Richard. For a time, the real power lay in the hands of Richard's uncles, most prominently John. In the first dream of *Piers* A, with the activities of Lady Mede (whether or not she is modeled on Alice Perrers) and Conscience, we can see this poet's vision of competing interests in and around the English court and London society in the 1360s. In the longer B version of *Piers* (ca. 1377–81: Kane, "The Text"), and in its revision in the C version (ca. 1381–85: Kane, "The Text"), we can trace the continuing effects of these events into and through the reign of Richard II.

Various episodes of *Piers Plowman* reflect political, social, and theological concerns of the later years of the reign of Edward III. Some of these are specific enough to have led scholars to conclude that the A version of *Piers Plowman* was probably composed during this latter stage in the long reign of Edward III, sometime after 1362 and before 1370. The evidence further suggests that the text of the poem was probably being fixed and copied in the period 1368–74 (Kane, "The Text"). From the present state of our scholarly knowledge, then, we may propose that 1368–70 would offer likely dates for the completion of the poem we title *Piers* A.

Some familiarity with the political, economic, and ecclesiastical backgrounds to the period will enrich a reader's appreciation of the poem and its critical and satirical intent. The prominence of Lady Mede in the first dream invites attention to economic conditions in mid-fourteenth-century England. The poem's idealization of a plowman reinforces this focus, inverting traditional social and economic hierarchies by giving moral authority to a member of the third estate (laborers), who ordinarily ranked below those who fought (the knightly aristocrats) and those who prayed (the clergy).* By beginning the first dream with Lady Holy Church and by naming his idealized plowman Piers (i.e., Peter), the poet makes us reflect on the leadership of the Catholic Church, whose head, the pope, was the successor of the apostle Peter, the "rock" upon which Jesus established his church and to whom he granted the "keys of the kingdom [of heaven]" (Matt. 16:18–19).

---

*For a useful discussion of the tradition of the three estates, and Chaucer's depiction of various representative members of each, and satirizing their failure to live up to the ideals expected of them, see Mann, *Estates Satire*.

The virulent wave of bubonic (and pneumonic) plague that devastated populations across Europe in 1348–49 had widespread social and economic effects. In England, as much as one-third of the population died in what became known as the Black Death, and those who survived found the value of their labor, particularly in the countryside, increased as landlords were forced to compete for labor in their fields and pastures. This competition put severe pressures on traditional feudal relations and tempted workers who had previously been bound to serve on the estates of their noble and aristo-cratic masters to seek offers of increased wages from others, or to join those leaving the land to work in cities like London. The traditional bonds of service in this feudal society had already, in any case, been weakening in the face of a growing money-based economy for military or agricultural service that in earlier days would have been taken simply as a duty (McKisack; Baldwin; Vance Smith, "National Noetic."). The Black Death aggravated this, and there were repeated attempts by Parliament and local authorities to control the movement of laborers and the rise in their wages. The Ordinance of Laborers (1349) was followed by the Statute of Laborers (1351), which attempted to force workers to stay home and work for their masters at wage levels that had existed before the plague. The need for repeated statutory legislation in the decades following attests to the failure to control the costs of labor and goods, which continued to climb in later years, especially after recurrent outbreaks of plague (e.g., 1361–62, 1368–69).

While these domestic economic and social difficulties compounded the costs of military efforts in France, relations between England and the church were also complicated by the political struggles with France, because the papal court had moved from Rome to Avignon in southern France in 1308 and was perceived to be more favorable to French interests. The English king and Parliament grew increasingly dissatisfied with the exercise of papal power in England, and there were repeated efforts to restrain, by statute (e.g., 1351 and 1354), the pope's prerogatives with respect to installing ("pro-viding") bishops and priests to posts in England. This, too, reflected the effects of the Black Death, which resulted in a shortage of clergy, particularly in the countryside (McKisack). Likewise, the increased costs of military actions abroad led to complaints about, and statutory actions controlling, both the clergy's freedom from mandatory taxation in England (although they quite regularly offered "voluntary" subsidies) and the payment of papal taxes by English clergy and, of course, their parishioners.

A growing English "nationalism" increased the ordinary levels of anti-clerical feelings that accompanied the rise of centralized ecclesiastical power in the High Middle Ages and played no small part in the increase in social and religious unrest that marks the decades after the 1360s. The Rising of 1381 (the so-called Peasants' Revolt) brought to a head complaints issuing from economic and social unrest that had been festering since the Black Death, as well as reformist anticlerical movements associated with John Wyclif and others, including those who will later be persecuted as Lollards and heretics. The pointed moral criticisms in *Piers* A are directed at the failures and ambitions of secular figures and clergy alike, and while they will appear consistent with more extreme views adopted by others in later decades, they are not themselves extreme. More constructive than revolutionary, perhaps, they are also more hopeful about effecting reform in contemporary society than dismissive about potential improvements in the status quo.

The Text

Editors have distinct choices to make when they approach any text, and these are multiplied when it is a text like *Piers Plowman* A. Its text appears in no authorial copy and is attested by a large number of surviving manuscripts; and the complex relations among these manuscripts are further complicated by the frequent overlapping among the witnesses to the various distinct versions of the poem. All these elements make it difficult for an editor to decide what approach to take. Nevertheless, an editor is required to make *a* choice. The manuscripts of the A version of *Piers Plowman* offer not only a choice of editorial methods but particular challenges as well. In producing any text that can justifiably claim to represent this work, such a choice will require consistent application of some clearly articulated principles. A survey of the options available to editors will allow us to place the present edition in its context.

The basic choice lies between producing in accessible form for modern readers a representative documentary artifact selected from among those texts that actually existed in the Middle Ages or, alternatively, reconstructing a more authoritative version of the work than survives in the available witnesses. Because we lack anything that can be identified as the poet's own "edition" of *Piers Plowman*, most recent editors have taken it as their goal to produce a version that is as close as they can get to the missing original, presumably authorial, text. Because this is a laborious and potentially controversial process, in which individual decisions about the text are each subject to critical scrutiny and (often) damning review (editorial scholarship being what it is), some editors will abandon an attempt at recovering an "original" and will instead (to mention one extreme) choose to offer a photographic or digital facsimile of one or more manuscripts to interested readers; this is particularly attractive when the primary audience is expected to be other scholars interested in the text.

This is an attractive way to document a particular artifact and make it more easily available to readers—and to protect the original from overexposure. This is particularly attractive when there is a unique manuscript of the text surviving, as is the situation with some of the most famous medieval English texts, such as *Beowulf* and the fourteenth-century Middle English *Sir Gawain and the Green Knight*. But the difficulties of simply reading such old texts (in the original or even in high-quality facsimile) inevitably reduce the size of their audience. Even if one becomes familiar with their odd letter forms, irregular (and often ambiguous) spelling, unusual spacing and word division, unconventional (to modern eyes) punctuation, and frequent use of abbreviations, there are other problems to contend with, such as the material depredations of time and use (or neglect). These, alone or in combination, can prevent those without specialized training from reading such texts intelligently or appreciatively.

One way to overcome these material difficulties with reading a primary artifact or even a high-quality facsimile of the text as it appears in its medieval manuscript is to produce a "diplomatic" or "documentary" edition, one that essentially reproduces the manuscript in a carefully exact transcription into print, using modern letter forms and noting or correcting obvious errors (such as a blatant misspelling or the omission of a crucial word) in the manuscript. The *Piers Plowman* Electronic Archive has begun producing such diplomatic editions of all the surviving manuscripts and accompanying them with good, full-color digital facsimiles of the actual manuscripts. Such an edition of MS. Rawl. poet. 137 (the base text for this present edition) is currently in preparation.

Once we move beyond editions that provide such reproductions (photographic or diplomatic) of individual manuscripts of a medieval work, we enter the world of what is usually called a "critical" edition, one that attempts to reconcile the differences among the variations in the texts found in the surviving manuscripts (or posited to have been in lost manuscripts). Here, the terrain gets even more varied, and the underlying principles guiding the editor's choices, and judgments, are contested, but it is possible to identify three main types of critical edition: the "best text," the "genealogical," and the "eclectic."

Editors who adopt the "best text" principle choose one manuscript as the best surviving representative of the poem and erect their edition on its text. Unlike the strict "documentary" editor, however, "best text" editors are willing to revise and correct the readings of their selected manuscript, on the basis of their understanding of the poem's language and metrics and sometimes of better "readings" found in (or inferred from) other witnesses. Some of the errors (e.g., the omission or repetition of words or lines) often can be easily identified and corrected from comparison with other manuscripts. Other unique, or unusual, word choices or phrasing may be less clearly in need of correction: a word in the base manuscript may make excellent sense and suit the immediate syntax and metrics, but it may be quite different from the wording that appears in other manuscripts. In a case like this, the editor will need to judge whether the word is an error or a scribal variant in need of correction, or whether it is an acceptable alternative reading that should be retained, on the principle that, if this is indeed the "best text," its readings should be given preference in all cases where they are not demonstrably corrupt or incorrect.

In the nineteenth century, attempts to apply principles of scientific (or logical) methods to the editing of texts produced hypotheses of the genetic, or genealogical, relations among surviving texts. On the principle—not always uncontroversial, of course—that all the surviving manuscripts of a given work were witnesses to a single, original text (or version) of that work, this editorial method set out to establish the family tree (or "stemma") of the surviving witnesses to the work, with an eye to establishing principles by which to select from among competing witnesses (actual or hypothetical) what were likely to be the words closest to the earliest text. While admitting that, in most cases at least, not every historical copy of the work has survived, an editor of this school would insist that, by careful comparison of the variations among those that do survive, it is possible to identify the relations among the surviving witnesses and establish a hierarchy among them. Crucial to this method of editing is the determination of "errors" in particular manuscripts, and by identifying manuscripts that shared individual errors, it would be possible to identify the genetic relations among the members of this subgroup of texts and further clarify this branch's relations to others in the genealogical tree. Of course, determining what is a shared "error" depends on the editor's sense (whether fixed or evolving) of the correct (i.e., original or authorial) readings. So there may be some circular reasoning involved in the arguments.

The logic of the genealogical method relies on the analysis of errors introduced into and sustained in the text during the process of scribal copying and earlier editing; to explain certain errors, it is helpful for an editor to be able to identify certain types of scribal practices that could result in major and minor errors. Similarities in letter forms in certain Middle English scripts (such as "e" and "o," or "c" and "t," or long "s" and "f," or "þ" [thorn] and "y") can explain certain differences in words. Eye-skip is another: a scribe copies from memory the last word of a phrase (such as "relations" in the phrase "genetic relations" toward the end of the preceding paragraph), but when he goes back to pick up the rest of the line, he starts at the same word, "relations," in the phrase "branch's relations" in the *next* line; the result may be the loss of an entire line of the earlier text and the production of a not very satisfactory sentence: ". . . it would be possible to identify the genetic relations to others in the genealogical tree." An editor attempting to reconstruct his edition from a "corrected" descendant of this latter manuscript would infer that the scribe has fallen prey to "eye-skip." When there are multiple witnesses to the text, informed emendations can sometimes be made, and the missing text supplied. But what if the error occurred at the earliest antecedent, or archetype, of *all* the surviving manuscripts, and some of their scribes attempted their own correction of what they perceived to be a nonsensical, or at least problematic, passage? Of course, what one scribe or later editor might see as an error, another scribe or editor might take to be the authorial original—or a later authorial revision—witnessed by the family (or individual manuscript) the other editor had relegated to a contaminated (and so illegitimate, or bastard) branch of the larger family.

In producing their genealogy of manuscripts, editors of this school would attempt to identify the relation of the text they were producing to the author's original. Not all would claim, however, that they were able to reach back as far as the first text of the work; most would acknowledge that the limits of their evidence would allow them only to identify the form of the *archetype*, that is, the earliest immediate ancestor of the surviving witnesses. Because not all the witnesses survive, and because the method aspires to scientific rigor, it may be that in particular cases the farthest the method can take an editor is to the ancestor of one particular branch of the surviving family tree—a consequence of all the witnesses of other branches having been lost or becoming irretrievably corrupt.

This genealogical method (also referred to as *recension*) requires us to accept some corollary principles, the most important of which is that the products of scribal activity are the results of largely automatic, unreflective copying by scribes, working with a single exemplar that they are reproducing. But (as recensionists usually realize) not all scribes were unsophisticated, mechanical, or successful transcribers of their exemplars. As a result, some practitioners of the genetic method entertain the possibility of more complex editorial activity by certain scribes. And, indeed, some scribes may have assumed for themselves the role of author or reviser of the work they were copying. This is clearly the case with at least some of the multiple manuscripts of *Piers Plowman* and arguably the case with many. Not all scribes considered themselves mere copyists; nor did all consider themselves editors or creative revisers. The range of scribal identities is broad and capable of shifting back and forth among the various potential roles.

The desire to establish a hierarchical stemma (or family tree) undergirds the work of editors in the genealogical school. By analysis of individual variants, they seek to identify certain manuscripts (or groups of manuscripts) as providing more trustworthy evidence of the authorial or archetypal original of the text. (This may be taken as a somewhat "abstracted" or "hypothetical" extension of the principles underlying the best-text edition.) The genealogical relationship among the surviving texts provides the basis for this kind of editing, and the confidence of its practitioners may at times become self-inspiring. If you are convinced of the axiomatic assumptions of the method, then you must agree to the conclusions that derive from application of its editorial (i.e., more or less scientific) principles. On these principles, a critical edition of *Piers* A was published in 1952, the work of Thomas A. Knott and David C. Fowler.

However, not everyone is convinced about the axiomatic principles behind the genetic analysis of the extant witnesses to a text. Critics of the genealogical method insist that establishing the required hierarchy of manuscripts is impossible in many (if not all) cases because all the witnesses are uniquely corrupt and the specific kinds of corruption are difficult to determine. What appears to be a shared error may arise from contamination: the scribe may have more than a single exemplar before him. Or it may be a coincidental error, deriving from two or more scribes' independently making the same mistake or unconscious "correction" of what is before them in the manuscript they are copying. It is clear, therefore, that not all shared variations (often identified as "agreements in error") explicitly reveal shared genealogies.

Similar criticisms may, of course, be made of *any* systematic "rules" for editing. Because the text and history of each work are unique and the interventions by others in the reception and transmission of its text are many and varied—we have almost no medieval literary text in the author's own hand or, for that matter, demonstrably overseen by its author—it is nearly inevitable that the particulars of the text do not always respond well to mechanical, systematic treatment because so many intermediate, and often rather independent, hands have been involved in transmitting the text to us.

George Kane, in the chapter on "Editorial Resources and Methods" in his introduction to the edition of the Athlone A version, lays the articulate foundations for what has come to be called his *eclectic* method of editing. An eclectic edition adopts much of the comparative method underlying recension but rejects the determinative structuring of the relations among the surviving witnesses that a genealogical tree establishes. As Kane noted, "*Piers Plowman* was especially subject to variation as a living text with a content of direct concern to its scribes. Its relevance to contemporary circumstances would not merely distract them from the passive state of mind ideal for exact copying but actually induce them, whether consciously or subconsciously, to make substitutions" (*A Version*, 115). For this reason he concluded, "Recension is not a practicable method for the editor of A manuscripts" (ibid.), and he severely criticized the principles underlying the Knott-Fowler edition. While scribes were prone to mechanical errors, some of what might seem to be errors were clearly deliberate. Although an editor is expected to discriminate between the two sorts of errors, as Kane points

out, "A sure means of determining whether these . . . were generally mechanical or deliberate does not, however, suggest itself" and "the editor is
brought to the difficult borderline between mechanical and conscious variation" (A Version, 125). In other words, while some scribal substitutions and
omissions are mechanical and subconscious—the result of misreading, ambiguity, haste, carelessness, or habit—some were quite conscious and individual, deliberate attempts to improve, correct, or extend what they were
copying. Identifying what kind of "error" is involved becomes an editorial
preliminary to choosing between authorial and scribal texts.

Because there are no simple, systematic relations to be derived from the
practices of individual scribes, the eclectic editor undertakes to examine each
variant separately and to make an individual determination about which one
is most likely to be "original." Sometimes this can lead to adopting a "harder
reading"—one that is not as likely to be supplied by ordinary scribal habit—
that survives in one manuscript that a genealogical editor would rank lowly.

Sometimes, however, an insightful editor can reconstruct as the authorial
original—from the range of manuscript variants and an understanding of
scribal practices—a reading that is supported by no extant manuscript at all.
In such cases, the quality of the editor's judgment becomes crucial, and this
can finally be assessed only when those "decisions" have been laid "open to
examination by full presentation of the evidence and an exposition of [the
editor's] grounds for determining originality" (Kane, A Version, 165). When
accompanied by the "full . . . evidence" and articulated "grounds," such
editorial judgments may win praise for their brilliance—or condemnation
for their being subjective: Kane and his coeditors in the Athlone series have
enjoyed or endured both.

In addition to adopting this eclectic method over that of recension, Kane
also holds that the revisions in the three versions that he has edited are the
product of a single author, William Langland, and as a result he has felt it
proper (as Knott and Fowler would not) to compare readings from manuscripts of all three versions in making decisions about the text of each one of
those. Nevertheless, despite their divergent methods and underlying editorial principles, it is notable that the two critical editions of Piers A—Knott-
Fowler's and Kane's—reveal few substantial disagreements between their
texts. This is all the more striking because the two editions issue from
radically different approaches to the science/art of editing and fundamen-
tally disagree about the number of authors involved in the production of the
versions. Despite their scholarly disagreements on these matters, both editions use the same manuscript (Trinity College, Cambridge, MS R.3.14) as
their base or copy text. This, of course, may account for many of the general
similarities between their texts.

As is generally the case in the scribal world of medieval text-production, we do not have any manuscript of *Piers* to which we may confidently attach authorial responsibility (as scribe or supervisor or corrector). In fact, the Athlone editors of the B and C versions (Kane and E. Talbot Donaldson for B; George Russell and Kane for C) are fairly confident that the archetypes of the extant manuscripts of those versions were not themselves "correct." In other words, the revisions carried out in B and C were not made to antecedent versions as they had been finally corrected by their author. Thus, the author/reviser of B was apparently revising a text that had already been altered in transmission by its scribes. If this is indeed the case, it leaves modern readers with understandable questions about who *is* responsible for the words on the page (or screen) before them. In the absence of an author's holograph, we cannot of course test our arguments over particular details; editorial, scholarly consensus has to provide whatever authority is required. In the meantime, it provides a source for scholarly disputation, conference papers, publications, and new editorial undertakings.

One of these undertakings, the parallel edition of the four versions of *Piers* by Schmidt, has now appeared. Any comparison of these versions will, however, lead a careful reader to think of the essential *Piers Plowman* as something like the New Testament Gospels: four distinct versions of an original's essential text, each adjusted to meet the preferred emphases of each of the discrete communities for whom these were the Word of God. As the debates of the early church councils and the proliferation of Christian denominations since the Reformation reveal, there is little agreement regarding the literal details of the essential Gospel. In an analogous fashion, the four versions of *Piers* make it almost impossible for readers and critics to achieve common understanding about its meaning, a consummation that will continue to be postponed, of course, as long as *a* specific textual referent for *Piers Plowman* is itself not agreed upon.

Another large-scale editorial project, the *Piers Plowman* Electronic Archive, is also attempting to inform our understanding of the authorial originals by providing in even fuller detail than the Athlone edition the evidence found in the surviving manuscripts. When completed, the PPEA will have produced a complete set of documentary editions of the surviving manuscripts and early prints of *Piers Plowman*, along with (it is to be hoped) new full-color digital facsimiles of the manuscripts. Beginning with the manuscripts of the B version, of which seven have already been published on CDs and others are soon to appear, the PPEA also has a team of editors using the detailed information produced in these documentary editions to provide a more complete foundation for a new critical edition of the B archetype, the purported original identifiable behind all the surviving manuscripts. This will not, as the Athlone editions did, aim to approximate the authorial original; rather, it will offer what the editors, following the principles of the genealogical method, view as the closest they can get to that on the basis of the textual witnesses that have come down to us. The PPEA team has also begun work on editions of the A manuscripts, and eventually these will be joined by documentary editions of C manuscripts, and critical editions of A and C.

This present edition originally aimed to update the Knott and Fowler edition, by revising its text to take account of the textual and literary scholarship of the intervening half century. But in the end, as a result of comments on this plan by colleagues, the present edition has adopted a different strategy. As mentioned already, the existing editions of the A version (including recently that in Schmidt's *Parallel-Text*) adopt the Trinity MS as their base text. This decision has considerable merit on the basis of its early date and high quality . The manuscript deserves an important position in any discussion of the A version, but although both genealogical and eclectic editors accord it primary status, it stands only marginally first among more or less equals.

In the interest of reintroducing to modern students and readers something of the textual variety of medieval manuscript culture and reopening discussion of the *forms* of the A version, this edition has been based not on the Trinity MS but instead on Bodleian Library, MS. Rawl. poet. 137, whose text (despite its containing the later added thirteenth passus) ranked highly in the stemma of Knott-Fowler and in what (to avoid the genealogical implication) Kane terms "[p]ersistent variational groups" (*A Version*, 85). Unlike Trinity (and two of its closest siblings, Harley 6041 and Chaderton), MS. Rawl. poet. 137 is arguably less affected by readings from B and C manuscripts and does not "complete" its text of *Piers* as these, and other, manuscripts do, with passūs from the C version. We may characterize this present edition, then, as a critically edited documentary edition of the Rawlinson MS, and thus it adopts sensible readings from this manuscript even when they are unique among the extant variants. (The textual notes will indicate where the edition diverges substantively from the MS. Rawl. poet. 137.) Where lines make sense in Rawlinson, we leave them to make their own sense; where they seem not to make any clear sense, we find ways to add to or emend them so that they do make good sense. In some respects, this edition shares characteristics of a best-text edition (like Bennett's partial edition of the B version), without adopting the underlying claim that it is "the best single copy of th[e] version extant" (Bennett, viii). If it succeeds in approximating the other principles of that edition, it will have more than achieved its aims.

The main reason for selecting the Rawlinson MS as the focus for the edition, if not to advance a claim that it is "the best single copy," is to present in accessible form one interesting and important manuscript of *Piers* A and to offer it as a reasonable (and readable) artifact of that version of the poem that was produced in the early fifteenth century. As neither the earliest nor the (claimed) closest to the author's original, it is nevertheless a representative text of *Piers Plowman* that deserves attention for itself and for what it can tell us about the transmission of an influential document of fourteenth-century English literary and intellectual culture.

The Language of *Piers* A, including Spelling and Punctuation

The period of *Piers Plowman* is one that sees, in and around the royal court in Westminster and various government offices (especially Chancery) in London, the beginnings of a standard, official "dialect" of written English. Because much of this standardization is for a considerable time limited to London and, in any event, postdates the creation and early copying of *Piers*, we find a rich variety of prestandard spellings of English in the surviving manuscripts of *Piers*, which are widely distributed in the southern half of Great Britain. The manuscripts of *Piers* A have the most expansive distribution and appear to be more distantly related (in both time and geography) to their original(s). As a result, the various manuscripts evidence more layers of dialect spellings and variations in scribal orthography than are apparent in the manuscripts of the later B and C versions. Many of the B manuscripts cluster in and about London and show in many cases evidence of efforts to standardize and fix the text; and the manuscripts of C are concentrated in the West, in Gloucestershire and the Malvern Hills (Samuels). The monumental *Linguistic Atlas of Late Medieval English* (McIntosh et al.) provides detailed accounts of the provenance and the main dialects of most of these manuscripts, and while there is strong influence of Southwest Midland forms in most witnesses to the A version, it is difficult to establish an underlying authorial dialect and orthography.

In the case of the MS. Rawl. poet. 137, the base text for this edition, however, we have persuasive evidence that points to its scribe's linguistic home as being in southwest Sussex. In fact, recent research has shown that we can go even further and identify the scribe by name, as a priest named Thomas Tilot (ca. 1382 to post-1436), who lived and worked in the diocese of Chichester (Horobin). Records show that in 1410 he was ordained deacon (September) and priest (December) with the support of the Augustinian priory at Hardham (Sussex) and was listed as a vicar at Chichester Cathedral in 1415. In addition to the Rawlinson *Piers*, he copied at least one other important Middle English text, the *Prick of Conscience* (Oxford, University College, MS 142). He signed both it and the copy of *Piers* in MS. Rawl. poet. 137: *Nomen scriptoris tilot* (Univ: *thomas*) *plenus amoris*.

Printed editions of a medieval English text are forced to make choices among the various options available for representing the language of that text. Our modern presumption that there is, or *should* be, a standard or correct spelling of words is by no means the operative principle in the later Middle Ages, though we may begin to see an evolution toward a standard orthography about the time the Rawlinson MS is being produced. In the absence of any fully standardized spelling of English in the time of *Piers Plowman*, editors contend with texts that reveal a variety of scribal practices in representing the *sounds* of the words that comprise them. Medieval scribes might represent the sounds of, say, spoken vowels in various ways, especially when a scribe is copying texts written in a dialect different from his own. Some, especially those who are professional scribes copying the Bible or legal texts, could be quite careful to reproduce the text before them exactly as it appears. Others, however—and this seems frequently the case with those writing down vernacular texts—might make the words their own, by inserting their own more familiar forms of words for those in their exemplar, the original they are copying.

Sometimes this results in entire words being replaced; more frequent, however, are the conscious or unconscious variations in spelling, the result perhaps of the scribes' silent pronunciation of the words they are reading and copying. So, for instance, we find Tilot's text varying between <a> and <o> (e.g., *balder* [4.92] vs. *bolder* [8.168]), or <e> and <y> (e.g., *byfel* [8.141] vs. *befel* [8.147]), or, in the case of consonants, between <c> and <k> (or <c> and <s>), or between <ssch> and <x> and <sk> (e.g., *assched* [1.71] vs. *asked* [5.58] vs. *axede* [5.148]). Which of these is his own preferred form, if indeed he has one, and which may point back to an earlier scribe's, or author's, preference, is difficult to settle decisively. Of course, similar variants continue to show up in transcriptions of modern English dialects, and the tension continues between "correct" spelling (as established by dictionaries, editors, and schoolteachers) and successfully communicative (if unconventional) spellings of contemporary spoken language, such as we find in, for instance, electronic text-messages. Even the iconic standards that did evolve and were purportedly settled by the eighteenth-century dictionaries proved by no means universal, and British and American spellings often differ: e.g., *neighbour* and *neighbor*, *quay* and *key*, and *-ise* and *-ize*. To the degree that modern English spelling reverts to attempts at representing the sounds of a speaker's language (influenced, for instance, by educational movements such as "phonics"), we can expect ourselves to be getting closer to the experience of scribes and early readers of *Piers Plowman*.

But the difficulty with interpreting Middle English spelling practices is not limited to how it represents the spoken language with the conventional letters of the English (or Latin) alphabet. Many, but not all, of the early manuscripts of *Piers Plowman* were produced by scribes who had available to them distinctive letters that have fallen out of the modern English alphabet.

Two of these, þ (thorn) and ȝ (yogh) go back to the earliest days of written English and appear regularly in medieval texts. In some late Middle English manuscripts, these letters were beginning to fall out of use, and many scribes favored, instead, letters in the Latin alphabet: as a result *th* can alternate with þ, and ȝ can be replaced, in varying situations, by <g> (*ȝiftis* ["gifts"]), <gh> (*nyȝt* ["night"]; *plouȝ* ["plough," or "plow"]), <s> (*folyȝ* ["fools"]), <w>" (*saȝ* ["saw," or "say"]), or <y>" (*ȝeres* ["years"]). As many other scribes do, Tilot offers the newer forms alongside the older ones in irregular variation.

Likewise, medieval scribes did not adhere to the modern spelling conventions that distinguish among <i>, <j>, and <y> (e.g., *my* vs. *mine* in Modern English, or *mi* and *myn* in Middle English) and between "u" and "v" (e.g., *vndir* ["under"], *vnlouely* ["unlovely"], *gyue* ["give"]). Many of these conventions have more to do with the letter's position in a word rather than any difference among the sounds they represent.

In his 1841 essay "Self-Reliance," Ralph Waldo Emerson firmly declared, "A foolish consistency is the hobgoblin of little minds." We might debate whether in our own time consistency in spelling should be considered "foolish"; there are distinct advantages to standardized spelling. It would certainly be unfair, however, to condescend to the inconsistent spelling practices of many medieval English scribes and fail to recognize the serious, if competing, principles that produce the scribal texts that survive for us to read and edit. While there is some growing tendency in the late medieval and early modern periods for spelling of English words to become standardized, as a result of institutional practices (e.g., in governmental agencies, such as the Chancery) and the rise of commercial publishers using movable-type printing in the later fifteenth century, it is not really until the dictionaries of the eighteenth century that we really begin to find an insistence on stable graphic representations of English words. Even two centuries after *Piers Plowman*, we have something like twenty different ways of spelling Shakespeare's name in documents from his own lifetime and immediate locale.

The relation of graphs (printed letters) to phones (spoken sounds) is often one that admits of multiple possibilities, and correct spelling is a fungible ideal: the "same" sounds can be accurately represented in various ways. And there was little or no sense that the written form of a word was an iconic ideal. So the scribe of MS. Rawl. poet. 137, Thomas Tilot, was almost certainly not a professional scribe. He was therefore perhaps less governed by any overriding word-based spelling conventions, such as those that were beginning to take shape in later fourteenth- and fifteenth-century English at official centers of legal and government documents, and could happily spell the plurals, or singular possessives, of nouns with endings like *-es* and *-ys*

(and, less frequently, *-is* and *-us*). One (or more) of these might of course
have been the preferred form(s) in the exemplar from which he was making
his copy, but nevertheless his text was not initiated, or corrected, to achieve a
strict regularity in these forms. The evidence of his own practice in regard to
these spellings does not unambiguously point to any demonstrable preference for a *single* form for each word. Some individual forms are no doubt
simply errors in production, the result of confusion or inattention; others
may be mechanical reproductions of forms in his exemplar, of words perhaps unclear or uncertain in meaning to the scribe.

Even in a single line, however, Tilot could offer diverse versions of the
unstressed vowels in these forms of the plural or possessive:

And summe men myrthes to make, as menstralys cunne

(Pr.33)

Pyryes and plomtreys were put to the erthe

(5.16)

Sygnes of Synay, and schellys of Galys

(6.8)

Chesibles for chapeles, cherchis to honoure

(7.19)

And fech the hom faukonys the foules to kylle

(7.32)

Chibolles and skalonys, and ripe cheries manye

(7.276)

Alle shul deye for his dedys, be downes and hilles

(10.175)

Some variants like these have been inventoried by scholars studying the
dialects of Middle English and employed to establish distinctions in regional
pronunciations and usage. A striking instance of this occurs in the third-
person singular forms of many present-tense verbs. Most modern English
dialects mark that form with a final *-s*: for example, I walk/she walks; you
dance/he dances. The ordinary mark of that form, going back to Old English
(and earlier), was *-eth* (or more usually *-eþ*), which survives in some modern
forms of English and is still prominent in texts of the Bible based on the King
James and other early modern translations. In the period during which manuscripts of *Piers Plowman* were being produced, there was a marked tendency
in culturally prominent places such as London for the *-s* form (coming from
the north of England) to gain priority over the *-eth* forms. Chaucer, for exam-

ple, seldom employs the latter. His contemporary, Thomas Tilot, the Sussex canon who wrote the text of *Piers* in the Rawlinson MS, uses both forms, sometimes in the same line:

The water is lyk to this world, that waxeth and wanyes

(9.35)

In at least one instance, even the same word appears with the two different endings in a single line:

The pound that sche weyes by weyeth a quarter more

(5.130)

Given this scribe's spelling practices, which are fairly representative of the variety of forms that we find in many medieval vernacular manuscripts, this edition has not attempted to simplify his forms or to adjudicate among them. In the case of this scribe's many abbreviations, which are expanded in this edition, when there are variant forms we have opted to expand the abbreviation with the more common of the forms used elsewhere. As a result, in the inflections for the plural or possessive, we expand the abbreviation with −*es*, which appears most frequently when those forms are not abbreviated. In cases, such as those given here, where the variant forms are fully spelled out, we have reproduced them as written.

In addition to variations in spelling and inflections, a few other differences from modern usage may be useful to note. The second-person singular of verbs (in the present and past indicative) have the usual −*st* ending (with various vowels preceding): for example, *Thou myghthist* (Pr.90), *sclepyst thou* (1.5), *thou wroughtest* (1.13), or *thou hast* (2.82). Also, the past participles of verbs are at times, but not always, marked by a prefixed <y> (derived from the earlier Germanic perfective prefix <ge>): for example, *gif* (2.82) and *ygif* (5.209).

A more frequent and more noticeable difference from Modern English can be seen in the Middle English pronouns, in subject (object; possessive) forms:

	Modern English	*Middle English*
SINGULAR		
1st:	I (me; my, mine)	I, y (me; my, mi, myn)
2nd:	you (your, yours)	thou (the; thi, thy, thin, thyn)
3rd:	he (him; his)	he (hym, him; his, hys)
	she (her, hers)	sche, she, he (hure, hire, here, her)
	it (it; its)	hit, it (hit, it; his, hys)

PLURAL

1st:	we (us; our, ours)	we (us; oure, our)
2nd:	you (your, yours)	ye (you, yow; your, youre, yowre)
3rd:	they (them; their, theirs)	thei, they, hy (hem, hym; here, her, hire)

Punctuation is very lightly used in medieval manuscripts, and this is true of MS. Rawl. poet. 137. This edition has followed more modern practice. It has done the same with respect to capitalization: readers will find modern punctuation and capitalization, along with the modern English alphabet.

The appearance of an asterisk in the left margin of a verse line indicates the presence of an explanatory note in the endnotes.

PIERS PLOWMAN: THE A VERSION

Prologue

Hic incipit liber qui vocatur Pers Plowman: Prologus. — "Here begins the book which is called Piers Plowman: Prologue."

In a somyr sesoun, whenne I south wente, — spring

I schop me a schroude, as I a schep were. — dressed myself in; woolen cloak; sheep

In abyte as an ermyte unholy of werkys, — habit; hermit

Y wente wyde in this worlde, wondrys to hure.

5* But upon a May morwe on Malverne hyllys — morning

Me byfel a ferly, of fayrye me thoughte. — There happened to me; an unusual thing; fantasy/enchantment; it seemed to me

I was wery forwandred; I wente me to reste — worn out with wandering

Under a brod banke by a burne syde. — broad; small stream's

But as I lay and lenede and loked on the waterys, — reclined/rested

10 I slombryd in a slepyng. I swevenede so merye, — dreamed

Ther gan I to mete a merwelous swovene: — did; dream; wonderful dream

That I was in a wildernysse, I wyste nevere where; — wilderness; knew

But as I behelde into the este, up to the sunne, — looked

I saw a tour in a coste, tryly ontyrid; — castle/fortress; hillside; excellently; decorated

15* A dep dale bynethe, a doungon therynne, — beneath; dungeon

With depe dykys and derke, dredful of syghth. — ditches; frightening; awe-inspiring; appearance

A fayr felde ful of folke fonde I bytwene, — found

Of alle maner of men, the mene and the riche, — kinds; lower class/poor; powerful/rich

Worchynge and wandrynge as this worlde askys: — working; moving about; requires

20 Somme putte hem to the plow, and pleyde ful selde, — themselves; played; very; seldom

In seed tyme of sowyng swonkyn ful harde, — worked

Wonne that thes wastorys now wyth glotonye destroyen. — To produce; what; idlers

Some putte hem to pride, and paralyde hem therafter: — devoted themselves; dressed up/decked out

In countenance of clothing they comyn dysgysed. — display; dressed

25 To prayere and to penaunce putte hem many, — penitential actions

	For the love of oure Lord lyvede ful strayte,	very strictly
	In hope for to have heveneryche blysse,	kingdom of heaven's
*	As ankerys and hermytes that lyven in her cellys,	recluses
	And coveytyn noughth in the countre to caryen aboute,	desire; not; travel
30	For none lykerous lyflode here lykamys to plese.	luxurious/dainty/self-indulgent; livelihood/lifestyle; bodies
*	And somme chosen hem to chaffare: they chevyd the betere,	trade/commercial business; succeeded
	As it ys sene to oure syghth that suche men thryven.	become rich
*	And summe men myrthes to make, as menstralys cunne,	entertainments; produce (in verse); are able to/know how to
	Gete gold with her gle, synneles, I trowe.	singing/music; believe
35	Ac japeris and jangeleres, Judacys chyldryn,	But; jesters; chatterers; Judas's
	Gon fyndyn meny fantasyes and foles hem makyn,	did; invent
	And han wit at her wille to worche what hem lykys.	intelligence/knowledge; if they wanted; work; it pleases
*	That that Poule precheth of hem I dar not provyn here:	Paul; preaches; apply/declare
*	*Qui loquitur turpiloquium* ys Lucyferes hyne.	"He who speaks evil"; servant
40	Beggeres and bydderes faste aboute yede,	beggars; everywhere; went
	Til her belyes and her bagges ware bredful crammed;	completely full (? full of bread)
	Thei flyteth for her foode, and fyghthen at the ale;	deceive
	In glotenye, God wot, go thei to bedde,	knows
*	And rysen up with rybaudye, as robertes knavys;	debauchery/lewd behavior; Robert's; servants
45	Sclep and slowthe sewyth hem evere.	sleep; laziness; pursue; always
*	Pylgrymys and palmeres plytyth hem togedere	professional pilgrims; contract/agree
*	For to seke Seynt Jame and seyntes in Rome;	search out
	And wente forth in her way with manye wyse talys,	clever; stories
	And hadde leve to lye al her lyf after.	permission; tell lies
50*	Hermytes on an hepe with hokede stavys	crowd; crooks/sticks with curved handles
*	Wente to Walsyngham, and her wenches after.	girlfriends
*	Grete lobyes and longe, loth for to swynke,	Big; lubbers/good-for-nothings; tall; unwilling; work
	Clothed hem in copys to be knowe fro othere;	clerical robes; recognized/distinguished
	Schopyn hem ermytes, here ese to have.	Dressed up; themselves; as hermits
55*	Vicars on fele halve fonden hem to done:	many; sides; establish themselves; act/provide service

Lederes thei be of lovedayes, and with the lawe medle.   *days for reconciling disputes; negotiate*

*   I fonde ther the freres, alle the fower orderes,
    Prechynge the peple for profyt of here wombys,   *their bellies*
*   Glosede the gospel as hem goud lykede,   *Interpreted; best; it pleased*
60   For covetyse of copys construd yt as thei wolde.   *greed; clerical robes; translated; wished*

    Many of tho maystres mown clothen hem at lykyng,   *may; as they liked*
    For her money and her marchaundyse metyn togederis.   *are made for each other*
    Sythe charite hath be chapman, and chef to shryve lordis,   *Since; salesman; especially; grant absolution to*
    Fele ferlis han falle in a fewe yerus;   *many; unusual things / wonders; occurred / taken place*

65   But holy cherche and they holdyn togederys,   *Unless; stand together*
    The moste myschef of this molde mounteth up faste.   *greatest; earth; will increase*
*   Ther prechede a pardoner, a prest as though he were,   *priest*
*   Broughthe forth bullys wyth busschopys selys,   *papal proclamations; bishop's*
*   And seyde hymself myghte asoyle hem alle   *absolve / grant absolution to*
70   Of falsnesse, of fastynge, of avowes brokyn.
    The lewde men leved hym wel, and lykyd his speche,   *uneducated / illiterate; believed*
    Come knelyng up to kyssyn his bullys;
    He blessed hem with his brevet, and blered here eyes,   *letter of indulgence; blinded*
    Raughthe hem with his rageman broches and rynges.   *Grabbed / raked in; from them; bull with seals; brooches*

75*   Thus ye geven yore gold glotonys to helpyn,
    And lenyn hit to loselys that lecherye haunten!   *hand over; to wasters; indulge in*
*   But were the byschop yblessed and worth bothe his erys,   *holy / blessed; ears*
    His selys schulde not be sent to disseyve the peple.   *deceive*
*   I trowe hit be not for the byschop that the boye precheth;   *believe; rascal / rogue*
80   But for the pardoner and the pariches prest departyn the sylver   *because; share*
    That the pore scholde departyn yif that thei ne were.   *ought; divide; did [not] exist*
*   Parsonys and parrys prestes playnen to her byschop,   *parish priests; complain*
*   That her parryssenys ben pore sithen the pestelens tyme,   *parishioners; have been; since; plague*
*   To have a lycence and a leve at Londoun to dwelle,   *freedom; permission*
85*   To synge for symonye, for sylver is swete.   *simony; sweet*
    Ther hovyd an houndred in howys of sylke,   *hung about; caps*
*   Serjauntis tho semede, pletede at the barre;   *Sergeants [of the law]; they; pleaded (cases in court)*

*   Thei pleted for penys and poundyt the lawe,   *money; expounded / pulverized*

Ac non for the love of our Lord opnyd here lyppys. — But; opened

90 Thou myghthist beter mete the myst on Malverne hyllys — measure

Than getyn a mum of her mowth tyl monye be schewyd. — mumbled word; mouths; money; shown

*   I saw ther byschops bolde and bacheleres of dyvyn — bachelors; divinity/theology

Bycome clerkes of acount, the kyng for to serven; — accounting

*   I saw ther archedeknys and denys, that dignyte havyn — archdeacons; deans; high office

95 To preche the peple and pore men to fede; — provide food for

They beth lopyn to Loundoun, thorw leve of here byschop, — gone/slunk off; with permission; their

*   And beth clerkes of the kynges bench, the cuntre to schynde. — become; destroy

Barounys and burgeysys, and bondeagys also, — great nobles; citizens of towns; serfs

I saw in that symble, as ye schul here herafter. — assembly

100* I saw ther bakesteres and brewesteres, bocheres and kokys, — (female) bakers; (female) brewers; butchers; cooks

Wollene webesteres, and weverys of lynene, — of wool; (female) weavers; weavers; linen

Taylowres, taverneres, and tynkeres bothe, — Cloth cutters/tailors; tavern keepers; tinkers/tinsmiths

Masounys, mynores, and many other craftys, — Stone masons; miners

As dykeres and delveres, that don here werk ylle, — ditchdiggers; diggers/farm workers; badly

105* To dryve forth the longe day with "Deusa Damme Eme." — waste; "Sweet Lady Emma" (song)

Cokys and her knawys cryden, "Hote pyes, hote! — servants; Hot pies

* Gode gees and grys! Go we dyne, go we!" — piglets; dine

Taverneres tolled hem, and tolde hem the same, — tavern keepers; beckoned; charged; likewise

* With "Whyt wyn of Oseye, and of Gascoyne, — White; wine; Auxerre; Gascony

110 Of the Ryn and the Rochel, that roost to defye!" — Rhine; La Rochelle; digest

This I saw myself, and seven sythes more. — times

Passus One

Passus primus de visione.

"The first step of the vision."

	Now what this fayre mounteyn may mene, and this derke dalys,	these
	And this felde ful of folk, fayre wil I schewe.	clearly
*	A lufly lady of lere, in lynene was yclothed,	lovely; face; linen
*	Cam doun fro the chyf, and called me fayre,	top (of the mountain); politely
5*	And sayde, "Sone, sclepyst thou? Seyst thou this peple,	are you asleep; Do you see
*	How bysy that thei be aboute the mase?	busy; disordered world
	The moste party of the peple that passyth on lyve,	greatest; portion; pass through / life
	Have thei worschepys of this worlde, thei kepe no bettre;	esteem; care for
	Of other hevene than here hold thei no tale."	account / importance
10	I was aferd of hire face, thow sche fayre were,	afraid; although
	And sayde, "*Mercy*, madame, what may this bymene?"	"If you please" / "Have pity on me" (in French); mean
	"The tour in toft," quod sche, "Trouthe is therinne;	on the hill
	Wolde that thou wroughtest as his word schewys,	He desires; behaved; reveals
	For he is fader of feyth, and formed us alle	father; created
15	With fel and whyt face, and a fyn wyt	skin; white; developed
	For to worschepe hym therwith, whyl that ye ben here;	
	Therfore he lyghthe into erthe to helpe us echone	descended
	Of wollene, of lynene, of lyflode at nede,	woolen; livelihood
*	In mesurable manere, to maken us at ese,	moderate
20	And commaunded of his cortesye in comoun thre thynges;	courtesy
	Are non nedful but tho, to mevyn hem I thenke,	those; mention
	And rekkene hem in resoun; reherse ye hem after:	recount; repeat
	"That on is vesture verylyche, from chele you to save;	one; clothing; truly; cold
	That other mete at your mel, for myschef of yourselve;	food; meal; lest you damage
25	Drynke when thou dryest—ac do hit not out of resoun,	become dry; but
	So that ye wyrche the worce when ye swynke schulde;	may perform; job; work
*	For Lot in his lyf dayes, for lykyng of drynke,	

Dede by his doughtryn as the devel lykyd, did; to/with his daughters; pleased

Delyted hym in drynke, as the devyl wolde, delighted; wanted
30   And lecherye hym laughthe, and lay by hem bothe; took hold of
And al he wyted the wyn, that wyckede dede. blamed; wine; deed
Dred delytable drynke, and thou schalt do the betere; intoxicating
Mesure is medycyne, they thou moche desyre; moderation; though
Al is not good to the gost that the gut askyt, soul/ghost
35   Ne lyfful to lykame, that lyf is to the soule. permissible/life-giving; body; dear
*   Lef not your lykame, for a lyer hem techys, Believe; body
That is this wreched worlde, the to betraye. wretched
For the fend and thy flesch folwyn togedere, fiend; come after; in each other's company

To schende thi sely soule; set hit in thyn herte. ruin; innocent
40   And for thou shuldist be war, I wisse the the beste." aware/wary; advise
*   "A, madame, *mercy*," quod I, "me lykes wel your "thanks"; please
           wordis;
Ac the money of this molde, that men so faste holdys, But; earth
Telleth me to whom that treasoure apendys." belongs
*   "Go to the gospel," quod sche, "that God seyde
           hymselve,
45   Tho the peple hym aposyd with a peny in the temple, When; questioned
Yif thei schulde worschep therwith Sesar the kyng. If; Caesar
And God asked of hem of whom spak the lettere, spoke
And ymage lyke, that therinne standys. likewise
'Sesar,' thei sayde, 'we sen wel echone.' each one
50   '*Reddite Sesari*,' quod God, 'that Sesar byfallyth, "Give to Caesar"; "to Caesar"; belongs (Matt. 22:21; Mark 12:17; Luke 20:25)

Et que sunt dei deo, or ellys ye do ylle.' "And what are God's, to God"
For rygthful resoun schal reule yow alle, just
And kende wit be wardeyn, yowre welthe to kepe, natural knowledge, warden; preserve

And tutour of your tresour, to take hit you at nede; guard; give it to you
55   For husbondrye and he holden togedere." good housekeeping
        Thanne I frayned hure fayre, for hym that hure made: asked; politely
"The doungoun in the dale, that dredful is of syghth,
What may hit bymene, madame, I the byseche?" beseech
        "That is the castel of Care; whoso cometh therto whoever
60   May banne that he bore was to body or to soule. curse
*   Therinne woneth a wyghth that was yhote dwells; creature; called

Fader of falshede—he fonde hit hymself.   *lies; instituted*

Adam and Eve he heggede hem to helle;   *urged on*

And conseyled Caym to kylle his brother;

65 Judas he japede with Jewene sylver,   *mocked; of Jews*

* And sythen on a eldere heng hymself after.   *then; elder; hanged*

He is lettere of love, and seyneth hem alle;   *hinderer/obstacle; puts his mark on; them*

That trustyn on his tresour betrayd ar sonere."   *Those who; sooner*

   Than had Y wonder in my wit what womman hit were   *mind*

70 That suche wyse wordes of holy wryt schewde;   *scripture*

* And assched her on the hye name, or then sche thenne yede,   *asked; in God's name; before; thence; went*

What sche were wyterly that wyssed me so fayre.   *truly; taught*

   "Holychurche I am," quod sche, "thou aughtys me to knowe;   *Holy Church; ought*

* I underfong the furst, and your feyth the taughthe.   *received*

75 Thou broughtest me borwys, my byddyng to wyrche,   *pledges; command; perform*

To love me lely, the whylys thy lyf duryth."   *loyally; endures*

   Thanne I knelyd on my kneys and cryed hure of grace,   *knees; begged*

Prayede hure pytusly to praye for my synnys,   *piously*

And ek teche me kyndely on Cryst to byleve,   *also*

80 That I myghthe wyrke his wille that wroughthe me to manne.   *do; created; as*

* "Teche me to no tresour, but tel me this ylke: *the following*

Hou I may save my soule, that seynt arn yholde."   *holy; regarded*

   "Whenne alle tresoures arn tried," quod sche, "trouthe is the beste;   *tested*

* I do hit on *Deus caritas* to deme the sothe;   *base; "God [is] love" (1 John 4:8,16); judge*

85 Hit is as derworthe a dreury as dere God hymselve.   *precious; treasure*

For whoso is trewe of his tonge, tellith non other,   *whoever; talks (about)*

Doth the werkes therwith, wyllyth no man ylle—   *desires*

* He is a god by the gospel, on grounde and alofthe,   *earth; in heaven*

And eke lyk to oure Lord, by Seynt Jamys wordys.

90 "Clerkes that hit knoweth schulde kenne hit aboute,   *teach*

For crystene and uncrystene cleymeth echone.   *non-Christian; proclaim*

* Kynges and knyghthes schulde kepe hit by resoun,   *in accordance with*

And ryde and rappe adoun in remys aboute,   *strike; down; realms*

And take trespasoures, and tyghe hem faste,   *bind*

95 Til truthe have termynyd here truthe to an ende.   *decided*

*   "For Davyt in his dayes dubbede knyghtes,   *created*

	And dude hem swere on her swerdys to serve truthe evere;	had
	This is the prophecye apertly that apendyth to kynghtes,	plainly; belongs
	And noughth to faste a Fryday in fyve score wynter;	one; years
100	But holde with hym and with hure that asketh the truthe,	desires
	And nevere leve hem for love ne for lachynge of sylver;	nor; taking/receiving
	And he so that pursewyt, he is *apostata* in her ordere.	pursues; "traitor"
*	And Cryst, kyngene kyng, knyghthede tene,	of kings
	Cherubyn and seraphyn, and such sevene othere;	Cherubim; seraphim
105	And gaf hem myghth in his mageste, the meryere hem thoughthe,	to them; it seemed
	And over his mayne made hem archangelys;	household
	Taughthe hem thorw the trinyte the treuthe to knowe;	
	To be buxum at his byddyng, he bad hem nought ellys.	obedient
	"Lucyfere with legyonys lered hit in hevene,	legions; learned
110	And was the lovelekyst of syghth, after oure Lord,	loveliest
	Tyl he brak buxsumnesse thorw bost of hymselve;	broke; obedience; boast
	Thanne fel he with his felawys, and fendys bycome.	companions
	Out of hevene into helle hoblede they faste,	stumbled; quickly
*	Summe in erthe and some in eyre, doun into helle depe;	air
115*	And Lucyfer lowest lyghthe of hem alle;	lies
	For pride that he putte oute, his payne hath non ende.	displayed; punishment/suffering
	And alle that worschepe with Wrong, wende they schulde,	travel
	After here deth day, and dwelle with that schrewe.	cursed one
	Ac tho that worche that word that holycherche techys,	But; those; do/act according to
120	And endeth, as I ere sayde, in parfyte workys,	before; perfect
	Mowe be syker that her soule schal wende into hevene,	may; sure/secure; go
	Ther Truthe is in Trinite, and trowen hem alle.	Where; Trinity; vouch for
*	"Forthy I seye, as I sayde ere, by sent of these tyxtes,	Therefore; say; before; agreement; texts
*	Whanne alle tresures be tryed, Truthe is the beste.	are tested
125*	Leryth thus lewyde men, for letteryd hit knowyn,	Let [them] learn; uneducated; literate/educated
	That Truthe is tresour, the tryeste on erthe."	most treasured
*	"Yut have I no knowynge," quod I, "ye mot me betere teche,	understanding/knowledge; must
	By what crafth in my cors hit cometh, and where."	(living) body
	"Thou dotede daffe," quath sche, "dulle are thy wittes!	stupid; dummy
130	Hit is a kynde knowynge that comes in thyn herte	natural understanding
	For to love thi Lorde lever than thyselvyn;	more dearly

	No dedly synne to do, thegh thou deye schuldest.	mortal; though; die
*	This, I trowe, be Truthe; who can teche the betere,	believe
	Loke thou suffre hym to say, and sythe lere after.	permit; speak; then; learn; in that way
135	For thus witnesseth his word (worche thou therafter):	behave in accord with that
	That love is the levyste thing that oure Lord asketh,	most precious; requires/desires
*	And the plente of pes, prechyd in thyn harpe	plant; peace; proclaimed
	Ther thou art merye at mete, when eny byddyt the yedde.	Where; meal; anyone asks; sing
*	For in kynde knowynge of herte ther cometh a merthe,	happiness
140	And that falleth to the fader that formede us alle,	is attributable
	Lokede on us with love, and let his sone deye	allowed; die
	Meklyche for oure mysdedys, to amende us alle;	meekly; redeem
	And yut wolde hym no wo that wroughthe hym that pyne,	(Jesus) wished; punishment; inflicted suffering
	But mekly by mouthe mercy bysoughthe,	meekly
145	To have pyte on that peple that pyned hym to dey.	tortured
	"Here myghthe thou se exaumples, in hymself one,	alone
	That he was mercyful and meke, and mercy gan graunte	did
	To hem that hengyn hym by, and his herte therled.	hanged; beside; pierced
	"Forthy I rede the thou riche, have reuthe on the pore;	Therefore; advise; you rich man; pity
150	Thow ye be myghthy to mote, beth meke of your workys.	issue orders
*	For the same mesure ye mete, amys other ellys,	distribute; badly or otherwise
	Ye schul be weye therwith, whenne ye goth hennys.	weighed; from here
	Forthy beth trowe of your tonges, and trewlyche wynne,	Therefore; properly; profit/gain wealth
	And ek be chast as a chylde that in the cherche wepys;	chaste/innocent; cries
155*	But ye love lely and lene the pore,	Unless; faithfully; give/lend to
	Of such gode as God sent goudlyche departyn,	wealth; generously; share/give alms
	Ye have no more meryte in masse ne in houres	benefit; masses; hours (divine office)
*	Than Malkyn of hire maydynhede, that no man desyres.	virginity
*	For Jamys the gentyl jugyd in his bokys,	noble; declared (as true)
160	That feyth withoute fet is febelere than noughth,	faith; deed; weaker; nothing
	And ded as a dorenayl, but yif the dede folwe.	doornail; unless
	"Chastite withoute cheryte worth schryned in helle;	charity; will be/deserves to be; enshrined
	Hit is as lewyd as a laumpe that no lyghth is inne.	useless; lamp; light
	Manye chapelaynes are chaste, ac cherite is awaye;	chaplains; but; absent

165 Are no men hardere than they whan they beth   less generous; promoted
        avaunsed.
    Unkynde to her kyn and eke to alle crystene,   relatives; also
    Schewen here cherite and chyden after more: display; whine
    Such chastyte withoute cherite worth schryned in helle. will be/deserves to be; enshrined
        "Ye curatures that kepe you clene of your body,   curates (priests); yourselves
170 Ye beth acombred with synne, ye counne nought out   weighed down; creep
        crepe,
    So hard hath avaryce hasped you togedere!   firmly; greed; latched onto
    That is no truthe of Trynite, but trecherye of helle,
    And a begynnynge to lewede men the latter to dele.   basis (? and encouragement); for;
                                                            uneducated; more slowly;
                                                            distribute [alms]

    For this are wordis ywryten in the Ewangelye: these; Gospel
175 'Date et dabitur vobis, for I dele you alle;   "Give and it will be given to you"
                                                            (Luke 6:38); give you everything
                                                            you need

    That is the lok of love that lateth oute my grace   act; allows
    To comforte the carfulle acombred with synne.'   anxious; weighed down
        "Love ys the levyste thyng that oure Lord asketh,   most precious; desires
    And eke the redyeste gate that goth into hevene.   most available; path
180* Forthy I seye as I sayde ere, by sent of these tyxtes, Therefore; agreement; texts
    Whan alle tresoures are tryde, Truthe is the beste.   tested
        "Now have I told the what Truthe is, that no tresour is than which
        betere,
    I may no longer lette; now loke the oure Lord."   stay; may (Our Lord) look after
                                                            you

Passus Two

Passus secundus de visione.　　　　　　　　　　　"The second step of the vision"

* Yut kneled I on my kneys, and soughthe hure of　　　knees; begged
　　grace,
* And sayde, "*Mercy*, madame; for Marye love of hevene,　　"Have pity"; for the love of Mary
　　　　　　　　　　　　　　　　　　　　　　　　in heaven
　That bare that blessede barne, that boughthe us on the　　child; redeemed; rood (cross)
　　rode,
　Ken me by soum crafte to knowe the Falce."　　　　teach
5* 　"Loke on thy lyfthe half, and loke where he standys,　　left; side
* Bothe Fals and Favel, and his feres alle!"　　　　False; Flattery (Deceit);
　　　　　　　　　　　　　　　　　　　　　　　　companions

　I loked on my lyfthe half, as the lady me taughthe　　side; instructed
* And was war of a womman wonderly yclothed,　　aware; impressively; dressed
　Ypurfyled with pellure, the puryste on erthe,　　fringed/trimmed; fur; finest
10　Ycorouned in a coroune, the kyng hath no betere:　　Crowned; crown
　Of the puryste perreye that prince wered evere;　　most exquisite; gems; wore
　In red scarlet robyd, rybaynyd aboute with golde;　　dressed; striped
* Ther is no quene queyntere that quyk is on lyve .　　queen; more elegant; alive
　　"What is that womman," quod I, "so wonderly　　wonderfully; dressed
　　atyryd?"
15* 　"That is Mede, the mayde, that hath noyed me ful　　harmed
　　ofte,
　And lacked my lore to lordys aboute.　　denigrated; teaching; lords
　In the popys paleys sche is prevy as myselve,　　pope's; palace; intimate
　And so schulde sche not be, for Wrong was hure syre;　　father
* Out of Wrong sche wexe, to wrotherhele manye.　　sprang; evil fortune
20　I aughthe be hyere than sche, for Y come of betere.　　higher; descend
　　"Tomorwe worth the maryage mad of Mede and of　　will be; contracted; False
　　Falce;
* Favel with fayre speche hath forged hem togedere.　　Deceit; joined
　Tomorwe worth the mariage ymade, as I telle;　　will be; contracted
　Ther myghthe thou wyte, yif thou wolt, whych thei ben　　understand; wanted
　　alle
25　That longeth to that lordschep, the lesse and the more.　　belongs; lordship; lesser; greater

Know hem ther yif thou canst, and kep the from hem
    alle, — *Identify; are able*

* Yif thou thenkest to wone with Truthe in his blysse; — *expect; dwell*

I may no lenger lette—Lord I the byteche, — *stay; commend*

And become a goud man for eny covetyse, I rede." — *in spite of; covetousness; advise*

30*   Al the ryche retenaunce that ryneth with Falce — *retinue; runs (? reigns)*

Were ybede to the bredale on bothe two sydys. — *invited; wedding*

* Syre Symonye is ofsent to sele the chartres — *Simony; sent for; seal; contracts*

That Fals other Favel by ony fyn holdeth, — *or; license/transfer fee; obtains*

And feffe Mede therwith, in maryage for evere. — *endow*

35* Ther nas halle ne hous to herberwe the peple — *was; not; provide accommodation for*

That ech feld nas ful of folke aboute. — *with the result that; was*

In myddes a mounteyne, at mydmorwe tyme, — *halfway up; midmorning*

Was pyghth up a pavyloun, proud for the nones; — *pitched; pavilion*

And ten thousand tentys tyghth ther bysydes, — *raised up*

40* Of knyghthys, of cortyeres, of comeres aboute, — *courtiers; visitors*

* For sysores, for somnerys, for selleres, for byggeres, — *jurymen; summoners; buyers*

For leryd, for lewyd, for laboreres, for threpis, — *learned; ignorant; villages/hamlets*

Alle to witnesse wel what the wryt wolde, — *official document; declared*

In what maner that Mede in mariage was feffed; — *endowed*

45 To be fastnyd with Fals the fyn is areryd. — *license/transfer fee; prepared/produced*

   Thanne Favel fettyth hire forth, and to Fals taketh, — *fetched*

* In forward that Falshede schal fynde hire for evere, — *agreement; falsehood; support*

* And sche be buxoum at his bode his biddyng to fulfylle, — *obedient; command; instructions*

At bedde and at bord, buxoum and hende, — *obedient; compliant/agreeable*

50 And at Sire Symonyes wille, to schewyn his heste. — *Simony's; show; command*

   Symonye and Syvyle standes up bothe, — *Civil Law*

And unfoldeth the feffyment that Fals hath makyd, — *unfurls; deed of endowment*

Thus bygynneth this gome and gretyth wel eche: — *man; addresses; everyone*

* "Wyten and witnessen, that woneth upon erthe, — *listen; dwell*

55 That I, Favel, have feffed Falsnesse to Mede, — *entrusted*

To be present in pryde, for pore or for ryche, — *poverty; wealth*

With the erledom of Envye evere to laste,

With al the worschep of Lecherye, in lengthe and in
    brede; — *high office; breadth*

With the kyngdome of Covetise I crowne you togedere,

60 And alle the vycys of Usures and Avaryce the faste; — *vices; Usury; strong/unyielding*

Glotonye and Gret Othis, I gyf hem togedere

* With alle the lytes of Lust the devel for to serve; — *estates*

In al the seygnorye of Scleuthe I sese hem togedere,   landed estate; Sloth; endow
They to have and holde, and here eyres after,   heirs
65* With al the portunances of Purgatorye, into the pyne of   appurtenances; as far as; pain(s)
    Helle:
Yeldynge for this thing, at on yeres ende,   Giving in return; one
Here soulis to Sathanas, and synke into pyne,   souls; Satan; torment
Ther to wone with Wrong, whilys God is in hevene."   reside; as long as
    In witnesse of which thing Wrong was the fyrste,
70* Peres the pardoner, Paulyns doctor,
And Bette the bydul, of Bokyngham schyre,   Bartholomew/Bertram; town
                                                                        crier/ herald in court of justice;
                                                                        Buckinghamshire
*   Randolf the reve, of Rokelond sokne,   steward; Rockland (? in Norfolk);
                                                                        jurisdiction
Mundy the mylnere, and many mo other.   miller; more
*   "In the date of the devel this dede I asele,   contract; seal
75* By seyt of Sire Symonye and sygnys of notories."   in the presence of; signatures;
                                                                        notaries

    Thanne tenyde hym Theologie, when he this tale   got angry; heard
        hurde,
*   And sayde to Syvyle, "Sorwe on thy bokys   Civil Law; A curse; books
Such weddyng to worche to werre with Truthe;   make; fight/wage war
And or this weddyng be ywroughth, wo the bytyde!   before; consummated; may woe
                                                                        befall you
80* For Mede is muliere of frendis engendryt;   (legitimately born) woman;
                                                                        relatives/friends
God graunteth to gyve Mede to Truthe,   intends
And thou hast gif hure to a gyloure!   deceiver
The tyxte telleth not so, Truthe wot the sothe: scripture; knows; truth
*   Dignus est operarius mercede.   "A worker deserves wages" (Luke
                                                                        10:7; 1 Tim. 5:18; cf. Matt. 10:10)
85 'Worthi is the werkman mede to have.'   wages/payment/reward
And thou hast fastned hure with Fals—fy on thy lawes!   joined
For al by lesynges thou lyvest, and lecherouse werkes;   lies
Symonye and thiself schendeth holy cherche;   harm
Ye and the notoryes noyghen the peple.   notaries; injure
90 Ye schul abyghe bothe, by God that me made!   shall; pay for; the two of you
    "Wel ye wyte, warnerdys, but yif your wit fayle,   know; deceivers; unless
That Fals is faytour, and fals of his werkes,   imposter
*   And as bastard ybore of Belsabuckes kynne.   born Beelzebub's kin
And Mede is muliere, a mayden of gode;   freeborn woman; property
95 Sche myghthe kysse the kyng for cosyn, yif sche wolde.   cousin; wanted

Worcheth by wysdoum, and by wit after: *Act according to*
* Ledyth hure to Londone, ther lawe is handlyd, *take; where; legal matters; conducted*

Yif eny leute wil loke they lygge togedere, *(to see) whether; right thinking; permit; lie*

And Justyse jugyn hure to be joynyd with False. *determine*
100 Yut be war of that weddyng, for witty is Treuthe; *wise*
For Conciens is of his conseyl, and knoweth you echone; *recognizes*
And yif he fynde you in the faute, and with the Falce holdyn, *error; linked*
Hit schal beset your soulys wel sore at the laste." *weigh on; very bitterly; end*
Herto asenteth Syvyle, ac Symonye nolde *To this; Civil; agreed; but; would not*

105 Til he hadde sylver for celys and sygnys. *seals; signatures*
* Thanne fette Favel forth floures ynowe, *fetched; florins; enough*
And bad Gile go gyve gold anon al aboute, *ordered; immediately*
And namlyche to the notoryes, that hem non faylede, *especially; so that; none of them; went without*

* And feffe Fals-witnesse with floures ynowe— *supply; florins*
110 "For he may Mede amastrye, and make at my wille." *win over; conform*
Tho this gold was ygyve, gret was the thankyng *When; distributed*
To Fals and to Favel for here grete gifthes;
And come to comforte fro care the Falce *from*
And "Certes" sayde, "sece schulle we nevere *Assuredly; cease; shall*
115 Tyl Mede be thy wedded wyf, thorw wit of us alle; *? vigorous effort/? cunning*
For we have Mede amaystryid with oure merye speche *won over; sweet talk*
That sche graunteth to go with a good wylle *agrees*
To Londone and loke yif that the lawe wolde *see whether*
Jugen you joyntlyche in lawe for evere." *Declare*
120 Thanne was Falce fayn, and Favel as blythe, *pleased; happy*
And let somone alle the seggis in scheres aboute, *summon; men; shires*
And alle beth bon, beggeres and othre, *ready*
To wende with hem to Westmynystre, to witnesse this dede.
Thanne caryd they for capelys to caryyn hem theder; *went; horses; carry; there*
125* Thanne fette Favel folys therof the beste, *foals/fools*
* Sette Mede on a schyrreve, yschod al newe, *sheriff; newly shod*
And Fals on a sysour that softly trotted, *juryman*
And Favel upon a fayre speche, fetysly atyryd. *handsomely/exquisitely; dressed*
Tho hadde notorijs none, anoyghed they were, *when/because; notaries; angry*
130 And Symonye and Syvyle schulde on here fet gange. *had to go; their*
* Than seyde Syvyle, and swore by the rode, *cross*

That "Somnores schulde be sadlyd and servyn hem   summoners; saddled
   echone—

* And let hem parayle the provysoures in palfray wyse;   outfit/dress up; holders of papal
                                                benefices; saddle horse; fashion

Sire Symonye himself schal syttyn on here backes
135* And alle the denys and subdenys as destreres hem   deans; subdeans; war horses;
   dyghthe,   prepared
For thei schulle bere these bisschopys and brynge hem   bear
   at her reste.

* Paulynus peple, for pleyntes in constorye,   Pauline's; complaints;
                                            ecclesiastical court

* Schulle serve myself, that Sevyle hatte;   shall; Civil; is; named
* And sadle the comysarye—oure cart schal he drawe,   bishop's officer
140* And fette in oure vytaylys of fornicatoures;   fetch; food; from fornicators
And makyn of Liere a long cart, to lede al this othere,   Liar; carry/convey; these others
As folys and faytoures that on here fet rennys;   fools; deceivers/pretenders; run
And Mede the maydyn, and al the mayne after."   company
*   I have no tyme to telle the tayl that hem folwyd,   enumerate; retinue; them
145 Of meny maner men that on this molde lybbys;   earth; lives
Ac Gyle was foregoere and gredde hem alle.   but; the advance man; called
                                              aloud to

Sothnesse seth hem wel and seyth but lytyl,   Truthfulness; watches; says
But prikede forth on his palfray, and pasede hem alle,   spurred
And cam to the kynges curt, and Conciense tolde,   court
150 And Concyense to the kyng carpede after.   spoke
    "By Crist," quod the king, "and I myghthe chacche   if; catch
Fals other Favel, other eny of his ferys,   or; companions
I wolde bewreke me of tho wrecchis that wroughthyn so   avenge; myself; on; bastards;
   ylle,   acted/behaved; badly/wickedly
And don hem hange by the hals, and alle that hem   have them hanged; neck; support
   manteynyth;
155 Schal nevere man on this molde meynpryse the beste,   earth; provide bail; (even) the best
                                            of them

But ryghth as the lawe loketh, lat falle on hem alle!"   provides
* And comandyth a constable—he come at the fyrste—   ordered; immediately
To "Take the tyrauntes, for eny tresour yhote;   arrest; despite; bribes; promised
Feteryth Falsnysse faste, for eny skynnes gyftys,   fetter; securely; in spite of; kind
160 And gaderyth of Gylis hed—lat hym go no ferther;   pull off; Guile's
And bryngeth Mede forth, maugre hem alle.   in spite of
Symonye and Sevyle, I sende hem to warde   Civil; prison
That holy chyrche for hem worth harmed for evere.   Because; on account of; would be
And yif ye lacche Lyere, lat hym naughth aschape,   get hold of; not; escape

165   Ere he be put on the pylory, for eny tresour yhote."
                                                                              before; pillory; no matter what
                                                                              bribes are promised

      Drede at the dore stant and that dome herde,
                                                                              stood; decision
      And wyghthlyche wente to warne the Falce,
                                                                              quickly
      And bad hym fle for fere, and his feres alle.
                                                                              told; fear; companions
*   Tho Falsnesse for fere fley to the freres,
                                                                              flees; friars
170   And Gyle doth hym to go, agast for to deye;
                                                                              prepares to leave; afraid; die
      Ac marchauntes mette with hym, and made hym abyde,
                                                                              but; merchants; got him to stay
      Beschette hym in here schoppes, the peple to serve.
                                                                              shut; shops; customers
         Lyghthlyche Lyere lepte away thennys,
                                                                              quickly; Liar; from there
      Lurkande thorw lanys, to be logged of manye.
                                                                              Skulking; alleys; sheltered /
                                                                              concealed; by

175   He was nowher welcome, for his many talys;
                                                                              because of; lies
      Overal yhonted and yhote trusse,
                                                                              everywhere; hunted; ordered to
                                                                              get moving

      Til pardoneres hadde pite, and pulled hym to house,
      Waschede hym and wyped hym and wounde hym in
                                                                              Washed; cleaned up; wrapped
         clothes,
      And sente hym on Sondayes with selys to cherche,
180   And yaf pardoun for pens, poundmele aboute.
                                                                              gave; indulgences; money; by the
                                                                              pound

*   Thanne lourede lechys, and letteres tho sente,
                                                                              frowned; doctors
      For to wone with hem, wateres to loke.
                                                                              dwell; waters (urine); examine
      Spysourys spak with hym, to aspye her ware,
                                                                              dealers in food stuffs; look over
      For he coude on her crafte, and knoweth many
                                                                              because; was knowledgeable
         gummys.
                                                                              about; tricks; aromatic gums
185   Menstralys and messageres mette with hym onys,
                                                                              once
*   And withheld hym half yere and enleve dayes.
                                                                              held him back; eleven
         Freres, with fayre speche, fetten hym thennys,
                                                                              friars; sweet talk; fetched; from
                                                                              there

*   For knowyng of comeres, copyd hym as a frere;
                                                                              to prevent his being recognized;
                                                                              visitors / strangers; dressed in a
                                                                              cloak

      Ac he hath leve to lepe in and out, as ofte as hym lykyth,
                                                                              but; come and go; it pleases
190   And ys welcome when he wol, and woneth with hem
                                                                              wants (to stop by); stays; a lot
         ofthe.
         Alle fleddyn for fere and flowyn into hernys;
                                                                              fled; fear; escaped; corners
      Save Mede the mayden, no mo dorste abyde.
                                                                              except; no one else dared hang
                                                                              around

      Ac treuly for to telle, sche tremelyd for drede,
                                                                              but; shook for fear
      And eke wep and wrong, when sche was atached.
                                                                              cried; wrung her hands; arrested

Passus Three

Now is Mede the mayde name of hem alle,   taken away; from

And with bedelys and baylifys broughth to the king.   by; heralds in the court of justice; bailiffs

The king called a clerk—I can not his name—   don't know

To take Mede the mayde, and make hure at ese:

5 "I wolde asaye hure myself, and sothly avise   examine; truly; consider

What man of this molde that hure were levyst;   earth; most desirable

And yif sche wyrke by wyt, and my wil folwe,

I wil forgyf hure the gylt, so me God helpe."

Curteysly the clerk than, as the king hyghthe,   commanded

10 Tok Mede by the myddel, and broughthe hure to chaumbere.   waist

And ther was merthe and mynstrasye Mede to plese;   minstrelsy

And tho that wone at Westmenstre worschepyn hure alle,   dwell; did her homage

Gently with joye; the justyse tosompne   courteously; justices; together in a group

Busked hem to the bour, ther the berde duellyth;   hastened; themselves; private room/antechamber; girl/bride; is staying

15 Comfortyth hure kyndely, by clergyes leve,   permission

And sayde, "Murne not, Mede, ne make thou no sorwe;

For we wil wisse the kyng and thi wey make,   advise

For al Concienses cast and craft, as I trowe."   contrivance; plotting; believe

Myldelyche Mede than mercyed hem alle   graciously; thanked

20 Of here gret goudnesse, and gaf hem echone   For their

Coupys and clene gold, and pecys of sylver,   cups; pure; pieces

Rynges with rubeys, and rychesses manye;   rubies; valuable things

The leste man of here mayne a motoun of golde.   household; French coin

Than laughthe thei leve, thes lordes at Mede.   took; from

25 With that come clerkes to comforte hure thanne,

And bode hure be blythe—"for we beth thyn owyn   told; happy; on your side

For to wyrche thy wylle, whyl oure lyf lasteth."   carry out your desires

Hendelyche sche thanne behyghth hem the same, *Courteously; promised*

"To love you lelly and lordys you make, *loyally*

30 And in constorye at the court calle youre names. *consistory (ecclesiastical court)*

Ther schal no lewednysse hem lette, the lede that I lovie, *ignorance; hinder; person*

That he ne worth furste avaunsed; for I am beknowe *will be; promoted; well known*

Ther counynge clerkes schul clocke behynde." *clever; should limp*

Than cam ther a confessour, ycoped as a frere; *dressed; friar*

35 To Mede the mayde meklyche he lowtede, *humbly; bowed*

And seyde wel softly, a schryft as hit were, *very; in; confession*

"They lered and lewed hadde loyn by the alle, *Though; learned [men]; ignorant; lain*

And thei Falsnesse hadde yfolwed the this enleve wynter, *even if; followed; these eleven years*

I schal asoyle the myself, for a sem whete, *absolve; eight bushels*

40 And eke be thi bawdekyn, and bere wel thin arnde *also; procurer/pimp; carry; message*

* Among clerkes and knyghthis, Conciense to felle." *kill*

Than Mede, for hure mysdedes, to the man knelyd,

* And schrof of her schrewedenesse, schameles, I trowe; *confessed; wickedness; without any shame; believe*

Tolde hym a tokne, and tok hym a noble, *plausible story; gave; noble (gold coin worth 6 shillings 8 pence, or one-third of a pound)*

45* For to be hure bedman, and hure baude after. *beadsman; procurer*

Than he asoyled hure sone, and swythe he sayde, *absolved; immediately; quickly*

* "We have a wyndowe at wyrchyng, wil stonde us hyghe; *being constructed; cost*

Woldest thou glase the gable, and grave ther thy name, *if you were to glaze; inscribe*

Sikyr schulde thy soule be hefne to have." *certain; heaven*

50 "Wiste I that," qwath the womman, "ther is no wyndowe ne auter *knew; altar*

That I ne schuld make and amende, and my name wryte, *construct; repair; inscribe*

* That ech segge schal se I am suster of your house." *so that; each person; order/community*

* And God alle gode folke such gravyng defendeth and seyth: *engraving; forbids*

"*Nesciat sinistra quid faciat dextera*: *"Do not let the left hand know what the right hand is doing" (Matt. 6:3)*

55 Let nought thy lyft half, late ne rathe, *side; early*

Wite what thy ryt half worchyt or delyth." *know; right side; is doing; distributes [in alms]*

And so pryvylyche parte hit that pride be not seye — *in secret/without fanfare; share; so that; seen*

Neyther in syth ne in soule; for God hymself knoweth — *visibly; spiritually*
Who is curteys or kynde, or coveytes or ellys. — *courteous; otherwise*
60 Forthi I rede you lordes, such wrytynges levyth, — *Therefore; advise; give up*
To wryte in wyndowys of your wel dedys,
* Or to gredyn after Godys men when ye gyve dolys; — *call loudly; alms*
* An auntere ye have your hyre ther of youre gode. — *by chance (= lest perhaps); will have; wages; good (deeds)*

For oure saveour seyde, and hymself preched.
65* Meyrys and maysteres, ye that beth mene — *magistrates; intermediaries*
Bytwythe the king and the common, to kepe the lawes, — *Between; preserve*
As punschin on pylorijs, and on pynnyng-stolys, — *pillories; stools for punishment*
* Breweres, bakeres, bocheres, and kokys— — *butchers; cooks*
For thes are men on molde that most harme werkyn — *earth*
70 To this pore puple that parcelmele beggen. — *bit by bit; buy*
For they poysone the puple pryvyly wel ofte, — *in secret; very*
And rechyn thorw regratyng, and rentes hem buggen — *get rich; selling at retail; revenue-producing properties; for themselves; purchase*

Of that the pore puple schulde pote in her wombes. — *with what; put; stomachs*
For ne tok he ontrewely, he tymbred not so hye, — *if he had not accumulated wealth wrongly; erected timber [frames for houses]*

75 Ne boughthe none bargayns, be thou wel certeyne! — *merchandise; very*
And Mede the mayden the meyr sche besowghthe — *mayor; begged*
Of alle suche selleres sylver to take, — *from*
* Or presentes withoute pens, as peces of sylver, — *cash; items*
Ryng or other rychesses, thes regrateres to meyntene. — *valuable items; buyers and sellers*
80 "For my love," quod that lady, "love hem ychone,
And suffre hem to selle sumdel ageyn resoun." — *somewhat against*
* Salomon the sage, a sermoun he made, — *Solomon*
To amende meyres and men that kepe the lawes, — *straighten out; mayors; preserve*
And tok hem this teme that I telle thinke: — *presented; theme; intend*
85 *Ignis devorabit tabernacula eorum qui libenter accipiunt munera.* — *"Fire will consume the tents of those who willingly accept gifts" (Job 15:34)*

Among these lettered men this Latyn amounthyth — *educated; signifies*
That fyre schal falle and forbrenne at the laste — *burn up completely; end*
The hous and the homes of men that desyren — *houses*
To have giftes of here servises in youthe or in elde. — *for; old age*
90 The king, for his counseyl, calde after Mede,

And ofsente hire swythe, with serjauntes hire fette,   *sent after; quickly; sergeants*

* And broughthe hire to boure with blysse and with joye.   *a private room*

    Curtaysly the king comseth to telle,   *commences; talk*

To Mede the mayden melus these wordes: *speaks*

95 "Onwyttyly wroughth hast thou wel ofte;   *Foolishly; acted/done; very*

And worse wroughthest thou nevere than tho thou Fals   *when*
    toke.

But I forgyve the that gylt, and graunte the grace   *amnesty*

Hennys to thy dethday—do thou so no more!   *From now on; if you do*

    "I have a knyght hyghth Conciens, come late fro   *named; recently; across the sea*
      byyonde;

100 Yif he wil the to wyve, wilt thou hym have?"   *is willing; marry*

*   "Ye, lord," quod that lady, "Lord forbede ellys;   *otherwise*

But I be holly at your heste, honge me ellys."   *unless; entirely; command; hang*

Than was Conciens cald and cam to apeyren   *appear*

* Byfore the king and his counseyl, clerkes and othere.

105 Knelyng, Concyens to the king louted   *humbly bowed (and asked)*

What his wille were, and what he don schulde.

    "Wil thou wedde this womman, yif I wil asente?

For sche is fayn of thi felaschep, for to be thy make."   *eager; companionship; spouse*

*   Qwath Conciens to the king, "Crist hit me forbede!

110 Ere I wedde such a wyf, wo me betyde!   *may sorrows oppress me!*

Sche is frethil of hure fleys, fykel of hure speche;   *foul; flesh; untrustworthy*

Sche maketh men mysdo manye skore tymes;   *do wrong*

In trust of hure tresour sche teneth wel manye.   *very; injures*

Wyves and wedues wantonnesse techeth;   *widows*

115 Lered hem lecherye that lovedyn hure giftes;   *taught*

* Your fader sche felde thorw falce behestes;   *killed; promises*

* Poysonede popys, apeyred holy chirche.   *popes; hurt/injured*

Is nought a beter baude, by hym that me made,   *there is*

Bytwen helle and hevene and erthe theygh men   *though*
    soughthe.

120 Sche is tykel of hure tayl, tallewys of hure tounge,   *wanton; tail; talkative*

* As comoun as the cartway to knave and to monke;   *cart track*

To menstralis and meselys, many tyme in hegges.   *lepers; hedges*

    "Sysoures and soumneres—suche men hire preyse;   *jurymen; summoners*

Schirreves and schyres were schent yif sche ne were.   *Sheriffs; shires; would be ruined*

125 Sche doth men lesyn here lond, and here lyf bothe,   *causes; lose*

And letyth passe the prysoneres, and preyeth for hem   *go free; makes appeals*
    ofthe,

And gyf the gayloures gold, and grotes togederes,   *gives; jailers; groats (silver coins worth 4 pence)*

	Text	Gloss
	And unfetereth the Falce, to fle wher hym luste:	lets loose; it pleases
*	He taketh Truthe by the top, and teygheth hym faste,	ties
130	And hangeth hym for hatered that harmed nevere.	hatred
	"To be cursed in constorye he counteth noughth a ryssche,	ecclesiastical court; rush
	For he copyth the comyssarye, and clotheth his clerkes.	[gives] cloaks
	Sche is asoyled as sone as hureself lykyth:	absolved; pleases
	Sche may ney as moche don in a monthe onys	nearly; once
135*	As your secret seel in sevene score dayes.	seal
*	Sche is privey with the pope, proveysoures hit knoweth:	intimate; papal appointees to benefices
	Sire Symonye and hureself seleth here bulles.	affix seals to
	Sche blesseth thus bischopys, they that he be lewde;	blesses / installs; bishops; they
	Provendres parsones, and prestes sche manteyneth	provides with prebends; priests; supports
140*	To holde lemmanys and lotebies al here lyf dawes,	concubines; paramours
	And brynge forth barnes agen forbode lawes.	children; against; laws that forbid this
	"Ther sche is with the king, wo is the rewme;	realm; in trouble
	For sche is favourable and false, and fouleth Truthe ofte.	tramples on
	Barounes and burgeyses sche bryngeth to sorwe;	Nobles; wealthy townspeople
145	By Jesu, with hire jewelys your justyces sche schendeth,	ruins
	And leyth agens the lawe, and lefteth hem ofte,	tells lies; against; abandoned
	That Feyth may not have his forth, hure floreyns goth so thicke.	faithful loyalty; way
*	Sche ledeth lawe as hure lust, and lovedayes maketh;	leads / practices; it pleases; sets up
	The mase for a mene man, thow he mote evere.	maze; poor; pleads
150	Lawe is so lordly, and loth to maken ende,	unwilling
	Withoute presentes or pens he pleseth wel fewe.	bribes; pennies; very
	Clergie and Covetyse coupleth hem togederes.	join themselves
	This is the lif of that lady—oure Lord yif hure sorwe!	give
	And al that manteyne hure men, myschauns hem bytide!	support; may misfortune come to them
155	For pore men have no power to pleyne, they hem nede,	poor; complain; even though necessity afflicts them
	Suche a mayster is Mede among men of gode."	property
	Than murnede Mede, and pleyned hure to the kyng,	was saddened; complained
	To have space and speche, spede yif sche myghthe.	to succeed
	The kyng graunted hure grace with a goud wille:	
160	"Excuse the, yif thou canst—I can no more segge—	Defend yourself; say
	For Conciens accuseth the, to conge the for evere."	dismiss

*   "Nay, lord," qwath that lady, "leve hym the werse   believe; less
      Whan ye wyte wyterly wher the wrong lyggeth.   know for certain; lies
      Ther that myschef is gret, Mede may helpe;   where; misfortune
165   And thou knowyst, Concyens, I cam nought to chyde,
      Ne to despyce thy persone wyth a proud herte.   Nor; defame
      Wel thou wost, Conciens, but thou woldest lye,   know; unless; choose to
*   Thou hast hangen on myn half ellevene tyme,   stuck to my side
      And grepyn my gold, and gyven hit when the lykyth.   grabbed; it pleases
170   Why thou wratthest the now, wonder me thynkyth;   become angry; extraordinary; it
                                                                seems

      Yit I may, as I myghthe, mylde the with giftes,   appease
      And mainteyne thy manhode more than thou knowest.
      "And thou hast famed me foule byfore the king here,   defamed; wickedly
      For kylled I nevere no king, ne counseyled therafter;
175   Ne dede as thou dost, I do hit on the king.   call the king as witness
*   In Normandye was he nought noyghed for me;   put in difficulties; because of
      And thou thyself, sykerly, schamed hym ofte,   certainly
      Crepe into a cabanne, for colde of thy naylys;   crept; cabin; fingernails
      Wenest thou that wynter wolde lasten evere,   you thought
180   And dreddest to be ded for a dym klowde,   you became afraid; because of;
                                                                dark

      And hastest the homward for hunger of thy wombe.   hurried back home; belly
      Withoute pyte, thou pelour, pore men thou robbedest,   thief
      And bore out bras on thi bak to Caleys to selle.   money; distribute
      And I lafte at home with my lord, his lyf for to save,   stayed
185   And made hym merthes, fro morwen til eve;   morning
      I batred hym on the bak, boldede his herte,   slapped; back; put courage in
      Dede hym hoppe for hope to have me at his wille.   made; dance
*   Had I be marchal of his men, by Marie love of hevene,   commander
      I dorste have leyde my lyf, and no lasse wedde,   would dare to bet; lesser wager
190   He schoulde have be a lord in that lond, in lengthe and
            in bredc,
      And eke king of that lyth, his kyn for to helpe;   country
      The leste barn of his blode a baronys pere.   child; equal
      Cowardlyche, thou Conciens, thou counseyledest hym   advised him against that
            thennes,
      To levyn his worschep for a lytel sylver,   abandon; estate
195   That is the rycheste of rewmys that regnes overhoves!   noblest; kingdoms; rains; hover
                                                                over

*   "Hit bycome a king that kepeth a rewme   is proper for; looks after; realm
      To geve his men mede that manlyche hym serven;   pay; bravely/generously
      To alienys, to alle men, to honoure hem with giftes.   foreigners

Mede maketh hym yloved and for a man holden. — regarded

200 Emperoures, erlys, and alle maner of lordes,

Thurgh giftes have yonge men to renne and to ryde. — run

The pope with his prelates gifthis underfongen, — received

And medyth men hymself to meynten hure lawes. — rewards; uphold

Servauntes for here servise—we sen wel the sothe— — see

205 Take mede of here maystres as thei mown acorde. — pay; from; masters; agree / contract

Beggeres for here byddyng byddeth men mede; — begging; pray / ask; people

Menstrales for here merthe, mede thei axin. — payment; ask

The king hath mede of his men to make pes in londes; — from his subjects

Men that ben clerkes mede of hym cravyth. — are; request

210 Prestes that prechin the peple to gode

Axin mede of messe pens and here mete also. — contributions; mass stipends; food

Alle kinde crafty men crave mede for here prentys; — craftsmen; seek; apprentices

Mede and marchaundise mot nede com togedere. — business; necessarily

No wyt, as I wene, withoute mede myghthe lybbe." — creature; guess

215 Qwath the king to Conciens, "Be Crist, as me thinkyth, — to me; it seems

Mede is worthi the maystrye to have!" — victory

* "Nay," quod Conciens to the king, and knelyd to the erthe,

"There arn two maner of medes, my lord, by your leve.

That on God of his grace gevyth, in his blysse, — one

220 To hem that worchen wel whiles thei ben here.

The prophete precheth hit, and put hit in the Sawter: — psalter

Qui peccuniam suam non dedit ad usuram. — "Who did not give his money to usury" (Ps. 14:5)

Tak no mede, my lord, of men that beth trewe; — loyal / faithful

Love hym and lene hem, for our Lordes love of hevene. — compensate

225 Godes mede and his mercy therwith myghth thou wynne.

"Ther is a mede mesureles that maysteres desyren; — immoderate; masters

To menteyne mysdoeres mede thei takyn. — support; criminals

And therof seyth the Sauter in a psalmes ende: — about that; Psalter

In quorum manibus iniquitates sunt; dextera eorum repleta est muneribus. — "In whose hands are iniquities; their right hands are filled with gifts" (Ps. 25:10)

230 And he that grypyth hure gyftes, so me God helpe, — takes / accepts

Schal abye ful bytterly, or the Boke lyes. — pay for it; Bible

Prestes and parsones that plesynges desyren, — pleasures

	Text	Gloss
	To take mede and mone for messes that thei synge,	money
	Schal han the mede of the molde that Mathew hath graunted:	
235	*Amen, amen, receperunt mercedem suam.*	"they have received their reward" (Matt. 6:2, 5, 16)
*	That laboreres and lond folk taketh of here maystres,	what; tenants
	Hit is no maner of mede, but a mesurable hyre.	kind of; reasonable wage
	In marchaundie is no mede, I may hit wel avowe;	business transactions
	Hit is a permutacioun, apertly, a peneworth for another.	exchange; clearly/simply; one penny's worth
240*	"Ac reddest thou nevere *Regum*, thou recreyede Mede,	but; did you read; "[Books] of Kings"; false/unfaithful
	How the vengauns fel on Saul and on al his chyldryn?	vengeance
	God sente hym to seye, by Samueles mouthe,	to tell
	That Agas of Amelek, and al his puple after,	
	Schulde deye for a dede that don hadde his eldren	his ancestors had done
245	Agens Israle, and Aaron, and Moyses his brother.	
	Samuel seyde to Saul, 'God sendeth the and hoteth	commands
	To be buxoum and bold his byddyng to fulfylle:	obedient; courageous
	Wend theder with thin ost wymman to kylle;	go; there; your army; women
	Children and chorles, schep hem to deye;	peasants; cause
250	Loke thou kylle the king, coveyte not his godes	see that; desire; property
	For eny milyouns of mone; morthere hem ychone,	thousands; money; kill
	Barnes and bestes, brene hem to dethe.'	children; burn
*	And for he kylde nought the king, as Crist hym bad,	did not kill; commanded
	Coveyted here catel, kylde nought here bestes,	cattle/goods
255	But broughte with hem the bestes, as the Byble tolde,	document
	God seyde to Samuel that Saul schulde deye,	
	And al his sed for that synne schenfullyche ende.	offspring/progeny; shamefully
	Suych a myschef Mede made the king to have,	misfortune
	That God hated the king for evere, and alle his eyres after.	heirs
260*	"The *culorum* of this kepe I not to schewe;	"final outcome"; hold back; show
	En aunter yif hit noyed me, an ende wil I make.	in case; harmed
*	In conciens knowe I this, for resoun hit me taughthe,	to me
	That resoun schal regne, and rewmes governe;	kingdoms
	And ryghth as Agas hadde hap, men schuld se sumtyme:	(mis)fortune
265	Samuel schal scle hym, and Saul schal be blamed,	slay (i.e., Agag); condemned
	And David schal be dyademyd and daunten hem alle,	crowned king; vanquish
	And o cristene king kepe us alle.	a single; protect
	Schal no more Mede be mayster on erthe,	longer

But love and lownesse and lewte togederes.   *humility; loyalty*

270 And whoso trespaseth trewlyche, and taketh agaynes   *transgresses; indeed*
         ryghth,

*   His wikke lewte schal don hym lawe, and lese his lyf   *perverse behavior; call down;*
         elles.   *upon him; will lose*

Schal no servaunt for his servise were no sylk gowne,   *wear*

Ne no ray robe with ryche pelure.   *striped cloth; fur*

     "Mede of mysdoeres maketh hem so ryche   *criminals*

275 That lawe is lord woxin, and lewte is pore.   *become; faithful service*

Wykkednysse is commaundour, and kyndenysse is   *natural behavior; banished*
         bansched.

And kynde wit schal come yit, and conciens togedere,   *natural wisdom*

And make of lawe a loburer, suche love schal areyse."   *laborer*

Passus Four

Passus quartus de visione. "The fourth step of the vision"

   "Sessyth now," seyde the king, "I suffre you no lengere. *cease; put up with*

Ye schul sawtlyn, for sothe, and serve me bothe. *be reconciled/make peace; in fact*

Cus hure," quod the king, "Conciens, I hote." *Kiss; command*

   "Nay, by God," quod Conciens, "conge me rathere; *send me away; before that*

5* But Resoun rede me ther-tille, arst wil I deye." *unless; advises; to[do] it; first*

*   "And I commaunde," quod the king to Conciens thanne,

"Rap the to ryden, and Resoun thou fecche; *haste; ride; fetch*

Commande hym that he come, my counseyle to here. *hear*

For he schal rewle my rewme, and rede me the beste *rule; kingdom; advise; (what is) the best*

10 Of Mede and of mo othere, what man schal hure wedde; *Regarding; many others*

And counte with the, Conciens—so me God helpe— *settle/weigh in*

How thou leryst the peple, lered and lewed." *teach; educated; uneducated*

   "I am fayn of that forward," seyth the feytz thenne, *pleased/happy; agreement; young man*

And ryght rennes to Resoun, and rownes in his ere, *directly; runs; whispers; ear*

15 Seyde hym as the king sente, and swythe tok his leve. *quickly; took*

   "I schal aray me to ride," quod Resoun; "reste the awhile"; *prepare*

* And calde Catoun his knave, curteys of speche: *called; Cato; servant; courteous*

* "Set my sadel upon Suffre-til-I-se-my-tyme, *saddle; Be patient; see*

And let warroke hym wel with ryghthful gerthes, *gird; secure; girths*

20 Hong on hym an hevy brydel and hold his hede lowe; *bridle; keep*

And yut we wil make many 'wehe,' ere we come there." *whinnies*

   Thanne Conciens on his capel caryeth forth faste, *horse; went away*

And Resoun with hym ryt, and rapith hym swythe; *rides; hastens*

* At on Were Wisdoum, and Witty his fere, *together; Wary; companion*

25 Folwede hym faste, for he hadde to done *followed; closely; had (business)*

In the Chekyre and the Chauncerye, to be discharged of thinges; *Exchequer; Chancery Court; business matters*

And ryde faste, for Resoun schulde rede hem the beste *(they) ride; would advise*

For to save hemself fro schame and fro harmes.

    Ac Conciens cam arst to the court by a myle way,   *but; arrived; first; mile's distance*

30 And rowned forth with Resoun ryght to the king.   *spoke in private/whispered; straight*

Curteysly the king than com in to Resoun,

* And bytwyn hym and hys sone set hym on benche,   *son*

And wordedyn a gret while wel wisly togederes.   *were in conversation; very*

*   Then com Pes into parlement, and put up a bylle,   *Peace; parliament*

35 How Wrong agens his wille hadde his wif take;   *against; taken*

And how he ravesched Rose, Raynaldes love,   *raped*

And Margrete of hure maydenhed, maugre hure chekys.   *virginity; in spite of; checks*

"Bothe my geys and my grys his gadelynges fecches;   *geese; piglets; henchmen; steal*

I dar not for fere of hym fytthen ne chyde.   *fear; fight back; complain*

He borwed of me Bayerd, and broughthe hym nevere agayn,   *borrowed; common name for a (bay) horse; back*

40 Ne no ferthing therfore, for nought I coude plete.   *farthing (one-fourth penny); no matter how much; was able to argue*

He maynteynes his men to murthere myn hynes,   *maintains; peasants/servants*

* Forstalles my feyres, fyttes in my cheping,   *obstructs; fairs; fights; market*

Breketh up my berne dores, and beryth awey my whete,   *barn doors; carries away; wheat*

And taketh me but a tayle for ten quarteres of otys.   *gives; receipt; eighty bushels; oats*

45 And yut he betyth me therto, and lyth by my mayden;   *in addition; beats; on top of that; lies [in bed]; with; maidservant (or daughter)*

And I am not so hardy onys for hym to loke."   *bold; once; oppose*

    Tho knew the king he sayde soth, for Conciens hym tolde.   *told the truth*

Wrong was aferd tho, and Wisdam he soughthe

To make his pes with his pans, and profrede manye;   *peace; pennies; offered*

50 And sayde, "Had I the love of my lord the king,

Lytel wolde I recche that Pes and his power pleyned hem evere."   *little; care; Peace; army; complained; again and again*

    Wysdam wan tho, and so dude Wit alse,   *wisdom; went; also*

For that Wrong hadde ywrought so wycked a dede,   *because; committed*

And warnede Wrong, wyth swych a wys tale: *wise*

55 "And who wercheth by wil wratthe maketh ofte;   *acts; willfully; causes anger*

I sey hit by myself, thou schalt hit sone fynde:

But Mede hit make, ther myschef is uppe;   *unless; settles; in this situation; misfortune; increased*

#	Text	Gloss
	For bothe thiself and thi lond lyth in his grace."	lie; at his mercy
	Wrong than on Wisdam wep to helpe hym at nede,	wept/begged
60	For ryght therof his handy-dandy payed.	immediately; bribe
	Than Wysdam and Wyt wenten togederes,	wisdom
	And tok Mede with hem mercy to wynne.	took
	Pes put hym forth his hede and his panne	pushed himself forward; head; skull
	Redly withouten gilt—"God wot, that is skathe!"	immediately; wrong
65	Conciens and the king knewe wel the sothe,	truth
	And wiste wel that Wrong was a schrewe evere.	knew; criminal
	And Wisdam and Wit were aboute faste	on the move
	To overcome the kyng with catel yif thei myghte.	win over; valuables/money
	The king swor by Crist, and by his crowne bothe,	also
70	That Wrong for his werkes shulde wo thole,	punishment; endure
	And comandyth a constable to caste hem in irenys:	commanded; chains
*	"He schal not this seven yer se his fet onys!"	years; see; feet; once
*	"God wot," qwath Wisdam, "that were not the beste;	would not be
	And he amendes mowe make, lat meynpris hym have	if; can; release on bail
75	And be borwe for his bale; and bryngen hym bote,	go bail for; wickedness; if; compensation/remedy
	Amende that mysdede, and evermore the betere."	misdeed
	Wit acordeth therwith and seyde the same:	agreed
	"Beter is that bote bale adoun brynge,	compensation; injury; reduce
	Than bale be bote, and bote nevere the betere."	wickedness; punished; compensation
	Than gan Mede to meke hure, and mercy bysoughthe,	did; humble/abase; herself; begged for
80	And profered Pes a present al of pure golde:	refined
	"Have this of me, man," qwath sche, "to amende thi skathe,	injury
	For I wil wage for Wrong, he schal do so no more."	pledge
*	Pees thanne pitousliche preyede to the king	with forgiveness in his heart
	To have mercy on that man, that mysdede hym ofte:	mistreated
85	"For he hath wagid me wel, as Wysdom hym taughte,	paid me
	I forgyve hym that gilt with a good wille,	
	So that ye assente. I can sey no more:	As long as
	For Mede hath mad my mendes, I may no more axyn."	Because; given me compensation; ask
	"Nay," quod the king, "so God gyve me blysse!	
90	Wrong wendeth not so away, er I wyte more;	does not get away; before; find out
	Lep he so lyghtly away, laughen he wolde,	if he were to get; easily; laugh

	Text	Gloss
	And after the balder be and betyn myn hynen.	afterward; bolder; beat; servants
	But Resoun have ruthe on hym, he schal reste in stokkes	unless; pity; stay; stocks
	As longe as I lyve, but more love hit make."	unless; repair / amend
95	Some men redde Resoun to have ruthe on that schrewe,	advised
	And to counseile the king and Conciens bothe;	counsel
	That Mede muste be meynpernour Resoun thei besoughte.	one who provides bail / surety
*	"Rede me nout," quod Resoun, "no ruthe to have,	advise; pity
	Til lordes and ladyes loven alle truthe;	
100*	Til Peronelys purfyl be put in her hocche;	Peronel's; fancy clothes; chest
*	Til childres chersyng be chasted with yerdes,	children's; cherishing; punished; canes
*	And harlotes almesse be holden for an hyne;	alms for an undeserving rascal; considered; thing of little value
	Til clerkes and knyghtthes be curteys of her mouthe,	their
	And hate to here harlotrye or mouthe hit hemselve;	be unwilling; dirty stories; speak
105	Til prestes here preching proveth hemselve,	live by
	And do hit in dede to drawe us to gode;	lead
*	Tyl Seynt Jame be ysoughth ther I schal asyne,	looked for; where; assign
	That no man go to Galys but yif he go for evere;	So that; Galicia (northwest Spain: site of the shrine of St. James); unless
*	And alle the Rome-renneres for robberes of byyonde	as / because of; in foreign lands
110*	Bere no sylver over se that sygne of king scheweth,	should carry; sea; image / inscription; displays
	Neyther grotes ne gold ygrave with kinges coyne,	silver coins; engraved; coin
	Up forfeture of that fee, who fynt hym dygnere,	upon; money; no matter who considers; deserving of respect (i.e., above the law)
	But hit be marchaunt or his man, or myssager with lettres,	unless; merchant; servant; messenger
	Or provysour or prest that the pope avaunseth.	provisor; priest; promotes
115	"And yut," quod Resoun, "by the Rode, I nel no ruthe have,	Cross; will not; pity
	Whil Mede hath the maystrye to mote in the halle.	power; plead; court
	And I may schewe you ensaumple, as I se other:	example; see
	I sey hit for myselve, and hit were so	say; if; happened
	That I were king with crowne, to kepe a rewme,	govern; kingdom
	Schuld never wrong in the world, that I wyte myghthe,	know
120	Be unpunsched by my power, for peril of my sowle;	unpunished; on

Ne gete my grace with giftes, so me God helpe; *nor; get; pardon*
Ne for no mede have mercy, but meknysse hit made. *bribe; unless; meekness; made it happen*

* For *nullum malum* the may mete wyth *inpunitum*, *"no evil"; maid; "unpunished"*
And bad *nullum bonum* be *irremuneratum*. *"no good"; "unrewarded"*

125 Let thi confessour, syre king, construe hit the this in *translate; for you*
    Englys.
And yif thou wirke hit in werk, I wedde bothe his erys *do; deed; bet; ears*
That lawe schal be a labourer and lede to felde dunge, *haul; field; manure*
And love schal lede thy lond, as the best lykes." *govern; it pleases*

*   Clerkes that were confessoures coupled hem *joined*
      togederes

130 For to construe the clause and declyned faste. *interpret; text; parsed carefully*
Ac whan Resoun among the renkes hadde rehersed tho *but; men; spoken aloud*
    wordes,
Ther nas man in that mothalle, more ne lasse, *was not; lawcourt; greater nor lesser*

That he ne held Resoun a mayster, and Mede a muche *not; victor; big loser*
    wrecche.
Love let of here lyght, and low hure to skorne, *esteemed; lightly; laughed*
135 And sayde hit so loude that Sothnesse hit herde,
That who wynne hure to wyve, for welthe of hure godys, *wins; wife; because of; property*
"But he be cokewald ycalde, cut of my nose!" *if not; cuckold; called; off*
    Onwarned Wysdom tho, Onwittes fere, *Ill-advised; Stupidity's companion*
Coude not warpen a word to withsegge Resoun; *utter; contradict*
140 But stareden and stodiede and stode forth as bestes. *stared dumbly; pondered; stood around; like beasts*

The king acorded by Crist to Resounes sawes, *agreed with; statements*
And rehersed that Resoun had ryghthfully schewed: *declared; what; accurately; demonstrated*

"Ac hit is ful hard by myn hed, hereto hit to brynge, *but; very; head; to effect this*
And alle my lyche ledes to ledyn hcm thus evene." *loyal subjects; govern / rule; fairly*
145   "By hym that raughthe on the rode," quod Resoun to *stretched; cross*
      the king,
"But yif I reule thus thy rewme, rent of my rybbys, *unless; rule; kingdom; tear out; ribs*

Yif hit be so that Buxumnesse be of myn asent." *As long as; Obedience; agreement*
    "And I asente," quod the king, "by Seynte Marie my
      lady,
Be my counsel ycome of clerkes and of erlys. *let; come; earls*

150   Ac redly, Resoun, thou schalt not ryde hennys;   but; soon; away from here
      For as longe as I lyve, love the I wille."
          "I am redy," quod Resoun, "to reste with you evere;   remain; always
      So Conciens be of your counseyl, kepe I no better."   as long as; care
          "I graunte," quod the king, "Godes forbode he fayle;   May God forbid; fail
155   As longe as I lyve, lybbe we togederes."   let (us) live

Passus Five

Passus quintus de visione.   "The fifth step of the vision"

*   The king and his knyghtes to the cherche wente
To here matynes and masse, and to the mete after. — *attend; morning prayers; mass; meal*

*   Than waked I of my wynkyng, and wo was withalle — *awoke; from sleep; very sad*
That I ne hadde sclepte sadder and yseye more. — *slept; more soundly; seen*

5   Ere I hadden fare a furlong fantasye me hadde, — *gone; one-eighth of a mile; delusion; took hold of*

That I ne myghthe ferther a fot, for defaute of slepyng. — *further; lack*
*   I sat softely adoun, and sayde my byleve, — *down; recited; creed*
*   And so I babled on my bedes thei broughthe me on slepe. — *as; mumbled; prayers; to*

*   Than saw I a mekel more than I before tolde: — *lot*
10   I saw the feld ful of folke that I byfore sayde, — *spoke about*
And Conciens with a cros com forth to preche. — *crozier; came out*
He prechede the peple to have pyte on hemselve, — *compassion; themselves*
*   And provede the pestelence was for pure synne, — *plague; because of; only*
*   And the southwest wynd on Saterysday at even — *wind; in the evening*
15   Was apertly for pryde, and for nothing ellys; — *plainly; because of; else*
Pyryes and plomtreys were put to the erthe, — *pear trees; plum trees; knocked*
In exsaumple, seyth God, ye schul do the betere! — *warning*
*   Beches and brode okes were blowe to the grounde, — *beeches; large oaks*
And turned up the tayl in toknyng of drede — *roots; sign; judgment*
20   That dedly synne er domesday schal fordo hem alle. — *mortal sin; before; doomsday; utterly destroy*

    Of this matere myghthe I mamele wel longe, — *about; babble; very*
Ac I schal say as I seyde—so me God helpe— — *but; said*
How Conciens with a cros comsede to preche, — *crozier; began; preach*
*   And bad Wastour go worche what he best coude, — *commanded; Waster/Idler; do what he knew best how to do*

25   And wynne that he had wasted with som maner craft. — *gain back; what; kind of job*
He prayde to Peronel hure purfyl to leve, — *requested of; fancy dress; abandon*

And kepe hit in hure cofre for catel at nede; — chest; as something to sell; in case of necessity

Thomas he taughthe to take two staves, — canes
* To fecche Felys hom fro wyvene pyne; — Felicia; from wives' (place of) punishment

30 He warnede Watte his wif was to blame, —
* That hure hed was worthe a marke and his hod not a grote; — head(dress); two-thirds of a pound (13 shillings 4 pence); hood; silver coin worth four pennies

He chargeth chapmen to chaste here children— — directed; merchants; chastise
"Let no wynnyng forweny hem whyles thei beth yonge." — profit; spoil; are
He prechede prelates and prestes togedere, — directed; bishops; priests
35 That thei preche the peple and prove hit hemselve— — put it into practice
"And lyve as ye lere us, for we wil love you the betere." — teach; so that
And swythe he radde religyus here reule to kepe— — then; advised; people in religious orders; rule

"Last the king and his counceyl your commounes apeyre, — Lest; provisions; will diminish
And stiward in your stede for ye be stywed betere, — oversee; place; so that; managed
40 And ye that seke Seynt Jame and seyntes at Rome, —
Sekyth Seynt Truthe, for he may save us alle, —
* Qui cum patre et filio, that fayre you mote byfalle." — "Who with the father and son"; so that; good things may come to you

* Than Repentauns rehersed his teme, — repeated; theme
* And made Wille to wepe water with his eye. — weep
45 Peronel Proud-Herte plat hure to the erthe, — threw down flat; herself
And lay longe er sche loked, and "Lord, mercy" cryed, — before; raised her head
And behyghte to hym that us alle made — promised
* Sche schulde unsewe hire serk and sette ther an heyre — take off; tunic; put on in its place; hair shirt

To afauten hire fleys, that fresch was to synne: — subdue/mortify; flesh; all too ready; sin

50 "Schal nere hey herte me hente, but holde me lowe, — never; proud; catch hold of; (I shall) keep myself in humility

And suffre to be mysseyd, and so dude I nevere; — allow (myself) to be spoken badly of/slandered; did

But now I wil meke me, and mercy byseke — humble myself; ask for
Of al that I have had of envye in myn herte." — everyone; any envy of
* Lecchour seyde "Allas," and on oure lady cryde — Lechery; called
55 To make mercy for his mysdede bytwethe God and hym, — sins

With that he schulde Satourdayes, seve yer after,   *Because; on Saturdays; seven years*

Drynke but with the goos and dine but onys.
   Envye, with hevy herte, asked after schryfte,   *confession*
And carfully his compte he gynnyth to schewe.   *anxiously; list of sins; reveal*
60 He was pale as a pelet, and paltyk he semede;   *pebble; palsied*
* He was clothed in a caury-maury, I coude hit not discrie: *dressed; rough cloth; describe*
A kyrtel and a curtepy, a knyf by his syde,   *jacket; short coat; knife*
Of a freres frog were the fore-slevys.   *habit; cuffs*
As a lyk that hadde yleye longe in the sunne,   *like; leek; lain*
65 So loked he with lene chekes, lowrynge foule.   *lean; scowling; foully*
* His body was bolned for wroth that he bot his lyppe,   *swollen; anger; so that; bit*
And wrothlyche he wrong his fyste, to wreke hym he thoughthe   *angrily; rubbed; avenge himself*
With werkes and with wordes, when he sey his tyme.   *saw*
   "Venym or verjous or vynegre, I trowe,   *venom; acid/juice of unripe fruit; vinegar; believe*

70 Walwyth in my wombe, and waxeth, I wene.   *rolls; belly; increases; guess*
I myghte not many a day do as a man myghthe,
Swych wynd in my wombe waxyth er I dyne.   *gas; belly; expands; eat*
I have a nehebour ny me, I noyed hym wel ofte,   *neighbor; near; harmed; very*
And blamed hym byhynde his bak to brynge hym in fame;   *said bad things about; back; into disrepute*
75 To apeyre hym by my power I pursued wel ofte,   *hurt; set out; very*
And bylowe hym to lordes, to do hym lese sylvere,   *lied about; make; lose; money*
And don his frendes to ben his fon, thurgh my falce tonge;   *cause; to be; enemies; lying*
His grace and his gode happes greved me wel sore.   *success; good luck; very deeply*
Bytwen hym and his mayne wratthe I made ofte;   *household; anger; caused*
80 Bothe his lyme and his lyf was lost thorw my tonge.   *limb(s)*
Whan I mette him in market that I most hated,   *whom*
I halsed hym as hendely as I his frend ware.   *embraced; courteously*
He is doughthier than I; I durste non harme don him.   *stronger; dared*
Ac haddyn I maystry or myghth, I wolde mourthre him for evere!   *but; if I had; superiority; power; would; murder*
85 "Whan I come to the cherche, and knele byfore the rode,   *cross*
To praye for the peple, as the prest me techys,
After thanne I crye on my kneys 'Oure Lady gyf hem sorwe
That bare away my bolle and my brode schete.'   *took; bowl; wide; sheet*
Fro the auter myn eye I turne and byholde   *altar*

90 How Hayne hath a newe cote—I wyssche hit were myn   *coat; own*
      owe;
   And al the wele that he hath greveth me wel sore.   *wealth; very grievously*
   Of his lesyng I smyle, and therof laugheth myn herte;   *At; losses; at it*
   And of his wynnyng I wepe, and weyle the tyme.   *profits; lament*
   I deme men ther thei do ille, and yut I do werse;   *condemn*
95 I wolde that ech wyghth were my knave;   *would like; every; person; servant*
   And whoso hath more than I, that angreth myn herte.   *whoever*
      "Thus I lyve loveles, lyk a lyther dogge,   *live; without any love; miserable/lousy*

   That al my brest bolneth for byter of my galle;   *swells; bitterness; bile/malice*
   May no sugre ne swete thing swete hit an unche,   *sugar; sweeten; ounce*
100 Ne no diapendion dryve hit fro myn herte;   *expectorant; expel*
*   Yif schryft shulde, hit were a gret wonder."   *confession; were able to; would be*
      "Yis, redly," quod Repentauns, and redde hym to   *Yes, indeed; advised*
      gode,
   "Sorwe for synne saveth wel manye."   *very*
*   "I am sory," quod Envye, "I am but selde other;   *seldom; anything else*
105 And that maketh me so mad, for I ne may me wenge."   *angry; because; myself; avenge*
      Than come Covetyse—I can hym not descrye—   *describe*
*   So angrey and so holwe, Sire Hervy hym loked: *shrunken; appeared*
   He was byter-browed and eke baberlypped, with two   *had shaggy eyebrows; also; with*
      blered eyen;   *large/drooping lips; watery/dim*
   As a lether purs lolled his chekes;   *like; purse; hung trembling*
110 In a tore tabard of twelve wynter age—   *coat; years*
   But yif a lous coude lepe, I may hit not trowe   *Unless; louse; knew how to; believe*

   That he ne schulde slyde theron, so was hit bare.   *threadbare*
      "I have yloved covetyse," quod he, "al my lyf tyme,
   And knowe hit here before Crist and his swete moder.   *acknowledge*
115* For sumtyme serwed I Symme at the noke,   *oak (tree)*
   And was his prentys yplyghth, his profyt to loke.   *apprentice; contracted; look out for*

*   Furst I lerned to lye a lef other tweyne;   *tell lies; page; two*
   Wyckedly to wynne was my furste lessoun.   *make a profit*
*   To Wynchestre and to Wy I wente to the feyre,   *Winchester; Weyhill*
120 To many maner marchaundie, as my mayster me het;   *kinds of; trade; ordered*
   Ne hadde the grace of gile go among my ware,   *if not; benefit; deceit; goods*
   Hit hadde be unsolde this seven yer, so me God helpe!   *would have; years*
*   "Than drow I me amonge draperis my Donet to lere,   *took; myself; cloth dealers; Donatus*

	To drowe the leser along, the lengere hit semeth.	stretch; strip of cloth
125	Among the ryche rayes I rendred a lessoun,	fine; striped cloths; learned
	Broched hem with a pak-nedle, and playted hem togedere,	pierced; thick needle; wove/ stitched
	Put hem in a pressour, and pynned hem therinne.	laid; cloth press; squeezed
	"My wyf was a wynnestre, and wollen cloth made,	wool winder
	And spak to the spynnestre to spynne hit so softe:	spinner (fem.); lightly
130	The pound that sche weyes by weyeth a quarter more	
	Than ony aunsel dede, when I weyed truthe.	any; weighing scales; accurately
*	I boughthe hure barly—sche brew hit to sale;	for her
	Penyale and pigwhey sche pured togederes	thin/poor ale; ? weak cider; poured
	For laboureres, for loth folk that lyveth by hemselve.	unpleasant
135	The beste in my bed chaumber lay by the walles,	
	And whoso boused therof boughth hit therafter:	drank; paid for
	A galoun for a grote, God wot, no lesse,	gallon; knows
	When hit come in coppe ale—that craft my wyf used.	cup measures; trick
	Rose the regrater was hure ryghthe name;	huckster; proper
140	Sche haldeth ostrye this ellevene wynter.	kept/owned an inn; years
	"And I swere now sothly, that synne schal I lete,	cease/leave
	Ne nevere weye wyckedely, ne no chaffare make;	commercial transactions
*	But wende to Walsyngham, and my wif after,	behind me
*	And bydde the rode of Bromeholme brynge me out of dette."	pray; cross; debt
145	Now begynneth Glotoun for to go to shrifte,	confession
	And carieth hym to churcheward, his synne to schewe;	takes himself; confess
	And Betoun the brewestre ther bad hym goud morwe,	brewer; morning
	And she axede of him whederward he wolde .	which way; was headed
	"To holy chyrche," quod he, "for to here masse;	attend
150	And sytthe I wil be shreve, and synne no more."	afterward; confessed
	"I have goud ale, gossyb," quod she; "Glotoun, wilt thou asaye?"	friend; try it
*	"Hast thou," quod he, "ony hote spyces?"	
	"Ye, Glotoun, gossyb, God wot, wel hote:	friend; knows; very spicy ones
	I have pepyr and pienye, and a pounde of garlyk,	peony
155	And a ferthingworth of fynkele sed, for fastyng dayes."	fennel
	Thanne goth Glotoun in, and grete othes after.	
	Sysse the sowestre sat on the benche,	seamstress
	Watte the wafrere, and his wif bothe,	wafer maker
	Symme the tynkere, and two of his knaves,	servants
160	Hycke the hakeneyman, and Hobbe the melnere,	stableman; miller
*	Clares of Kockes Lane, and the clerk of the cherche,	

Dawe the dykere, and a doseyn othere; *ditchdigger*

A ribaud, a ratoner, a rakere of Chepe, *wastrel/strumpet/entertainer; rat catcher; street sweeper; from;*

A ropere, a redyng-king, and Rose the dyschere, *rope maker; ? lackey; dish seller*

165 And upholderes an hep, erly by the morwe, *secondhand dealers; in; morning*

Gevyn Glotoun with glad chere goud ale to drynke.

Clement the cobelere cast of his cloke, *shoemaker; threw off*

* And at the newe feyre nempneth hit to selle. *offered*

Hicke the osteler hitte his hode after, *stableman; threw*

170 And bad Bette the bocher to be on his syde. *asked; Bartholomew/Bertram; butcher*

Ther were chapmen ychose, the chaffare to preise; *dealers; merchandise; appraise*

And whoso hadde the hode schuld have amendes of the cloke. *the difference for*

Thei resyn up in rape, and rownede togederes, *haste/hurry; whispered*

And preysede the peneworthes apertly by hemselve; *appraised; values; in the open*

175 Ther were othes on an hep: thei cunne not yut juge, *in*

Ne by here conciens acorden togederes, *agree*

Til Robyn the ropere was rad up to ryse, *rope maker; asked; get up*

And nempnyd for a nounpere, that no debat ware. *nominated; umpire; so that; might be*

Hicke the ostler than hadde the cloke, *stableman*

180 In covenaunt that Clement the cuppe schulde fille, *agreement*

And have Hickes hod the osteler, and holde him yserved; *consider; satisfied*

And whoso repented rather sholde rise afore, *objected; first*

And grete Sire Glotoun with a galoun of ale.

Ther was laughyng and lowring and "Let go the coppe!" *scowling*

185 Bargeynes and beveryches begunne to ryse, *deals; drinks; increase*

And setyn so til evesong, and sunge sumwhyle, *they sat; vespers*

Til Glotoun hadde ygolped a galoun of ale. *gulped down*

* He pisside a potel, in a *pater noster* while, *pissed; half gallon; Lord's Prayer; time*

And blew the rounde rowet at the riggebonys ende, *bugle; backbone's*

190 That alle that herde that horn held here nose after, *with the result that; their*

And wisshed it had be waxed with a wisp of fersen. *plugged; small handful; furze*

He hadde no strengthe to stonde, ere he his staf hadde, *grabbed*

And thanne gan he go sumtyme o syde and sumtyme o rere, *sideways; backward*

As whoso layde lynes to lacche wilde foules. — like one who; lines; catch/trap; birds

195* When he drow to the dore, than dymmed his eyen; — approached; door
He stumbled on the thresfold, and fel to the erthe, — threshold; ground
That with al the wo of the world, his wif and his daughter
Beryn him to his bed, and broughthe him therinne. — carry
And after al that surfet, an axces he hadde, — overindulgence; fever
200 That he slep Saturday and Sunday, til sunne yede to reste. — went

Thanne waked he of his wynkyng, and wyped his eyen; — from; sleeping; rubbed
* The furste word that he spak was "Where is the bolle?" — bowl (of ale)
His wif blamed him thanne, of wickednesse of synne. — accused
Than was the shrewe ashamed, and schraped his erys, — sinner; rubbed
205 And gan to gretyn grymly, and gret dol made — did; weep; miserably; sorrow
For his lether lyf, that he lyved hadde, — wicked
And vowed to faste, for hunger or for therste: — despite
* "Shal nevere fysch on Fryday defye in my mawe, — be digested; stomach
Er Abstinence myn awnte have ygif me leve; — before; granted; permission
210 And yut have I hated hure al my lif tyme." —

Slouthe for sorwe fel doun on sowne, — laziness/inertia; down; in a swoon
* Til Vigilate wile fecche water to his eyne, — "Be watchful"; bring
And flapte hit on his face, and faste on him cried, — threw/slapped; loudly/insistently
And sayde, "War, for wanhope wil the betraye. — Beware; despair; thee
215 'I am sory for my synne,' sey to thiself thanne, —
And bet thiself on thi brest, and byd him of grace." — pray to/ask him for
Than sat Slouthe up, and shryved him faste, — went to Confession
And made a vow to veri God, for his foule slouthe: — true
"Shal no Sunday be this seven yer, but syknesse hit make, — unless; causes
220 That I ne shal do me er day to the parysch cherche, — take myself; parish
And here masse and matines, as I a monke were; — attend; as if
* Shal non ale after mete holden me thennys, — meal; keep from there
Til I have evesong herd, I behote the rode. — vespers; promise; cross
And yut wol I yelde agen, yif I so moche have, — also; pay back
225* Al that I wickedly bywan, syn I wit hadde; — obtained; understanding; attained
And thei my lyflode fayle, lette yut I nelle — even though it leaves me short; hold back; will not

That every man shal have his, er I hennys wende; — so that; what belongs to him; from here; depart

      *   And with the residue and remenaunt—by the rode of   cross; Chester
              Chestre—
            I wil seke Truthe, or I se Rome."   before
230*   Roberd the robbere on *Reddite* lokede,   "Pay back"
            And for ther was not wherwith, he weped wel sore;   because; the means; very
                                                    sorrowfully

            And yit the synful shrewe sayde to himselve: still
            "Crist, that on Calvery on the cros deyde,
      *   Tho Dismas my brother bysoughth the of grace—   When; asked; for mercy for
                                                    himself

235   And thou haddest mercy on that man for *Memento*   "Remember"
              sake—
            Thi wil wirche upon me, as I have wel deserved,   let [thy will] work; justly
            To have helle for evere yif that hope ne were.   there were no hope
            To rewe on this Roberd, that red non ne haveth,   have pity; means of help
            Ne never wenyth to wynne with craft that he knoweth;   expected; earn (his living); skill
240   But for thi moche mercy, mitygacioun I beseke: great pardon; reduction; ask for
            Dampne me not at domysday, for that I dede so ylle."   because; acted; badly
      *   Ac what byfel of this feloun, I can not fayre shewe;   But; sinner; clearly
            Wel I wot he wepte faste water with his eyne,   know; a lot
            And knowliched his gilt to Crist yit eftsone,   admitted; soon after
245   That *Penitencia* his pik shulde pulche newe,   pike; polish; again
      *   And lep with him over lond, al his lif tyme;
      *   For he hadde leye by *Latro*, Luciferes aunte.   lain; "Thief"
              A thousand men and mo tho thrunge togederes,   more; then; crowded
            Wepyng and weyling for here wyckede dedis,   lamenting
250   Cried upward to Crist, and to his clene moder,   pure
            "To have grace to seke Truthe, so God leve that ye mote."   if God allowed

Passus Six

Passus sextus de visione.   "The sixth step of the vision"

*   Ac ther were fewe men so wise that thei thedir coude,   but; there; knew (the way) to it
    But blustred forth as bestes over valeys and hulles,   rush about; aimlessly
    Til late and longe that thei a lede mettyn,   person
*   Yparayled as a paynym, in pilgrymys wise.   dressed; pagan/heathen; fashion
5*   He bare a burdoun ybounde with a brod lyste;   pilgrim's staff; wound about; wide strip of cloth

*   A bagge and a bolle he bar by his side;
*   An hundred of ampollus on his hat seten,   small flasks (of holy water or oil); lay/were attached

*   Sygnes of Synay, and schellys of Galys,   souvenirs; from; (scallop) shells;
    And many a cros on his cloke, and keyghes of Rome,   keys; from
10   And the vernicle him byforn, for men schuld hym knowe   Veronica's veil; in front of; so that
    And sen by his synes whom he soughth hadde.   see; which saints
      This folke freyned hym fayre whennes that he come.   questioned; nicely; from where
      "Fro Synay," he sayde, "and fro the sepulcre;   Mount Sinai; Holy Sepulcher
*   Ac Bedlehem and Babyloyne, I have be in bothe;   but
15   In Ermonye, in Alisaundre, and many other places.   Armenia; Alexandria
    Ye mow sen by my synes, that sytten on myn hat,
    That I have walked wyde, in wet and in drye,   widely
    And soughth gode seyntes for my soule hele."   health
      "Knowest thou a corseynt," quod thei, "that men calle Truthe?   holy saint
20   Canstu wisse us the wey wher that he duelleth?"   Can you; point out
      "Nay, so me God helpe," sayde the gome thanne,   so help me God; fellow
*   "I sey nevere palmere, with pik ne with skrippe,   pilgrim; pointed staff; bag
    Axen after him, ere now in this place."   Ask about
*   "Peter!" quod a plowman, and putte forth his hed,   stuck out
25   "I knowe him as kyndely as clerkes done her bokes;   naturally
    Clene conciens and wit kennyth me to his place,   directed
    And dude me to sure him for to serve him evere,   made; assure
    Bothe now and sithe whil I swynke myghthe.   afterward; as long as; work
*   I have be his folwere al this fourty wynter;   disciple; years

30	Bothe sowen his sed, and sewed his bestes,	herded
	And kepid his corn, and caried hit to house;	looked after; grain
	Dyken and dolven, and don what he hyghthe,	made ditches; dug; commanded
	Wythinne and withoute, to wayte his profyte;	look out for
	Ther is no labourer withinne his lordschep that him lyketh betere,	pleases
35	For though I sey hit myself, I serve him to paye.	his satisfaction
	I have myn hire of hym wel, and otherwhile more;	receive; pay; regularly; sometimes; a bonus
	He is the prestyste payghere that pore men knoweth.	promptest; payer
*	He ne halt no hyne his hyre that he ne hath hit at eve;	keep from; servant; wages; so that; at the end of the day
	He is as low as a lomb and lovely of speche;	meek; lamb; loving
40	And yif ye wil wite where that he duelleth,	know; dwells
	I shal wisse you wel, ryghth to his place."	direct; straight
	"Ye, leve Peres," quod the pilgrymys, and profered him hire.	Okay!/Great!; dear; offered payment
*	"Nay, by the peril of my soule," quod Peres, and gan for to swere:	on
	"I nolde fonge a ferthing, for Seynt Thomas shrine;	would not take; farthing (one-fourth of a penny)
45	For Truthe wolde love me the worse a long tyme after.	
	Ac ye that wil wende theder—this is the weye:	but; want to go there
*	Ye mote go thorw Meknysse, bothe maydenis and wyves,	
	Til ye come into Conciens, that Crist wyte the sothe,	about which; knows
	That ye love him levere than the lyf in your hertes,	so that; more dearly
50	And thanne your neyghbores nixte in none wyse apeyre	next; manner; injure
	Otherwise than ye wol men wroughthe to yourselve.	want; people; did
*	"And so boweth forth by a broke, Be-buxum-of-speche,	direct yourself forward; stream; obedient
	Forth til ye fynde a ferde, Your-faderes-honowre;	onward; until; stream-crossing
	Wadeth in that water, and ways you therinne,	Wade; wash yourself
55	And ye schulle lepe the lyghtlyere al your lyf tyme.	skip/trot; more nimbly
	So shul ye se Suere-nought-but-hit-be-for-nede-	Swear; necessity
	And-namly-on-ydel-the-name-of-God-almyghthy.	especially; vain
	"Than shal ye come by a crofte, cometh not therinne;	small enclosed field
	That croft hatteth Coveyteth-not-mannys-catel-ne-here-wyvys-	is called; property; their
60	Ne-none-of-here-servantes-that-noyghe-hem-myghthe;	harm
	Loke ye breke no bowes there, but thei be your owyn.	boughs; unless
	"Two stokkes stondeth, but stynt you not there;	tree trunks; stop

Thei hatte Stel-not, Ne-sle-not; but strik forth by bothe. — are named; slay; go straight past

Lef hem on thi lyft half, and loke not theraftter, — back at them

65 And hold wel thin halyday, hey til the eve. — holy day; solemnly

* "Than shalt thou blenchen abak Ber-no-fals-witnesse; — turn sharply; back from

He is frithed in with floreynis, and other fees manye; — hedged; gold coins

Loke thou plucke no plantes ther, for peril of thi soule.

"Than shalt thou se Sey-soth-so-hit-be-to-done- — tell

70 And-loke-thou-lye-not-for-no-mannys-byddyng. — tell lies; request

* "Than shalt thou come to a court, as clere as the — bright

sunne;

The mot is of Mercy, the maner al aboute, — moat; manor; completely surrounding

* And alle the walles beth of Wit, to holde Wil theroute; — are; keep; outside

The cornelys beth of Cristendoum, that kynde to save, — crenellations; are; nature; preserve

75 And butrased with Lef-so-or-thou-best-not-saved. — buttressed; Believe; will be

Alle the howses beth heled, halles and chaumbres, — are covered/roofed

With no led but with Love and Lownesse, as brethren of o — lead; Humility; a single

wombe.

The toure ther Truthe is himself is up to the sunne; — where; as high as

* He may do with the daysterre what so him lykyth; — day star; whatever

80 Deth dar not do nothing that he defendes. — anything; forbids

"Grace hatteth the gateward, a goud man forsothe; — is the name of; gatekeeper; indeed

His man hatte Amende-you, for meny men him — servant; is named

knoweth;

Tel him this tokne: 'Truthe wot the sothe: — password/sign; knows; truth

Y parformed the penauns that the prest enjoyned; — assigned

85 I am sory for my synnes, and so shal I evere, — shall be

Whan I thinke theron, thow I were a pope.' — on them; even if

"Byddyth Amende-you mekyn him to his maistre, — Instruct; humble himself

Ones to wynne up the wyket that the wyght shette, — at once; fling; small door (in a larger one); man (Adam)

Tho Adam and Eve etyn oure bane; — When; deadly fruit/poison

90 For he hath the keyes and the clyket, thow the king — latch-key; even if; is asleep

slepe.

And yif Grace graunte the to gon in on this wyse, — in; way

Thou schalt se Truthe himself sytte in thyn herte;

And lere the for to love, and his lawes halde. — teach; keep

Ac be war of Wratthe-nouth, that wykkede shrewe, — but

95 For he hath envye to him that in thin herte sytteth.

And loke for no pride to preyse thyselve. — seek out

The boldnesse of that buffet maketh the blynd thanne,   *blow*

And so worth the dryve out as dew, and the dore yclosed,   *it will; deserved*

Ykeyghed and ycleketed to holde the theroute   *Locked; latched; keep out; of there*

100 Happily an hundred wynter, er thou eft entre.   *Perhaps; years; before; again*

Thus myghthe thou lese his love to lete wel by thiselve,   *think well of*

And gete hit agen thurgh grace and thurgh nothing   *back; besides*
    elles.

*   "Ac ther arn sevene doughtres that serve Truthe
    evere,

And beth porteres to the posternys that to the place   *doorkeepers; side doors; belong*
    longeth.

105 That on hatte Abstinence; Humylite is another ;   *is named*

Charite and Chastite beth her chef maydens;   *are*

Pacience and Pees, mekil peple thei helpen;   *many*

Largenesse the lady lateth in wel manye.   *Generosity; allows; very*

Ac who is sib to the sustres—so me God helpe—   *related*

110 He is wonderly wolcome and fayre underfonged.   *especially; well/nicely; received*

But he be sib related to some of thes sevene sustres,   *Unless; is*

Hit is wel hard, by myn hod, ony of you alle   *very*

To gete ingate at eny gate, but grace be the more."   *gain entrance; unless; is; stronger*

"By Crist," quod a cuttepurs, "I have no kyn there!"   *pickpocket; relatives*

115 "Ne I," quod a pelour, "by oughth that I knowe!"   *Nor; robber; anything*

"Wite God," quod a waufrere, "wiste I that the sothe,   *May [God] know; wafer or cake*
    maker; if I knew that was the truth

Shulde I nevere ferther a fote, for no freres prechyng."   *Would go*

"Yis," quod Peres Plowman, and poked him to gode,   *urged; toward virtue*

* "Mercy had a mayden there: she myghte over hem alle;   *has power*

120 She is sib to alle synful, and hure sone also;   *kin; sinners*

And thorw the help of hem two—hope thou non other—

Thou myght se grace there, so thou go bytyme."   *as long as; soon/early*

Passus Seven

Passus septimus de visione. — "The seventh step of the vision"

"This were a wickede weye but whoso hadde a gide — *would be difficult journey unless someone; guide*

That myght folwe us eche fote, til we were there." — *who; might arrive; in that place*
   Quod Perkyn the Plowman, "By Seynt Thomas the apostel, — *Piers*

* I have an half akre to ere, by the hyghe weye; — *acre; plow; main road*

5 Had I ered myn half akre, I wil with you til ye be there." — *plowed; will go*

*   "This were a long lettyng," quod a lady in a sleyre; — *would be; delay; veil*

"What shul we wynne and wyrke the whyle?" — *produce; work at; while we wait*

*   "Some shul sowe the sak, for sheding of the whete; — *to prevent spilling*

And wyves that have wolle, werchen hit ye shole, — *women; wool*

10 Spynneth hit spedly, spareth not your fyngres, — *efficiently; rest*

But yif hit be holy day, other holy even. — *Unless; or*

Loketh forth your lynene, and laboureth theron faste; — *Look after; work; on it; attentively*

The nedy and the naked, nym hede how thei lyen: — *pay attention; are housed*

Casteth hem clothes for colde, for so wil Truthe. — *provide; on account of; that's what; desires*

15 For I shal lene hem lyflode, but yif the lond fayle, — *provide; what they need to live; unless; give out*

As longe as I lyve, for the Lordes love of hevene.

And ye lovely ladyis, with your lovely fyngrys, — *fingers*

* That have sylke and sandel, soweth hit when tyme is: — *who; fine cloth; sew something; there is*

Chesıbles for chapeles, cherchis to honoure; — *chasubles (priest's liturgical robes); chapels; adorn*

20 And alle maner men, that by the mete libbes, — *what they eat*

Help hem wyrche witly that wynne your fode." — *hard / actively; produce*

*   "By Crist," quod a knyght, "thou kennest us the beste, — *teach*

And on this teme truly taught was I nevere; — *team / subject*

Kene me," quod the knight, "I wil leye ther to ere." — *instruct; make an effort; plow*

25   "By Seynt Poule," quod Perkyn, "for thou proferest the so lowe, — *because; volunteer yourself; humbly*

* I schal swynke and swete, and sowe for us bothe, — *toil; sweat*

And laboure for your love al my lyf tyme,

In covenaunt that thou kepe wel holy cherche right   *with the agreement; protect / properly*

And me fro wasteres and wikke men that me wolde distroye;   *idlers; wicked; want*

30   And go hunte hardily the hare and fox,   *vigorously*

And to bores and buckes, that breke myn hegges,   *after; boars; deer; destroy; hedges*

And fech the hom faukonys the foules to kylle,   *take home with you; falcons; birds*

For thes come to my croftes and croppe my whete."   *small enclosed fields; devour*

*   Curtesly the knight conseyvede his words: *received*

35   "By my power, Peres, I plyghte the my trouthe,   *pledge; troth / faithful word*

To fulfylle my forward, whilis I may stonde."   *part of the bargain; as long as*

*   "And yut a poynt," quod Perkyn, "I praye the more: *another matter; in addition*

Loke thou tene no tenaunt, but Truthe wil acorde;   *see that; trouble; unless; agree*

And they pore men profre the presentes and giftes,   *Even if; offer*

40   Nym hit nought, in aunter thou mow hit not deserve;   *Accept; in case; may*

For thou shalt give hit agen at on yeres ende,   *repay*

In a wel perliousere place that Purgatorie hatteth.   *much more terrible; is named*

And mysbede not thi bondemen—the beter thou myght spede;   *mistreat; "bound" laborers; / succeed*

And be trewe of thi tonge, and talis thou hate,   *stories / gossip*

45   But hit be wisdam other wit thi werkmen to chaste.   *Unless; or; discipline*

Hold with none harlotes, ne here non of her tales,   *Hang around; low-lifes; listen to; / stories / lies*

And namlyche at mete suche men eschue;   *especially; meals; avoid*

For hit arn the develes dishoures, I do hit the understonde."   *they are; devil's storytellers; take it / from me*

      "I asente, by Seynt Jame," seyth the knight thanne,

50   "For to worche by thi word, whil my lyf dureth."   *lasts*

      "And I shal aparayle me," quod Perkyn, "in pilgrimys wyse,   *dress myself; garb*

And wende with you the wey, til we fynde Truthe."

*   He caste on his clothes, yclouted and hole,   *put; patched*

His cokeres and his cuffys, for colde of his nayles,   *boots; gloves; on account of; / fingers and toes*

55   And heng his hopur on his bak, in stede of his skrippe—   *seed basket; place; wallet*

*   "A busshel of bred corn bryng me therynne,

For I wil sowe hit myself, and swythe wil I wende;   *quickly; set off*

And whoso helpeth me to erye, or eny thing swynke,   *plow; work at*

Shal have, by oure Lord God, the more hire in hervest,   *greater reward; at*

60 And make him merye with the corn, whoso hit
    begrucche.
no matter who; might dislike

    And alle skynnes crafti men that cunne leve with
    Truthe,
manner of; skillful; know how; to live

    I shal fynde hem fode, that feyfully lybbe,
provide; food; honestly

*   Save Jacke the jogelour, and Jonet at the stewes,
except; brothels

    And Robyn the ribaudour for his rusti wordes.
foul mouth; on account of; lewd

65 Truthe tolde me thus onys, and bad me telle hit ferther,
elsewhere

    Deleantur de libro, I shulde not dele with hem;
"Let them be stricken from the book" (Ps. 68:28)

    For holy chyrche is holde of hem no tithes to taken:
obliged; from; accept

    Et cum iustis non scribantur.
"And with the just let them not be inscribed" (Ps. 68:28)

*   They beth askaped godes aunter—God hem amende."
have been freed [paying tithes]; with good fortune; may God make them better

70*   Dame Worch-whanne-tyme-is Perys wyf hatte;
is named

    His doughter hatte Do-ryghth-so-or-thi-dame-schal-the-
    bete;
is named; exactly; mother; beat

    His sone hatte Suffre-thy-soveraynys-to-have-here-wille-
is named; superiors

    And-dem-hym-nought-for-yif-thou-dost-thou-schalt-hit-
    sore-abye.
judge; seriously; pay for

*   "Let God wyrche therwithalle, for so his word teches;

75* For now I am olde and hore, and have of myn owe,
gray; can be my own boss

    To penaunce and to pylgremage wyl I passe with othere.
go

*   Forthy I wyl, or I wende, do wryte my bequestes.
Therefore; before; set off; last will and testament

    " 'In dei nomine, amen: I make hit myselvyn.
"In the name of God, Amen"

    For he schal have my soule that best hath deserved,

80 And defende hit fro the fend, for so is my byleve,
protect

    Til I come to his acountes, as my crede me techys,
accounts; faith

    To have reles and remyssyoun on that rente I leve.
release; debts; leave unpaid

*   " 'The cherche schal have my careyne, and kepe my
    bonys;
corpse; look after

    For of my corn and my catel he craveth the tythys.
property; [the church] required; tithes

85 I payde hem aprestly, for peryl of my soule;
promptly

    He is byholde, I hope, to have me in mynde,
obliged

    And monne me in his memorie among alle Crystene.
recall

    " 'My wyf schal have al that I wan truly, and no more,
gained honestly

    And dele among my frendys and my dere chyldryn;
share it with

90 For though I deye today my dettes beth yquytted:
settled/paid

	Text	Gloss
	I bar home that I borwed or I to bedde yede.'	returned; before; went
*	And with the resydue and the remenaunt—by the rode of Chestre—	remainder; cross
	I wolde worschepe therwith Truthe by my lyve,	
*	And be his pilgrym at the plow, for pore menys sake.	
95	My plow schal be my pyk-staf, and pyke up the rotes,	pikestaff; pry
	And helpe my culter to kerve and close the forwys."	plow blade; cut open; furrows
	Now is Peres and the pilgrimys to the plow fare;	has; gone
	To herye the half-akere helpyn hym manye.	plow
	Dykeres and delveres dyggyng on the bankes;	ditchers; diggers
100	Therwith was Perkyn apayde, and preysed hem yerne.	pleased; eagerly/warmly
	Other werkmen ther were that wroughthyn ful faste;	worked; very hard
	Everey man on his manere made hym to done;	own way; set himself; do his job
	And some, to plese Perkyn, gaderyd out the wedys.	picked
*	At the hey prime Peres let the plow stande,	midmorning; stop
105	To oversey hem hymself: whoso best wroughthe	check out/look over; whoever; worked
	Schuld be heryed therafter, when hervest tyme come.	praised
	Thanne sete ther some, and sunge at the ale,	sat down; sang
*	And helpen to erye that half akre with "Dusa Damme Eme!"	plow; "Sweet Lady Emma" (song)
*	"By the prince of paradys," quod Peres tho in wratthe,	
110	"But ye ryse the rather and rape you to werche,	Unless; very quickly; hasten
	Schal no greyn that her groweth glade you at nede,	grain; fill; when you need it
	And they ye deye for dol, the devel hange that recke!"	even if; grief; may the devil hang whom he wants
	Thanne were faytourys aferd, and fayned hem blynde;	fakers/idlers; pretended; themselves
*	Some leyde the leg alery, as suche loselys counne,	akimbo; loafers; know how
115	And pleyned hem to Peres with suche pytous wordis:	complained
	"We have no lymes to labore with, Lord ygraced be ye!	We're disabled and can't work; blessed
	Ac we praye for you, Peres, and for your plow bothe,	but; also
	That God for his grace youre greyn multyplye,	increase
	And yelde you for your almesse that ye gyve us here.	repay; alms; what
120	For we mowe nother swete ne swynke, such febelnysse us eyleth."	neither sweat nor work; weakness; afflicts
	"Yif hit be soth," quod Peres, "that ye seye, I schal hit sone aspye.	true; what you say; discover
	Ye beth wastores, I wot wel, and Truthe wot the sothe;	are; parasites; knows
	And I am his olde hyne, I aughte hym to warne	long-time servant; warn him against

Swyche wastores in this worlde his werkmen to
    destroyin.

125   Ye eten that I schulde ete that erye for us alle; — *what; plow*
Ac Truthe schal teche you hys teem for to dryve, — *team (of oxen)*
Bothe to sette and to sowe, and to save his tilthe, — *plant; harvest; crops*
Chace gees from the corn, and kepe his bestis, — *Chase; geese; look after*
Or ye sculle eten barly bred, and of the brok drynke. — *Before; shall*

130   But he be blynd other brokeschankyd, other bedred — *Unless; one; broken-legged; lies*
    lygges, — *bedridden*
Ye schulle as I, so me God helpe, — *shall have what I have*
Til God of his grace gere hem to aryse. — *cause*
Ankeres and ermites that holdeth hem in her sellys, — *Anchorites; hermits; keep themselves*

Ye schal have of myn almesse, al the while I lybbe, — *some of my alms*
135   Ynow eche day at non, ac no more ar morwe, — *noon; before tomorrow/morning*
Lest his flesch and the fend foulyd his soule; — *defiled*
Onys at non is ynowgh that no werk ne usyth; — *physical work; enough for one who; performs*

He abydeth wel the betere that bommeth not to ofthe." — *remains/exists; much; who drinks; often*

*   Than gan the wastores aryse, and wolde have — *wanted to fight*
    yfoughte;
140* To Pers the plowman he proferyd his glove; — *one presented (as a challenge to fight)*

A Bretonyr, a braggere, bostede hym also, — *Breton; braggart; addressed arrogantly*

And bad hym go pysse hym with his plow—pylede — *piss himself; hairy bastard!*
    schrewe!
"Wille thou, nelle thou, we wil have oure wil — *Willy-nilly, we will get what we want*

Of thy flour and thy flees, fette away whanne so us — *meat; [we] will take; whenever it*
    lykyth, — *pleases us*
145* And make us merye therwith, maugre thy chekys!" — *in spite of*
    Thanne Peres Plowman pleyned hym to the — *complained*
    knyghthys,
To kepe hym, as covenaunt was, from cursede schrewes, — *protect; agreement; damned troublemakers*

Fro wasteres that wayte wynneres to schende. — *look; productive workers; ruin*
*   Curteysly tho the kynghth, as his kynde wolde, — *nature required*
150 Warnede wastores, and wyssede hem betere— — *advised*
"Or ye schal abyghe by the lawe, by the lord that I — *pay in accord with; profess*
    welde."

"I was not woned to worche," quod wastores, "now   accustomed
   wil I not bygynne."
And let lyth of the lawe, and lasce of the knyghth,   made light; less
And countede Peres at a pese, and his plow bothe,   worthless (the value of a pea); also

155   And mancede hym and his men, whanne thei nyxt   threatened
   mette.
   "Now, by the peril of my soule," quod Peres, "I schal   bring harm to
   apeyre you alle!"
*   And hopyd after Hounger, that herde hym at the fyrste: whooped; who; right away
   "Awrek me on thes wastores," quod Peres, "that this   avenge; destroy
   worlde schendis!"
   Hounger in haste thenne hente wastores by the   grabbed; stomach/belly
   mawe,
160   And wrang hem by the mawe that alle watered her eyen,   squeezed; so that
   And buffeted the Bretoner abouthe the chekys,   slapped
   That he loked as a lanterne al his lyf after.   so that; like; lantern
   He bet hem so bothe, and brak nere here mawes;   beat; burst; nearly
*   Ne hadde Peres with a pese lof prayed hem belyve,   if Piers had not; a bread made from peas; asked; quickly
165   And with a bene bach he hadde bytwene,   of beans; wad
   And hitte Hounger therwith amydde his lyppys—   between
   And bledde into the bodyward a bolle ful of grouuel—   poured; stomach; bowl; watery porridge

   Ne hadde the fesysyoun defended hem water   if not; doctor; forbidden
*   To bate the barly bred and the benys ygrounde,   wash down (? soak)
170   Thei hadde ben dede by this day, and dolven al warme.   would have; buried
   Faytoures for fere flowyn into bernys,   fakers/idlers; rushed
   And flappyn on with flaylys, fro morwe til eve,   beat; flails; morning; night
   That Hounger was not so hardy onys on hem to loke,   so that; brave enough
   For a potel of pesyn that Peres hadde ymaked.   Because of; half gallon; peas; prepared

175   An hep of ermytes hente hem spadys   crowd; picked up; for themselves
   And dolven dryt and donge to dryve Hounger out.   dug; manure; dung
   Blynde and blereyed were aboute a thowsand   bleary-eyed
   That leyghe blynde and broke-legged by the hye waye.   lay; main road
   Hounger hem helede with an hot cake,   cured; loaf
180   And manye lame mennys lymes were lythed that tyme,   made whole/cured
   And bycomen knavys to kepe Peres bestes,   servants; look after
   And prayde for cherite with Peres for to dwelle,   love of God

      And for covetyse of his corn, to chace away Hounger. — *out of a desire to have some of*

      And Peres was proud therof, and putte hem into offys, — *useful jobs*

185 Gaf hem mete and mone as they myghthe aserve. — *food; money; deserve*

        Thanne hadde Peres pyte, and prayde Hounger to wende — *begged; go away*

      Home into his owen yerd, and holde hym ther evere— — *own garden; keep himself; always*

      "And yut I praye," quod Peres, "or thou passe ferther, — *before; go away*

*   Of beggeres and bydderes what is best to done? — *panhandlers*

190 For I wot wel, be thou went, they wil worche ylle; — *know; if you were gone; badly*

      Myschef hit maketh, they beth so meke nowthe, — *hardship; causes; obedient; now*

      And for defaute of fode thus faste they wyrche; — *because of; lack; hard*

      And hit beth my blody brethryn, for God boughthe us alle. — *were; [related by] blood; redeemed*

      Truthe taughthe me onys to love hem echone,

195 And helpe hem of al thing, what that hem nedyth. — *in; in whatever for them was necessary*

      Now wolde I wyte yif thou wystyst what were the beste, — *want to know; know*

      Hou I myghthe amastrye hem, and make hem to wyrche." — *keep them in line*

        "Here now," quod Hounger, "and hold hit for a wysdom: — *Listen*

      Bolde beggeres and bygge that mowe her bred byswynke, — *may earn by labor*

200 With houndys bred and horse bred hold up her hertes, — *food for dogs and horses; spirits*

      And bayte hem with bonys, for swellyng of her wombys; — *relieve; husks; to prevent; bellies*

      And yif the gromys grucche, byd hem go and swynke, — *men; grumble; tell; get to work*

      For he schal soupe swetter when he hath hit deserved. — *enjoy his food more; earned*

      Ac yif thou fynde ony freke that fortune hath apeyred — *but; person; harmed*

205 With fyre other with falce men, fonde suche to knowe; — *or; seek out*

      Comforte hym with thy catel, for Cristes love of hevene; — *goods*

      Love hem and lene hem, for so the lawe of kynde wolde. — *support; nature; wants [it]*

      And alle maner of men, that thou myghthe aspye, — *kinds; discover*

      That nedy beth or naked, and noughth have to spende, — *nothing*

      With mete or with mone lat hem be the betere. — *food; money*

210* Lat make the frendys therwith, and so Mathew us techys: — *Make yourself friends in this way*

      Facite vobis amicos iniquitatis et cetera." — *"Make for yourselves friends of iniquity etc." (Luke 16:9)*

        "I wolde not gryve God for al the gold," quod Peres, "that groweth on this grounde. — *offend; earth*

	Myght I synneles don as thou seyst?" seyde Peres thanne.	without sin; asked
	"Ye, hardyly," quod Hunger, "or elles the Byble lyes;	certainly
215*	Go to Genesys the geaunt, engendrour of us alle:	giant; originator
	'*In sudore vultus tui* swynke thou shalt thi mete,	"In the sweat of [your] face" (Gen. 3:19); you will work for your food
	Tile and laboure for thi liflode,' as oure Lord hyghte.	Cultivate; livelihood; promised
*	And Sapiens seyth the same—I se hit in the Bible:	Wisdom
	'*Piger propter frigus* no felde nolde tilie;	"The idler on account of cold" (Prov. 20:4); would not cultivate
220	He shal bygge and begge, and no man bete his hunger.'	buy; beg; shall relieve
*	Mathew with the mannes face thes wordes thus mowtheth:	intones
	That *servus nequam* had a name, and for he ne wolde hit use,	"wicked servant" (Luke 19:22); talent; because
	He hadde maugre of his mayster evermore after;	ill will
	And bynam him his namme, for he ne wolde worche,	he took away; talent
225	And gaf hit him in haste that hadde ten ther byfore;	to him
	And sitthen hit seyde, that his mayster hit hadde:	afterward; got it back
*	'He that hath shal have, to helpe ther nede is,	
	And he that nought hath shal not han, ne no man him helpe;	nothing; get
	And that he wenyth wel to have, I wil that hit be him bereved.'	what; expects confidently; hold on to; from him; taken away
230	"Kynde wit wolde that eche wight wroughthe	wants; person; worked
	Or with teching or tellyng, or travalyng of hande,	either; working
	The Sauter seyth, in the psalme of *Beati omnes*,	"Blessed (are) all" *(Ps. 127)*
	Labores manuum tuarum quia manducabis, et ceteru:	"The works of your hands you shall eat, etc." (Ps. 127:2)
	He that get his fode here with trauayl of his handes—	obtains; work
235	God gevyth hem his blessynge that here liflode here so wynne."	living; earn
*	"Yit I praye the," quod Peres, "for charite, yif thou kennys	know
	Eny lyf of lechecraft, ken hit me, my dere.	page; medicine; teach
	For somme of my servauntes ben sek otherwhile,	are; sometimes
	Of alle the wyke worcheth not, so here wombe aketh."	for the entire week; so much; belly; aches
240*	"I wot wel," quod Hunger, "what syknesse hem eyleth:	afflicts
	Thei han manged overmykel; that maketh hem grone ofte.	eaten too much; causes

Ac I hote the," quod Hunger, "as thou thin hele weldest,   *but; command; as long as; (good) health; are in*

That thou drynke no day er thou ete sumwhat;   *before; something*
And not ete er hunger the take, and sent the of his sauce   *you*
245 To savoure thi lyppus; and kep sum til super tyme,   *lick; hold back*
And syt not longe: arys up er Apetyt have his fylle.   *get up; before*
Let not Sire Surfet sit at thi bord;   *table; Excess*
Lef not him: he is a lechour, and liberous of his tunge,   *love/believe; gluttonous*
And after many maner metes his mawe is alonged.   *types [of] foods; stomach; eager/craving*

250   "And yif thou diete the thus, I dar leyn myn armes,   *regulate (your) eating; wager*
That Fysyk shal his furred hod for his fode selle,   *Medicine*
And eke his cloke with calabre, and the knottes of golde,   *also; a kind of fur (associated with Calabria [in southern Italy]); cloak*

And be fayn, by my fay, his fysyk to letyn,   *content; medicine; put aside*
And lerne him laboure with lond, last his lyflode him fayle.   *on the; lest he lose his livelihood*
255* Ther are mo lyeres than lechys—God hem amende!   *more; doctors; reform them*
They don men deye with her drynke, ere destene wolde."   *cause; before; destiny; intended*
    "By Seynt Poul," quod Peres, "thes are profytable wordes;   *helpful*
This is a lovely lessoun; Lord hit the foryelde!   *attractive; amply repay*
Wend now when thy wil is, for wel be thou evere."   *Leave; may [you] be*
260* "I behote God," quod Hunger, "hennys ne wil I wende   *promise; from here*

Ere I have dined by this day, and ydrunke bothe."   *during; also*
    "I have no peny," quod Peres, "poletes to bugge,   *money; young hens*
Neyther ges ne grys; but tweyne grete cheses,   *piglets; only; two; large*
A fewe cruddes and crem, and an aver cake,   *curds; oat*
265 A lof of benys and bren ybake for my children;   *bran*
And yut I sey, by my soule, I have no salt bakoun,
Ne no cokeney, be Crist, colloppes to make.   *small egg; bacon and eggs*
Ac I have parsely and poret, many cool plantes,   *but; leeks; cabbage*
And eke a kow and a calf, and a cart mare   *also*
270 To drawe afelde the dunge, whil the drouthe lestyth.   *manure; as long as; dry weather*
By this liflode I most lyve til Lammasse tyme;   *on these provisions; early August (harvest) time*

By that I hope to have hervest in my croft;   *By then; (small enclosed) field*
Than may I dyghthe thi dyner as the dere lykyth."   *prepare; best; it pleases*
*   Al the pore puple the pesecoddes fetten,   *people; peapods; gathered*
275 Benys and bake applys thei broughte in her lappes,   *beans; aprons*

Chibolles and skalonys, and ripe cheries manye,   onions; scallions
And profred Peres this present, to plese therwith   offered
   Hunger.
And Hunger ete this in haste, and asked after more.   for
Than this folk for fere fetten him more   brought for him
280* Grene poret and pesyn, to poysone him they thoughthe.   cabbage; peas; dose him
By than hit neyhed hervest, and newe corn come to   approached; grain
   towne;
Than were folk fayn, and fedde Hunger with the beste.   content
With goud ale and glotonye, thei gere him to slepe.   overeating; put
   Tho wolde Wastour not wyrche, but wandre aboute,
285 Ne no beggere ete bred that benyn come inne,   beans
But coket and clerematyn, or of clene whete;   two kinds of fine white bread;
                                                 nothing but

Ne non halpeny ale on none wise drynke,   cheap; way
But of the beste and the brouneste that brewesteres   darkest brown; brewers
   sellyn.
   Laboureres that have no lond to lyve by but her
   handes,
290 Deyneth not to dyne o day nyghth-olde wortes.   condescend; last night's
                                                 vegetables

Ther may no peny ale hem paye, ne no pece of bakoun,   weak; satisfy / please
But hit be fresch flesch, other fysche yfryed,   unless; fresh meat; or fried fish
Bothe chaufed and *plus* chaufed, for chillyng of here   warmed; very warmed; to avoid;
   mawe.   stomach
* But he be heylyche hered, ellys wil he grucche,   unless; paid very good wages;
                                                 otherwise; complain

295 That he was ewere man wrought warie the tyme,   ever; created; curse
And curse the king, and al his counseyl after,
Suche lawes to loke laburers to chaste.   enact; punish
Ac whil Hunger was her mayster her non wolde chide   but; complain
Ne stryve agen the statute, so sternely he lokede.   Nor agitate against
300   I warne you, werkmen, wynneth whil ye mowe;   earn
For Hunger hiderward heyeth him faste.   hastens; quickly
* He shal awake thorw watur wastoures to chaste;   by means of; punish
Er fyve wynter be fulfyld, such famyn shal arise,   before; years; completed; famine
Thorw flod and foule wederes, cornes shul fayle;   grain crops
305 And so seyth Saturne, and sent you to warne.   predict; sends

Passus Eight

Passus octavus de visione.   "The eighth step of the vision"

*   Truthe herde telle therof, and to Peres sente
       To takyn his tem, and his erthe tylie;   team; soil/land; till
*   And purchas him a pardoun *a pena et a culpa*,   obtain; indulgence; "from
                                                                 punishment and from guilt"

*   For him and his eyres, evermore after.   himself; heirs
5   And bad him holde him at home, and eryen his layes;   keep himself; plow; unplowed
                                                                 lands
       And al that shul helpe to erie and to sowe,   plow
       Or ony maner myster that myghthe Peres helpe,   trade
       Part in that pardoun the pope hath ygraunted.   share; indulgence
          Kinges and knightes that kepeth holy cherche,   protect/defend
10   And ryghthfully the rewme rewlyth, and the peple,   justly; kingdom
       Have pardoun thorw purgatorie to passe ful sone,   indulgence; very quickly
       With patriarchis in paradis to pleye therafter.
*   Bysshopis that blessen, and bothe lawes kunne,   give blessings; understand
       Loke on that o lawe and lere men that other,   Watch over; teach
15*   And bere bothe on here bak, as her baner sheweth,   carry
*   And prechen hire parsonys the peril of synne,
       How that the shabbede shep shul here wolle save,   diseased; protect/keep
       Have pardoun with the aposteles when thei passen   from this life
          hennys,
       And at the day of dome at here deys to sitten.   judgment; high table
20*   Marchauntes, in that margyn, hadden manye yeres,   margin of that document; received
                                                                 years (of indulgence)
       But none *a pena et a culpa* the pope nolde graunte;   from punishment and from guilt
*   For thei holde not her holydayes, as holy churche techys, keep/observe
       And for thei swere by here soule, and so God mot hem   because
          helpe,
       Agens clene conciens, here catel to selle.   goods
25   And under his secret sel Truthe sente hem a lettre,
       And bad hem begge baldely what hem best lykede,   buy; confidently; it pleased
       And swythe selle hit agen, and save the wynnyng,   quickly; keep; profit

* And make *meysoun deu* therwith, mysese to helpe, — build; "house of God" (i.e., hospital); illness

* Wyckede weyes wytly to amende, — unsafe roads; actively; repair
30 And thinke on brygges aboute that tobroke were, — bridges; broken to pieces
* Maryen maydenys also, or make hem nounnes; — make it possible for (them) to marry; become

* Pore widues that wiln be wyves non after—
Fynden suche here fode, for oure Lordes love of hevene; — provide
Sette scholeres to scole, or sum kennys craftes; — students; kind of
35 Releyve religious, and renten hem betere— — provide support for; religious orders; support

* "And I shal sende myself Michael, myn aungel,
That no devel shal you dere, deye when ye deye, — So that; threaten; whenever you die

That I ne shal sende your soule saf into hevene,
And byfore the face of my fader for me you sette. — before
40 Usure, avarice, and othes I defende, — forbid
That no gile go with you, but the grete truthe." — so that
   Than were marchauntes merie and some wepe for joye,
* And gaf Wille for his wrytyng wollene clothes;
* For he copiede thus hire clause, hy konne him gret mede. — copied; offered
45 Men of lawe hadde leve, for lered thei ben alle; — permission; are
And so seyth the Sauter and Sapience bothe: — Psalter; (book of) Wisdom
* *Super innocentem munera non accipies. A regibus et principibus erit.* — "You shall not accept bribes/gifts against the innocent" (Ps. 14:5). "From kings and princes will be [their reward]" (cf. *Ecclus. 38:2*)

Of prynces and of prelates here pencioun shal arise, — payment
And of no pore peple no peneworth to take. — not a penny's worth
50* Ac that spendith his speche to speke for the pore, — he who employs
That innocent is and nedy, and no man apeyre, — injures no one
Shal no devel, at his deth-day, derie him a myte, — harm; bit
That he ne worth saf sykerly, and so seyth the Sauter. — so that; will be saved; surely
   Ac to bugge water, ne wynd, and wit is the thridde, — buy
55 Wolde nevere holy writ—God wot the sothe! — wanted; Holy Scripture; truth
These thre for thralles beth proved among us alle, — bound servants; are; provided
To waxen and wanyen, the while God lyketh. — grow/increase; lessen/decrease; it pleases

His pardoun in purgatorye wel petit is, I trowe, — very small; believe

That ony mede of mene men for motyng reseyven. — *Who; payment; from; poor; pleading in a lawcourt*

60 Ye legisteres and lawyeres, ye wyte yif I leye! — *advocates; know*
Syn ye se hit is thus, sheweth the beste. — *since*
    Alle lyvynge laboroures, that lyven by here handes,
That trulyche taken and trulyche wynnen, — *justly; obtain; earn*
And lyve in love and in lawe for here lowe herte, — *on account of; humble*
65 Hadde the same absolucyoun that sent was to Peres. — *received; forgiveness*
    Beggeres and bydderes beth not in the bulle, — *panhandlers; are not included in; papal document*

*   But the suggestionys be soth that him nede to begge. — *unless; allegations; genuine; it was necessary for him to beg*

For he that beggeth or biddeth, but yif he have nede, — *asks; unless*
He is fals with the fend, and frawdeth the nedy, — *like; deprives*
70 And eke gileth the gyvere, ageyns his wille. — *also; deceives; [to act] against*
They lyve not in love, ne no lawe holden; — *obey*
They wedde no wymmen that thei with delyn; — *have [sexual] relations*
* But as wilde bestes with "whehe," and worth up togederes, — *like; whoopee; mount one another*
And brynge forth barnys that bastardes ben yholden. — *children; are considered*
75 Or his bak or his bon thei brekyn in his youthe, — *Either*
And gon and fayten with her fauntes for evermore after. — *beg under false pretenses; children*

Ther beth mo mysshape amonges hem, whoso take hede, — *disabled; pays attention*
Than of alle other maner man that on this molde wandryn. — *kind of; earth*
Tho that have thus here lyf mow lothe the tyme — *Those; their; may hate*
80 That evere he was man wroughth, when he shal hennys fare. — *from here; depart*
    And olde men and hore, that are helples of strengthe, — *gray-haired*
And wymmen with childe, that wyrche nc mowc, — *rnay*
Blynde and blereyde, and broken here membres, — *with poor eyesight; limbs*
That taketh here myschef mekely, as meselis and othere, — *accept; misfortune; humbly; lepers*
85 Have as pleyn pardoun as plowmen hemselven; — *full*
Of here lowe herte oure Lord hath hem ygraunted — *for; humble*
* Here penaunce and here purgatorie upon this pleyn erthe. — *bare/flat; earth*
*   "Peres," quod a prest, "thi pardoun most I rede; — *look over*
I shal construy every clause, and telle hit the on Englys." — *interpret; explain; to you*
90   And Peres, at his prayer, his pardoun unfoldeth, — *request*

* And I, byhynde hem bothe, behelde al the bulle.   *papal document*

In two lynys hit lay, and not a lettere more;   *lines; consisted*

Hit was wryten ryght thus, in witnesse of Truthe: *just*

* *Et qui bona egerunt, ibunt in vitam eternam;*   *"And those who did good deeds, they will go into eternal life"*

95 *Qui vero mala, in ignem eternum.*   *"Those, however, who did wicked deeds, into eternal fire"*

* "Peter!" quod the prest tho, "I can no pardoun fynde,   *then*

But 'do wel and have wel, and God shal have thi soule;   *only*

And do evyl and have evyl, trust thou non other,   *nothing else*

Than after thi deth-day thou shalt wende to helle.'"

100* And Peres tho, for tene, pulled hit asunder, and seyde,   *then; anger; tore it in pieces*

* "*Si ambulavero in medio umbre mortis, non timebo mala, quoniam tu mecum es.*   *"If I should walk in the middle of the shadow of death, I shall not fear evil, because you are with me" (Ps. 22:4)*

* I shal sece of my sowyng," quod Peres, "and swynke not so harde,   *stop; work*

Ne aboute my lyflode so busy be no more;   *food / sustenance*

Of prayeres and of penaunce my plow shal be hereafter,   *from now on*

105 And beloure that I bylowe ere, they liflode me fayle.   *(I will) frown at; what; laughed at previously; even if I had no food*

* "The prophete his peyne hath in penauns and in wepyng,   *punishment*

By that the Sauter us seyth, and so dude many othere;   *according to; tells*

That loveth God lelly his lyflode is the more: *one who; faithfully; food*

Fuerunt mihi lacrime meae panes, die ac nocte.   *"My tears have been to me my food, by day and by night" (Ps. 41:3)*

110* And but yif the Boke lye, he telleth us another,   *unless; Bible*

By foules that are not busey aboute the bely joye: *birds; pleasures*

Non soliciti sitis, he seyth in his gospel,   *"Do not be anxious" (Matt. 6:25; cf. Luke 12:22)*

And sheweth hit us fayre by on exaumple oureselve to wisse.   *to us; clearly; teach*

The foulis in the firmament, who fynt hem in wynter?   *birds; provides [for]*

115 Whan the frost freseth, fode hem behoveth;   *freezes; for them; is necessary*

They have no gerner to go to, but God fynt hem alle."   *granary / storeroom; provides [for]*

Quod the prest to Perkyn, "By Crist! as me thenketh,   *so; to me it seems*

Thou art lerned a lytel. Who lered the on boke?"   *educated; taught; in books*

"Abstinence myn aunte myn A B C me taughthe,

120   And Conciens com after, and taughthe me moche
        more."
        "Were thou a prest, Peres, thou myght preche whan   *it pleased you*
          the lykede:
*   *Quoniam literaturam non cognovi* myghthe be thi teme."   "Because I do not have book-
                                           learning" (Ps. 70:15); subject

        "Lewed lorel," quod Peres, "litel lokest thou on thy   *ignorant; wretch*
          Byble;
    On Salomonys sawes litel thou beholdest: *sayings; gaze*
125   *Eice derisores et iurgia cum eis, ne crescant."*   "Cast out the mockers and
                                           quarrels along with them, so that
                                         they do not increase" (Prov. 22:10)

*   The prest and Perkyn aposed here eyther other,   *debated; each of them the other*
*   And thorw here wordes I awok, and wayted aboute,   *looked around*
    And saw the sonne evere south sytte that tyme.   *still sitting in the south*
        Meteles and moneyles upon Malverne hullys,   *Without food; without money*
130* Mamelyng on this metelys made me to studie,   *Babbling; dreams*
    And for Peres men the plowman, wel pensyf in herte,   *on account of; remembrance; very*
    For that I saw sleping, yif hit so be myghthe.   *Because of what; whether it might*
                                           be true

*   And Catoun construith hit nay, and canonistres bothe,   *Cato; concludes it (is) not so;*
                                         canon lawyers; also

    And jugyn hemselven, *Sompnia ne cures, et cetera.*   *hold the view; for themselves;*
                                         "Pay no attention to dreams, etc."

135   And for the Bible bereth witnysse how   *because*
*   Daniel demede the dremys of a knyghth,   *interpreted*
    That Nabagodonosor nemned this clerk;   *named*
    Danyel seyde, "Sire king, thi swevene is to mene   *dream; mean (signify)*
    That unkyd knyght shal come thi kyngdoum to cleyme;   *unknown; take over*
140   Among lowere lordes thi kingdam shal be departed."   *divided*
    As Daniel demed, in dede hit byfel after: *interpreted; fact; happened*
    The king les his lordschep; lasse men hit hadde.   *lost; sovereignty; lesser; took over*
*   And Josep mette mervelyusly hou the mone and the   *dreamed; wonderfully; moon*
          sunne
    And the enlevene sterres hayled hym alle.   *eleven stars; honored*
145   "Bew sire," quod his fader, "for defaute we shulle,   *Fair; lack (of food) / famine*
    I myself, and my sones, sekyn the for nede."   *search for; out of necessity*
    And hit befel as the fader seyde, in Pharaoys tyme,   *occurred*
    That Josep was justise, Egypt to kepe.   *judge; protect / rule*
        Al this maketh me on metelys to thinke,   *dreams; reflect*
150   Many tymes at mydnyght, when men shulde slepe;   *people*

On Peres plowman, whych a pardoun he haveth, *what kind of*

And hou the prest enpugned hit, al by pure resoun; *challenged; reason alone*

* And demed that Dowel indulgence passyth, *declared; surpasses*

* Byenales and trienales, and bisshopes lettres. *biennials (two years of masses);*
triennials (three years)

155* Dowel at the day of dome is dignelyche underfonge; *worthily received*

He passeth al the pardoun of Seynt Petres cherche. *surpasses; indulgences*

   Now hath the pope power pardoun to graunte *indulgences*

The peple with a penauns to passe to joye.

This is a lef of oure byleve as lettred men us teche: *page; faith; educated*

160 *Quodcumque ligaveris super terram, et cetera.* *"And whatever you shall bind*
upon earth, etc." (Matt. 16:19)

And so I leve lely—Lord forbede ellys— *truly; I don't*

That prayeres and pardoun and penauns ben salve *indulgences; are a cure*

To soules that have synned sevene sythes dedly. *times; mortally*

Ac to truste on this tryenales, truly me thinketh, *But; three years of masses; it*
seems to me

165 Hit is not so syker for the soule, certus, as is do wel. *safe; certainly; doing*

   Forthi I rede ye ne thinketh, ye that ben on erthe, *Therefore; advise; are*

Upon trust of your tresoure trienales to have:

Be thou nevere the bolder to breke the ten hestes! *commandments*

And namly ye maystres, as meyres and juges, *especially*

170 That have the welthe of this world, and wise men be *whoever; are considered*
   yholde,

To purchace pardoun and the popes bulles! *obtain; indulgences; documents*

At the day of dome whan ded shul arise

And come alle byfore Crist acountes to yelde— *settle*

How thou ledest thi lyf here, and his lawe keptest, *observed*

175 What thou dedust day by day: the doum wil reherse! *judgment; make public*

* A poke ful of pardoun there, ne provinciales letteres, *bag*

Though thou be founde in the fraternite of alle the foure *installed*
   orderes,

And have indulgence dublefold, but Dowel you helpe, *unless*

I nolde gyve for the patent of thi pardoun o fleis hele! *official document; one; fly's heel*

180   Forthi I conceyle alle Cristen to crie God mercy, *Therefore; advise; to beg God*
(for) mercy

And Marie his moder to ben mene betwynne, *intermediary*

That God gif us grace her, er we gon hennys, *here before; from here*

Suche werkes to worche, while we ben here, *perform; are*

That, after oure deth-day, Dowel reherse *may declare*

185 That, at the day of dome, we dude as we aughthe. Amen.

Explicit hic Visio Willelmi de Petro, & cetera.

Et hic incipit Vita de Dowel, Dobet, & Dobest secundum wit & resoun.

"Here ends the vision of William about Peter, etc."

"And here begins the life of Dowel, Dobet, and Dobest, according to wit and reason."

Passus Nine

* *Vita de Dowel, Dobet, & Dobest secundum Wit & Resoun*
   [Prologus]

Thus yrobed in russet I romed aboute, *dressed; working clothes*
Al a somer sesoun, for to seche Dowel; *spring*
And I frayned wel ofte, of folk that I mette, *inquired; frequently*
Yif ony wiste where Dowel was at inne, *If anyone; knew; lodging*
5 And what man he myghthe be, of meny man I frayned. *inquired*
    Was ther nevere wyghth, as I wene, that me wisse *person; believe; advise/instruct*
      cowde
    Wher this lode longeth, lasse ne more, *fellow; dwelled*
* Til hit fel on a Fryday, two freres I mette, *happened; friars*
    Maysteres of the Menoures, men of gret wyt. *Theologians; Franciscans*
10 And I haylsed hem hendely, as I hadde lerned, *greeted; courteously*
    And prayde hem for cherite, er thei passide ferthere, *asked; charity*
    Yif thei knewen ony countre or costes aboute, *places/regions*
    Wher that Do-wel duellyth, doth me to wisse. *let; know*
      "Marie," quod tho maystres, "at hom with us he *Mary; those; at home; lives*
        duelleth;
15 And evere hath, as I hope, and evere shal hereafter." *always has; believe*
*   "*Contra*," quod I as a clerk, and gan to disputen: *"On the contrary"; like a college student; began; debate*

"*Sepcies in die cadet iustus & cetera.* *"Seven times in a day the just man will fall, etc." (Prov. 24:16)*

'Sevene sythes on the day,' seyth the Book, 'falleth the *times; Bible; righteous*
  rytful.'
And whoso synnes," I sayde, "certes, me thinkes, *certainly; it seems to me*
20 That Dowel and Do-evel mow not duelle togederes; *may*
    Ergo, he is nowt alway at hom among you freres; *"Therefore"*
    He is otherwhile elleswher to wissen the peple." *sometimes; teach/direct*
      "I shal sey the my sawe," seyde the frere thanne, *tell; story*
      "How sevene sythes on the day the sadde man synnes; *good/just*
25* By a forebysne," quod the frere, "I shal the fayre shewe: *example; clearly demonstrate*
    Let brynge a man in a bot, amyddes a brod water; *boat; in the middle of; wide lake*
    The wynd and the water and the waggeng of the bote *rocking*

Maketh the man many tyme to falle and to stande; — get up

For stonde he nevere so styf, he stumbleth in the
wagging. — no matter; how steady/straight; rocking

30 And yit he is saf and sound, and so him behoves, — as is right for him

For yif he ne arise rather, and raughthe the sterne, — more quickly; takes hold of; rudder

The wynd wolde with the water the bot overthrowe. — capsize

Ther were the mannys lyf ylost, for lachesse of
himselve. — In that case; would be; negligence

"Ryght thus hit fareth," quod the frere, "with folk here
on erthe: — just so; goes

35 The water is lyk to this world, that waxeth and wanyes; — rises; falls

The godes of the grounde beth lyk to the wawes, — goods; earth; are

And as wyndes and wateres wawes abowte; — go back and forth

The bot is lik to the body, that brotel is of kinde, — fragile; by nature

And thorw the fend and the flesh, and the falce world, — deceiving

40 Syneth the sadde man sevene sithes on the day. — Sins; good; times

"Ac dedly synne doth he not, for Dowel him helpeth, — but; mortal

That is Charite the champioun, chef helpe of alle; —

Agen sevene to stonde, he steryth the soule, — Against seven (deadly sins); maneuvers

That they the body bowe, as a bot doth on the water, — So that; though; bob up and down; boat

45 Ay is the soule saf, but thou thiself wilt — Always; unless; assent to

Folwe thi fleschly wil, and the fend after, — desire

And do dedly synne, and drenche thy soule. — mortal; drown

God wil suffre the to deye so, for thou hast the maystry." — allow; control

* "I have no kinde knowyng," quod I, "to conseyve thi
wordes; — natural knowledge; understand

50 And yif I may lyve and loke, I shal go lere ferther. — be able to; investigate; learn more

I bykenne the Crist, that on the cros deyde." — commend you to Christ

And thei seyde the same—"Save the fro myschauns, — misfortune

And gif the grace on this erthe in goud lyf to ende." — give you

Thus I wente wide-wher, Dowel to seche, — here and there; search for

55 And as I wente by a wode, walkyng myn one, — wood; on my own

Blysse of the bryddes made me to abyde, — Happy sounds; stop

And under a lynde upon a launde lened I me a stounde, — linden tree; meadow; lay down; myself; for a while

To lythen the layes the lovely bryddes madyn. — listen to; songs; created

Blisse of the bryddes broughte me aslepe; — Harmony; put

60 The mervelyouste metyng mette me thanne, — most magical dream; came to [me] as a dream

That evere dryght in doute drempte as I wene. — *a man; fear/anxiety; dreamt; think*
A meke man, me thoughthe, lyk to myselven, — *humble; it seemed to me*
Com and calde me by my ryghthe name. — *called; proper*
   "What art thou," quod I, "that my name knowest?"
65   "That wost thou wel," quod he, "and no wyghth — *know; person*
      betere."
     "Wot I," quod I, "who art thou?" "Thought," than he — *do I know*
      seyde;
*   "I have served the this sevene yere—sey thou me no — *did you see me no sooner*
      rather?"
     "Art thou Thought," quod I, "thou coudest me telle — *if you are; would be able*
Wher Dowel dwelleth, and do me to wisse." — *make; understand*
70*   "Dowel," quod he, "and Dobet, and Dobest the
      thridde,
Are thre fayre vertues, and beth not fer to fynde. — *attractive; are; difficult*
Whoso is meke of his mouth, and mylde of his speche,
Trewe of tounge, and of his two handis,
And thorw the labour of his handes his lyflode wynneth, — *living; earns*
75 And trosty of his taylende, taketh but his owyn, — *trustworthy; accounting; only*
And is not drunkelew ne deynous, Dowel hym folwyth. — *drunkard; arrogant*
    "Dobet thus doth, ac he doth moche more: — *but*
He is as low as a lomb, and lovely of speche; — *meek; lamb; charitable*
Whil he hath of his owyn he delyth ther most nede is: — *enough for himself; distributes; where*
80 The bagges of the bigerdelys he hath broke hem alle — *purses; torn open*
That Erle Avarous hadde, and his eyres;
*   And with Mammonas mone he hath mad him frendes, — *Mammon's money; for himself*
And is ronne to the relygious, and hath rendred the — *has gone into the religious life;*
    Bible, — *translated*
And precheth the peple Seynt Powles wordes:
85 *Libenter suffertis, et cetera.* — *"Willingly endure, etc." (cf. 2 Cor. 11:19–20)*

'The wise suffreth the onwise with you for to lybbe.' — *allow*
And with glad wil do hem good, for so God him hyghte. — *commanded*
   "Dobest is above hem bothe, and bereth a bisshopes — *crosier*
    crose,
Yhoked at that on ende to holde him in good lyf; — *curved; keep*
90 A pyk in the potent to pycche adoun the wickede, — *spike; pointed end of the staff; pitch*

That haunteth eny wickednesse Dowel to tene. — *indulge in; trouble*
And as Dowel and Dobet don him to understonde, — *cause*
They have crouned a king to kepin hem alle; — *protect*

And yif Dowel and Dobet dedyn agenst Dobest,   acted
95   And were unbuxoum at his biddyng, and bold to don   disobedient to; commands;
            ille,   fearless; act badly
      Than the king shulde come and caste hem in prisoun,
      And putte hem ther in penauns withoute pite or grace;   punishment
      But yif Dobest prey for hem, abyde ther for evere.   And unless; (they will) stay
            "Thus Dowel and Dobet and Dobest the thridde
100   Crouned on to be king, and by his counseyl wroughthe,   one; acted
      And rewlen the rewme by red of hem alle;   kingdom; consultation among
      And otherwise and elles not, but as thei thre assente."   are in agreement
            I thanked Thoughth tho, so that he me taughthe: who taught me in this way
      "And yit savoureth me not thi seggyng, so me God   suit my taste; message
            helpe!
105* More kynde knowing I coveyte to lerne,   natural understanding; desire
      How Dowel and Dobet, and Dobest don on this erthe."   act
            "But Wit counne wisse the," quod Thought, "where tho   Unless; can teach
            thre duellyn,
      Ellys wot no man that now is on erthe."   otherwise; knows
*   Thought and I thus thre dayes we yede,   went
110   Disputyng on Dowel day after other;   debating about
      And er we war were, Wit gan we mete.   before; aware of it; did
      He was long and lene, lyk to non other,   no one else
      Sad of his sembland, and of a sad speche.   Sober; appearance; serious
      I durste meve no matere to make him to jangle,   dared; raise; subject; argue/
                                                                chatter

115   But as I bad Thought tho be mene bytwynne,   asked; then; to be an intermediary
      To putte furth soum purpos to proven his wittes.   proposition; test
            Thanne Thoughth in that tyme sayde these wordes: at
      "Where that Dowel and Dobet and Dobest were in
            londe,
      Here his wil wolde I wite, yif Wit coude teche."   know

Passus Ten

Passus primus de Dowel.   "The first step of Dowel"

*   "Sire Dowel dwelleth," quod Wit, "not a day hennys,   *from here*
In a castel that Kynde made of foure kennys things: *Nature; kinds of*
Of erthe and of eyre hit is made, medled togederes   *mixed; fire (i.e., ether)*
With wynd and with water, enjoyned wittily.   *wind; joined together; skillfully*
5   Kynde hath closed therin, craftily withalle,   *Nature; enclosed*
A lemman that he loveth lyk to himselve.   *girlfriend*
Anima hit hatteth; to here hath envye   "Soul" is named
A proud prykere of Fraunce, *Princeps huius mundi*;   *horseman;* "Prince of this world" (John 12:31, 14:30, 16:11)

And wolde wynne hure away with wyles yif he myghthe.   *tricks*
10   And Kinde knoweth this wel, and kepith hure the betere,   *Nature; protects; all the more*
And do hure to Sire Dowel, duk of the marches.   *entrusts; borders*
Dobet is hure damesele, Sire Dowelis doughter,   *maidservant*
And serveth this lady lely bothe late and rathe.   *diligently; early*
Thus Dowel and Dobet and Dobest the thridde
15   Ben maystres of this mare, this mayden to kepe.   *protect; borderland; protect*
    "The counstable of the castel, that kepyth hem alle,   *protects*
Ys a wys knyght withalle, Sire Inwit he hatteth;   *Intelligence / Understanding; is named*

*   And hath ſyve ſayre sones by his furste wyve:
Sire See-wel and Sey-wel, and Here-wel-the-ende,
20   Sire Wyrch-wel-with-thyn-hond-and-with-man-of-strengthe,   *power / force*
And Sire Godfrey Go-wel: grete lordes alle.
These syxe beth yset to save the castel;   *are installed; defend*
To kepe this wymman wise men ben charged,   *protect; are appointed*
Til Kynde come or sente and kepe here himselve."   *Nature; protect*
25   "What calle ye that castel," quod I, "that Kynde hath ymaked?   *Nature*
And of what kennys thing, conne ye me telle?"   *sort of; do you know*
    "Kynde," quod he, "is creatour of alle kynnes bestes;   *Nature; kinds of*
Fader and formere, the furste of alle thinges.   *creator*

And that he is grete God, that gynnyng hadde nevere,   beginning
30   The lord of lyf and of lyt, of blysse and of peyne.   life; light; punishment
Aungelys and al thing arn at his wille,
*   And man is him most lyk of mark and of shappe;   humankind; to him; similar;
                                                       appearance

For thurgh the word that he warp waxe forth bestes,   through; uttered; grew
And al, at his wille, was wrought with a speche: word
35   *Dixit et facta sunt, et cetera.*   "He spoke and they (i.e., things)
                                         were made, etc." (Ps.148:5; Ps.
                                         32:9)

Save man that he made ymage to himselven,
Gaf him of his godhede, and graunted him blysse,   divine nature
Lyf that ay shal laste, and al his lynage after.   always; descendants
That is the castel of Kynde made—*Caro* hit hatteth;   by Nature; "Flesh/Body"; is called
40   As moche to mene as man with the soule;
Thurgh myghth of the mageste man was ymaked: power; created
Faciamus hominem ad ymaginem nostram.   "Let us make humankind in our
                                           image" (Gen. 1:26)

"Inwit and alle wittes enclosed ben therinne,   Understanding; senses; are
For love of that lady that Lyf is ynempned;   named
45   That is *Anima*, that over al the body wandreth,   "Soul/Spirit"; is diffused
Ac in the herte is hure hom, heyest of alle;   most especially
Sche is lyf and ledere, and lemman of hevene.   guide; beloved
Inwit is the help that *Anima* desyret;
After the grace of God, Inwit is the grettest.
50   "Inwit in the hed is an help to the soule,
For thurgh his cunnyng is kept *Caro et Anima*   knowledge; protected; "Body and
                                                  Soul"
*   In reule and in resoun, but reccheles hit make.   proper order; unless;
                                                       recklessness; mars

He eggeth eye syght and hering to gode;   urges; toward
Of speche and of going he is bygynnere;   walking; originator
55   In mannys brayn he is most and myghthiest to knowe—   most powerful; strongest
Ther is his boure bremest, but hot blod hit make.   dwelling; strongest/most evident;
                                                     unless; destroys

For whan blod is bremere than brayn, than is the wit   stronger; good sense; restrained
    bounden,
And ek wantoun and wilde, withouten ony resoun.   careless; out of control; rational
                                                   control

"In fauntes and folys—in hem fayleth Inwit;   children; does not operate;
                                               Understanding

#	Text	Gloss
60	And ek in sottes thou myght se, that sytten at the ale—	drunkards; alehouse
	Thei helden ale in here hed til Inwit be drenchid,	soak up; Understanding; is drowned
	And ben brayned as bestes, so here blod waxit.	are inclined to act like; when; emotion; took control
	Than hath the pouke power, Sire *Princeps huius mundi,*	devil; "Prince of this world" (John 12:31, 14:30, et al.)
	Over swiche maner men, myghtis in here soulys.	kinds of; powers
65	And in fauntes and folys the fend hath no wit,	children; power/strength
	For no werk that thei werchyn, wikked or ellys;	in respect to; action; perform; otherwise
	But the fader and the frendes for fauntes shul be blamed.	children; responsible
	And thei be pore and catelles, and kepyn hem from ylle,	If; are; without property/destitute
	Than is Holy Cherche awenge to helpe hem save	obliged
70	Fro folyes, and fynden hem, til thei ben wisere.	support; until; are more mature
	"Ac ech wight in this world that hath understondyng	But; person
	Is chef soveren over himself his soule to yeme,	care for
	And chefveschyn for ony charg, whan childhod passeth,	keep (himself) clear; blame; leaves
	Save himself fro synne, for so him behoveth;	Preserve; for him; it is proper/necessary
75	For werche he wel other wrong, the wit is his owen.	or; power
	"Than is Dowel a duk and destroyeth vices,	
	And saveth the soule, that synne hath no myghth	so that; power
	To route ne to reste ne to rote in thin herte.	settle down; remain; take root
	And that is drede of God: Dowel hit maketh;	fear/awe; inspires/causes
80	And is gynnyng of goudnesse God for to dowte.	beginning; fear
	Salomon hit seyde for a soth tale:	true
	Inicium sapiencie, timor domini, et cetera.	"The beginning of wisdom [is] fear of the lord, etc." (Ps. 110:10; Prov. 9:10 [and cf. Prov. 1:7]; Ecclus. 1:16)
	"For doute men doth the bet, for drede is such a mayster	fear; dread
	That he maketh men mylde and mek of her speche,	considerate; humble
85	And alle skynnys skoleres in scole to lere.	kinds of; students
	Than is Dobet to be war for betyng of the yerdes,	wary/watchful; to avoid beating with rods
	And ther seyth the Sauter—the psalme thou myght rede:	
	Virga tua et baculus tuus, et cetera.	"Your rod and your staff, etc." (Ps. 22:4)

Ac yif clene conciens acorde and thiself do wel, — *agrees*

90 Wille thou nevere in this world why for to don betere; — *desire (to know); reasons why*

* For *Intencio iudicat hominem.* — *"Intention judges the person"*

With counseyl of conciens, acordyng with Holy Cherche — *advice; in agreement with*

Loke thou wisse thi wit, and thi werkes after; — *direct; judgment; accordingly*

For yif thou comsest agayn conciens thou combrest thiselven; — *begin (to act) against; burden*

95 And so witnesseth Godis word and holy writ after:

* *Qui agit contra conscienciam, ed. ad[us?]. de., et cetera* — *"Whoever acts against conscience, . . ., etc."*

"Ac yif thou werche by Godes word, I warne the the beste,

Whatso men wondryn of the, wratthe the nevere. — *about; become angry; yourself*

Catoun conceylyth so—tak kepe of this thing: — *thus; advises; pay heed to; text*

100* *Cum recte vivas, ne cures verba malorum.* — *"As long as you live righteously, do not pay attention to the words of the wicked"*

But suffre and sit stille, ne seke thou no ferther, — *endure/be patient; quietly; look around*

And be glad of that grace that God hath the sente;

For yif thou comsest to clymbe, and coveytest hyere, — *begin; climb; want; (to go) higher*

Thou myght lese thi lownesse for a lytel pride. — *humility; on account of*

105 I have herd, when lewed men have lered here children, — *ignorant; taught*

That selde men se the marbel mosy that ofte men tredyn; — *people; walk on*

And ryght so be renneres, that rennyth aboute — *exactly; gadabouts; who*

From religioun to religioun—rechelys thei ben evere; — *religious order/house; thoughtless; are completely*

Ne men that cunne alle craftes—as clerkes and other— — *know; educated men*

110 Trift or thedam with tho is selden yseye: — *Thriftiness; smart money management; them; infrequently*

* *Qui circuit omne genus, et cetera .* — *"He who embraces every kind (of thing), etc."*

"Poul the apostel in his pistel wrot hit,

In exaumple that swiche shulde not renne abowte;

And for wisdom is writen and witnessed in cherche: — *affirmed*

115 *In eadem vocacione qua vocati estis.* — *"In the same calling to which you were called" (1 Cor. 7:20)*

Yif thou be man maried, monk other chanoun, — *are*

Hold the stabele and stedfast and strengthe thi soule — *yourself; firmly; in place*

To be blessed for thi beringe, ye, beggere thei thou were! — *conduct; truly; even if you were a beggar*

"Loke thou grocche not on God, thei he geve the litel;   *grumble not against; though*

120 Be payd with the porcyoun, povere other riche.   *satisfied; allotted share; or*

For thus in sufferauns se thou myght how soveraynes arise.   *enduring difficulties; you may observe; rise up*

And so lerned us Luk, that lyghede nevere: *taught; deceived*

Qui se humiliat exaltabitur.   *"Whoever humbles himself will be raised up" (Luke 14:11, 18:14; cf. Matt. 23:12)*

And thus of dred and of oure dede Dobest ariseth,   *from fear; actions*

125 Whych is the frut and the flour fostred of bothe.   *flower; generated*

   "Righth as a rose, that red is and swete,

Out of a ragged rote and as a row brere   *spiky/thorny; root; rough briar*

That spryngeth and spredeth, that spiceres desiren,   *shoots up; apothecaries*

Or as whete out of wed waxeth out of the erthe,   *grows from*

130 So Dobest out of Dobet and Dowel gynnyth springe   *does grow*

Among men of this molde that meke ben and kynde;   *earth; are*

For love of her lounesse oure Lord gyft hem grace   *their humility; gives*

Such werk to werche that he his wit payed;   *action; perform; pleased*

Formest and ferst to folk that ben wedded,   *Foremost; are married*

135 And lyven as here lawes wiln, hit lyketh God almyghthi;   *pleases*

That thorw wedlak the world stant, whoso wil hit knowe.   *is established; whoever; wants*

Thei ben the rychest of rewmes, and the rote of Dowel;   *noblest; conditions*

For of here kyn thei comyn that confessoures ben nemled: *from their families; professed believers; are called*

Bothe maydenys and nunnes, monkes and ankeres,   *anchorites*

140 King and knyghthes, and alle kennys clerkes,   *every kind of*

Barounes and burgeys, and bondemen of tounes.   *Noblemen; citizens of towns; indentured servants*

   "And falce folk and feythles, thevys and lyeres,

Ben conseyved in cursed time, as Kaym was of Eve,   *Are conceived; Cain*

After Adam and Eve eten the appel

145 Agen the heste of him that hem of nought made.   *command; out of nothing*

An aungel in haste het hem to wende   *commanded; depart*

Into the wrecchede world to wone and to libbe   *dwell*

In tene and in travayle into here lyves ende;   *trouble; suffering/labor*

In that cursede constellacyoun thei knewe togederes   *planetary alignment; had sexual intercourse*

150 And broughthe forth a barn that muche bale wroughthe.   *child; misery; caused*

Kaym thei him calde, in cursed tyme engendred;

And so seyth the Sauter—se hit whan the lykyth: *look it up; pleases*

Concepit dolorem et peperit iniquitatem.

"He conceived sorrow and gave birth to iniquity" (Ps. 7:14; Job 15:35)

"Alle that come of that Kaym Crist hated hem after,
155 And manye milyonys mo of men and of wymman   thousands
That of Seth and his suster swithe forth come;   subsequently
* For thei maried hem with curses to men of Kaymes kynne.
For al that come of that Kaym, acursed thei were,
Forthi he sente hem to seye, and seyde him by an aungel,   therefore; to them; told; to him
160 To kepe his kynrede fro Kaym, that thei cople not togedere.   kin; so that; join
And sythe Seth and his soster were spoused to Kaymes kyn,   since; married
Agayn Godes heste gerles thei getyn;   command; children
And God was wroth with here werkes, and sayde these wordes: actions
Penitet me fecisse eos .i. homines.

"I regret that I created them (i.e., human beings)" (Gen. 6:6–7)

165 And is as moche to mene, amonge us alle:
'That I man maked, now hit me forthenketh.'   it causes me regret
* And cam to Noe anon, and bad him not lette   then; delay
Swythe to shapyn a ship of shides and of bordes.   quickly; construct; planks; boards
Himself and his sones thre, and sythen here wyves,   in addition
170 Buskede to that bot, and byde therynne,   hastened; stayed
Til fourty dayes were fulfyld, that flode have ywassche   completed; until; had washed
Clene away the cursed blod that Caym hath ymaked—   produced
    " 'Bestes that now ben shal banne the tyme   curse
That evere cursede Kaym com to this erthe;
175 Alle shul deye for his dedys, be downes and hilles,   because of; actions; hills
Bothe fysshes and foules, forth with the bestes,   birds; along
Outtake eighte soules, and of eche beste a couple,   Except; pair
That in the sengle ship shul be ysaved;
Ellys shul alle deye and to helle wende.'   Otherwise; go
180   "Thus thurgh cursed Caym come care upon alle;   through; sorrow/trouble
And al for Seth and his children spoused here eyther other,   because; married each
Agen the lawe of oure Lord leyghen togederes,   lay
And were maried at myschef, as men do now here children.   in sin

	Text	Gloss
	For some as I se now, soth for to telle,	truly; say
185	For covetyse of catel unkyndely be maried.	property; unnaturally; are
	A carful concepcioun cometh of swich a weddyng,	unfortunate / damnable
	As fele of this folk, as I before shewyd.	happened to; people
	"Hit is an uncomly couple, by Crist, as Y wene,	unsuitable; joining; believe
	To geve a yong wenche to an old feble,	girl
190	Or wedde ony wedue for ony wele of godes.	increase; property
	In jelosye joyeles and janglyng abedde	arguing in bed
*	Many a peyre syn the pestilens han plyghth hem togedere.	plague; contracted in marriage; themselves
	The frut that thei brynge forth arn many foule wordes;	
	Thei have no children but chost, and choppys betwythen.	strife; blows; between them
195*	Thei thei hiden hem to Donmowe, but yif the devel helpe	Even if they took themselves; unless
	To folwe after the flesche, fecche thei hit nevere;	compete for; Flitch; win
	But yif thei bothe be forsworn, that bakoun thei tyne.	unless; commit perjury; will lose
	"Forthi I counsel alle Cristen, thei coveyte not to be wedded	therefore; desire; married
	For covetise of catel or for kynrede riche;	greed for wealth; relations; noble
200	But maydenys and maydenys, yow to same takyn;	virgins; together
	Wedueres and wedues, werche ye also.	Widowers; act in the same way
	Thanne glade ye God, that alle godes sendeth;	please
	For in my tyme treuly, bytwen man and womman	
	Shuld no bedburd be, but they were bothe clene	bed play / sexual intercourse; unless; chaste / pure
205	Of lyf and of love and of lawe also.	in
	That derne dede do no man ne shulde	secret; one
	Ac bytwen sengle and sengle: swich lawe hath ygraunted	Except; unmarried; such a; permitted
	That every man have a make in mariage of wedlok,	person; partner
	And wirche on his wif and on no wymman ellys.	besides
210	"That othergates beth ygoten, gadelynges ben holdyn;	those who; otherwise; are conceived; bastards; are considered
	And tho ben false folk and false eyres also,	are; heirs
	Fundelynges and lyeres ungracious to gete love, or eny goud ellys,	Orphans; unsuccessful; other
	But wandryn as wolves and waste yif thei mowe;	roam about like; destroy; might
	Agen Dowel thei don eyvel, and the devel plese,	evil
215	And after here dethday shul duelle with the same,	

But yif God gif hem grace here to amende.   Unless; reform

    "Than is Dowel to dredyn and Dobet to suffren,   therefore; fear; be patient

And so cometh Dobest aboute, and bryngeth doun   [the] proud

    mody,

And that is wicked wil, that manye werkes shendeth."   destroys

Passus Eleven

	Poem	Gloss
	Passus secundus de Dowel.	"The second step of Dowel"
	Thanne hadde Wit a wif, was hote Dam Stodie,	(who) was called
	That lene was of lych, and of low chere.	thin; body; humble appearance
	She was wonderly wroth that Wit thus me taughthe,	extremely; angry; in this way
	And al sternely starynge Dam Stodie sayde:	glowering
5	"Wel art thou wys, Wit," quod she, "my wisdam to telle	
	To flatereres or to folys, that frentyk ben in wittes!"	insane
	And blamed him and banned him, and bad him be stille,	cursed; quiet
	With swyche wise wordes to wissen eny folys.	teach
	And seyde, "*Noli mittere,* man, margeri perlys	"Do not throw" (Matt. 7:6); margarite pearls
10	Among hogges that havyn hawes at wille;	hogs; have; hawthorn berries
	Thei don but dravelyn therupon; draf were hem levere	only; slobber; garbage; would be; to them; preferable
	Than al the precious perre that in parades waxeth.	gems; paradise; grow
	I sey by tho," quod she, "that shewe by here werkes	about
	That hem were levere lond than wirchepe on erthe,	to them; preferable; good name
15	Or rychesse or rentes, and reste at here wille,	wealth; rental income
	Than the soth sawes that Salomon seyde evere.	true sayings
	"Wisdam and wit now is not worth a roysche,	straw
*	But hit be carded with conciens, as clotheres don her wolle.	Unless; combed; cloth makers; wool
	That can construe deseytes and conspiren wronges,	One who; compose; deceptions; plot evils
20	And lede forth the loveday to lette the truthe—	preside; at a day of reconciliation; hinder
	That swich an kan is cleped to counseyl,	One who; such a thing; knows how to do; called
	And is served as a sire that serveth the devel:	lord

*Quare impiorum via properatur; bene est omnibus qui prave
    et inique agunt?*

> "Why does the way of the wicked prosper; [why] is it well for all those who behave perversely and wickedly" (Jer. 12:1; cf. Job 21:7)

And he that hath holy writ ay in his mowthe, — *always*

25 And can telle of theologie and of the twelve apostolys, — *talk about*

Or prechin of the penans that Pilatus wroughthe — *suffering; inflicted*

To Jesu the jentyl that Jewys todrowe — *On; stretched out*

On cros upon Calwarie as clerkes us techyn—

Lytel is he loved or late by, that such a lessoun teches, — *paid attention to*

30 Or daunseld or drawe forth; this disoures wite the sothe. — *honored; storytellers know*

For yif harlotrie ne holpe hem betere—so have God my truthe— — *scurrilous gossip; word of honor*

More than musyk or makyng of God almyghthi, — *music; versifying; about*

Wolde nevere king ne knyght, ne chanoun of Seynt Powlys,

Geve hem to here yersgeve the value of a grote! — *for their annual bonus; groat (= 4 pence)*

35   "Ac menstracie and merthe among men is nowthe — *people; now*

Lecherie and losengrie and brothelles talys, — *flattery; brothel's*

And glotonye with grete othes—thes are gamenys nowodayes. — *entertainments*

And yif thei carpen of Crist, thes clerkes and thes lewed, — *talk about; ignorant [ones]*

At mete in here merthe whan menstrales faylen, — *meal; are not available*

40 Than telle thei of the Trinite, how two slowe the thredde, — *chatter*

And bryng forth a balled tokne, Bernard to witnes, — *unconvincing evidence; as a*

And putten forth presumpcioun to proven the sothe. — *faulty arguments; truth*

Thus thei dravelyn at here des, the deite to knowe, — *blabber foolishly; high table; deity; explain*

And gnawe God in the gorge, when here throtes fullen. — *chew on; gullet; they fill*

45   "Ac the carful may crien and carpe at the gate, — *burdened with cares; call out; complain*

Bothe for hunger and for thrist and for chele qwake; — *cold; shiver*

Ther is non to nemle him in, ne angwys amende, — *no one; invite; suffering; lessen*

But honushe him as an hound, and hote him go thennys. — *spurn; dog; order; from there*

Lytel loveth he that Lord that leneth al that blysse — *offers*

50 That thus parteth with the pore a parcel whan him nedeth. — *shares; crumb; for him; it is needed*

Ne were mercy in mene men more than in riche, — *if not; poor*

Manye mendynauns metelys myght go to bedde. — *beggars; without a meal*

God is mechel in the gorge of thes grete maystres, — *throat*

And among mene men his mercy is in werkes. — lower-class
55 And so seyth the Sauter—sek hit in *Mementote*: — "Remember" (Ps. 131:1)
Ecce audivimus eum in Eufrata; invenimus eam in campis — "Behold we heard it in Ephrata; we
silve. — found it in the fields of the forest"
(Ps. 131:6)

Clerkes and kedde men carpen of God faste, — intelligent; speak; a lot
And han him mechel in her mowth, and mene men in
herte.
"Freres and faytores han founde up suche questiouns — con artists; invented; arguments
60 To plese with prude men syn the pestelens tyme, — proud
That defouleth oure feyth als at festes ther thei sytten; — who; betray; in this way; where
For now is ech boye bold, and he be riche, — nobody; if
For to telle of the Trinite to ben holde a sire, — chatter about; important man
And fyndeth forth fantasies oure feyth to apeyre, — proclaims; useless speculations;
injure
65 And eke defame the fader that us alle made, — also; blaspheme
And carpen agen clergie crabbede wordis: — speak; learning; complaining/
peevish

'Whi wolde our saveour suffre such a werm in his — savior; allow; serpent; paradise
blisse,
That begiled the womman, and the wey after, — deceived; man
Thurgh which werk and wille thei wente to helle, — As a result of
70 And al oure sed for that synne the same wo suffred?' — progeny; punishment endured
"Swiche notes thei mevyth, this maystres in here — points/opinions; raise; arrogance
glorie,
And make men to misbileve that mousen in here — cause; believe wrongly; reflect on
wordes.
Ac Austyn the hore for alle swiche precheth, — Augustine; gray-haired; against
And for suche tale-telleres such a teme shewyth: — against; text; presented
75* *Non plus sapere quam oportet sapere.* — "Not to know more than it is
proper to know" (Rom. 12:3)

That is to say, wilneth nevere to wyte why — desire; understand
That God wolde suffre Satan his sed to bygile; — permit; creatures; seduce
Ac bylef lely on that lord of holy cherche, — faithfully in
And pray him of pardoun and penauns by thi lyve, — for
80 And for his moche mercy to amende us here. — great
For al that willeth to wyte the weyes of God almyghthi, — desire; understand
I wolde his eye were in his ers and his hele after — ass; heel
That evere wilneth to wyte why — desires; understand
That God suffrede Satan his sed to bygile, — allowed; descendants; seduce
85 Or Judas the Jew Jesu betrayede—
Al was as he wolde: Lord, yworcheped thou be, — willed

And al worth as thou wilt, whatso we telle!　　　　　　　will be; desire; no matter what; say

　　"And now cometh a conioun, and wolde cacche of my　stupid fellow; (he) wants to find
　　　wittes　　　　　　　　　　　　　　　　　　　　　out; from

What is Dowel fro Dobet—now def mote he worthe!　　deaf; become

90　Swithe he wilneth to wyte which thei ben alle:　　　Quickly; wants; find out; what; are

But yif he leve in the leste day that longeth to Dowel,　unless; live; last; what belongs

I dar be his bolde borwgh that Dobet wil he nevere,　will risk; confident guarantor

Thow Dobest drawe on him day after day."　　　　　Even if; attracts

　　And whan that Wit was war how his wif tolde,　　clear; was speaking

95　He bycome so confous he coude not mele,　　　　　disconcerted; speak

And also dom as a dore drow him asyde.　　　　　　just as; silent; door; took himself
　　　　　　　　　　　　　　　　　　　　　　　　　off to the side

Ac for no carping that I cowde, ne knelyng to the　　words; on
　　grounde,

I myghte gete no greyn of his grete wittes;　　　　　knowledge

But al laughinge he loutede and loked upon Stode,　　he bowed his head; turned his
　　　　　　　　　　　　　　　　　　　　　　　　　eyes toward

100　In sygne that I shulde seken hure of grace.　　　　ask from her; some

　　And whan I was ware of his wile, to his wif gan I　did
　　　knele,

And sayde, "Mercy, Madame, your man shal I worthe,　If you please; servant; become

For to werche your wil whil your lyf durith,　　　　do; what you wish; lasts

To kenne me kyndely to knowe what is Dowel."　　　guide

105　"For thi meknesse, man," quod she, "and for thi mylde　humility; humble
　　speche,

I shal kenne the to my cosyn, that Clergie hotuth.　　guide; who; Learning; is called

He hath wedded a wif withinne this wykes sexe,　　woman

Is syb to the sefne ars, that Scripture is ynempled.　　(Who) is sister; seven (liberal)
　　　　　　　　　　　　　　　　　　　　　　　　　arts; named

Thei two, I hope, after my beseching,　　　　　　　expect; at my request

110　Shul wisse the to Dowel, I dar wel undertake."　　direct; firmly believe

　　Than was I as fayn as foul of fayr morwen,　　　happy; birds; on; fine morning

Gladdere than the gluman that gold hath to gifte,　　happier; minstrel; in payment

And axked hure the heyway wher Clergie wonde—　　main road; to where; dwelt

"And tel me sum tokne of him, for tyme is that I　　sign; set off
　　wende."

115　"Axke the heyway," quod she, "fro hennys to Suffre-　Look for the main road; here

Bothe-wel-and-wo-yif-that-thou-wilt-lerne,　　　　　good times; hard times

And ride forth by Rychesse—rest the not therinne ;　　don't stop there

For yif thou couple the with him, to Clergie comest thou　attach yourself; learning
　　nevere.

"And ek the longe launde, that Lecherie hatteth,　　also; wide meadow; is called

120	Lef him on thi lyft half a large mile and more,	left side; full
	Til thou come to a court Kep-wel-thi-tounge-	
	Fro-lesynges-and-lieres-speche-and-lykerous-drynkes.	lies; liars'; inebriating
	Than shalt thou se Soberte and Symplenesse-of-speche,	Seriousness; Honesty
	That iche wight be in wille his wit the to shewe.	so that; each person; will be
		intent; knowledge
125	So shal thou come to Clergie, that can many thinges;	Learning; who knows
	And sey him this signe: I set him to skole,	to him; password; school
	And that I grete wel his wyf, for I wrot hure the Bible,	warmly
	And sette hure to Sapience, and to the Sawter yglosed;	Wisdom; commented on
	Logyk I lerned hure, and al the lawe after,	taught
130	And al the mosouns of mosyk I made hure to knowe.	measures; music; understand
	Plato and poete, I putte hem furst to boke;	poets; reading
	Aristotle and other mo I taughthe furst to argue;	many
	Grammere for gerles I gar furst wryte,	children; first taught to write
	And bet hem with a baleys but yif thei wolde lerne.	hit; rod; unless; were willing
135	And alle kenne craftes I construed here to lerne:	explained; teach
	Tolus of carpenteres and kerve, I taughthe ferst masouns,	Tools; carving
	And lerned hem lyne and level, thow I lokede dymme.	taught; had poor eyesight
	"And theologie, that tened me ten skore tymes:	annoyed
	For the more I muse theron, the mistlikere hit semeth,	more; contemplate it; more
		mysterious; appears
140	And the deppere I devyne hit, the deppere me hit thoughthe.	more deeply; examine; to me; seems
	Hit is no sciens for sothe to sotile therinne;	in truth; to go deeply into
	Ne were the love that lyth therinne, a wel lewed thing hit were.	if there were not; resides; very useless; would be
	Ac for hit laft best by love I love hit the betere;	But because; remained; with
	For ther that love is lord balketh nevere grace.	refuses / hesitates
145	Leve lely theron, yif thou thinke Dowel;	Believe; faithfully
	For Dobet and Dobest ben drawe of loves scole.	are descended from
	"In other sciens hit seyth—I say hit in Catoun:	
*	*Qui simulat verbis nec corde est fidus amicus;*	"One who deceives neither with words nor in heart is a trustworthy friend"
	Tu quoque fac simile: sic ars deluditur arte.	"Act similarly, yourself: thus art is deceived by art"
150	Ac Theologie techeth us not so, whoso taketh hede;	
	He kenneth us the contrarie agen Catounys wordes,	teaches; opposite
	And byt us ben as brethren, and blesse oure enmys,	instructs

And loven hem that lyen on us, and lene hem at oure   *lie about; give to; in*
    nede,

And do good agens evyl; God himself hotes,   *commands*

155   And seyde hit himself in exaumple of the beste:

Necesse est ut veniant scandala.   *"It is necessary that obstacles come" (Matt. 18:7)*

    "Ac astronomye is hard thing and evel for to knowe;   *difficult; devilishly hard; understand*

Gemettrie and gemessie is greful of speche.   *Geometry; divinations by use of figures or lines; difficult*

That thinketh werche with tho thre thryveth wel late;   *One who intends; gains success; very*

160   For sorcerie is the soverayn boke that to that sciens   *most important; belongs*
    longeth.

*   Yut are thre fybicches of forels of manye mannys wittes,   *(there) are; three; tricks; boxes; a man's*

*   Of experimens of alkonomye, of Albertes makyng,   *invention; alchemy*

Nigramauncie and permancie, the pouke to reyse;   *conjuring the dead; divination by fire; devil*

Yif thou thinke Dowel, del therwith nevere.   *intend to*

165   Al these sciences, sikerly, I myself founded—   *certainly*

Founded hem formest folk to deseyven.   *invented; in the first place*

I bekenne the Crist," quod she, "I can teche the no   *entrust to*
    betere."

    I sayde, "Gramercy, Madame," and mekly hure grette,   *Many thanks, My Lady; humbly; said goodbye*

And wente witly my way withoute more lettyng,   *quickly; further delay*

170   And fond as she fayre tolde, and forth gan I wende,   *discovered; plainly; did go*

And er I cam to Clergie coude I nevere stynte.   *before; understanding; pause*

I grette the gode man as me the gode wif taughthe,   *said hello to; woman*

And tolde him the toknes as me taughth were;   *said to him; passwords*

Was nevere gome upon the grounde, syn God made   *there was; man; earth; created*
    hevene,

175   Fayrer underfonged, ne frendlikere mad at ese,   *better received; nor more warmly made to feel home*

*   Than myself sothly, so sone as she it wiste   *truly; as knew*

That I was of Wittes hous, and his wif Dam Stodie.   *from*

And I seyde him sikerly, "Thei sente me hyder   *told; confidently; here*

To lere at yow Dowel, and Dobet therafter,   *from*

180   And sithe afterward to se soumwhat of Dobest."   *then*

    "Hit is a wel lely lyf," quod she, "among the lewyd   *very faithful; uneducated*
    peple;

Actyf hit is yhoten, hosbondes hit usen; *called*

Trewe tilieres on erthe, talioures and souteris, *plowmen; tailors; shoemakers*

And alle kynde crafty men that konne her craft wynne, *every; skillful; know how; produce/earn*

185 With ony trewe travayle telye for here fode, *honest; work; plow*

Dykyn or delven, Dowel hit hatte. *ditch; dig; is called*

*   "To breke beggeres bred, to baskyn hem with clothes, *distribute to; dress/cover*

Comforte the carful that in the castel ben fetrid, *troubled; are imprisoned*

And sekyn out the seke, and sende hem that hem *look after; sick; provide them what*
   nedeth, *they need*

190 Obedient as brethren and sostren to óthere— *brothers; sisters; each other*

This beth tho that Dobet; so bereth witnesse the Sauter: *These are they*

Ecce quam bonum et quam iocundum habitare fratres in *"Behold how good and how*
   unum. *pleasant it is for brothers to dwell*
   in harmony" (Ps. 132:1)

Syk with the sory, syng with the glade: *grieve; sorrowful; happy*

Gaudere cum gaudentibus, flere cum flentibus. *"Rejoice with those who rejoice,*
   weep with those who weep"
   (Rom. 12:15)

195* God wot, this is Dobet. *knows*

          "Sire Dobest hath benefyces and so is best worthi, *holds; church offices; most*

By that God in gospel graunteth and techeth: *in accordance with what; proclaims*

Qui facit et docuerit, magnus vocabitur in regno celorum. *"Whoever shall act and shall teach*
   will be called great in the kingdom
   of heaven" (Matt. 5:19)

For this Dobest is a bisshopes pere, *equal*

200 Prince over Godes peple, to preche and to teche.

          "Dobet doth ful wel, and Dowel he is also, *very*

And hath possessiones and pluralites for pore mennys *properties/worldly goods; many*
   sake. *church offices*

For mendinant at myschef tho men were ydewed; *To (help) beggars; in trouble; endowed*

And that is rightful religioun—none renneres abowte, *proper behavior of religious; gadabouts*

205 Ne none leperis over lond ladijs to shrive. *roamers over the land; give absolution*

*   "Gregori the grete clerk, a goud pope in his tyme,

Of religioun the rewle he reherseth in his *Morales*, *religious orders; explains*

And seyth him in example that men shulde do the *himself; as; perform*
   betere:

*   'When fisshes faylen the flod, other the fressche water, *are deprived of; sea*

210   Thei deyen for the drouthe, when thei drye longe;   die; on account of; without water; remain

       Ryghth so by religioun: hit roxlet and stervyth,   just so [is it] with a member of a religious order; stretches thin; dies

       That out of covent in cloystre coveyteth to libbe.'   cloistered community; desires
       But now is religioun a ridere, and a rennere by stretes,   a professed religious; gadabout; along

       A ledere of lovedays and a lond byere,   convener; days of reconciliation
215   Popreth on a palfray fro towne to towne,   trots about; saddle horse; settlement

       A bedew or a baselard he beryth by his syde;   curved dagger; dagger; carries
*   Godes flesch and his fet and his fyf woundes   feet
       Arn more in his mynde than the memorie of his
           foundour.
       This is the lyf of thes lordes that shulde lyve with Dobet,
220   And wel-a-wey werse, and I wolde al telle."   very much; if; wanted to; everything; reveal

       "I wende kinges and knightes and keyseris with erlys   thought; emperors
       Were Dowel and Dobet and Dobest over hem alle;
       For I have sey hit myself, and swithe yrad after,   seen; often; read
       How Crist counseyleth the comoun, and kenneth hem   instructs; crowd; teaches; words
           this talis:
225   Super cathedram Moysi sederunt principes qui dicunt facite.   "On throne of Moses will sit princes who say 'Do [this]!' " (cf. Matt: 23:2–3)

       Forthi I wende that tho weyes were Dobest of alle."   therefore; believed; men
       "I wolde not skorne," quod Scripture; "but skreveynis   speak dismissively; unless; scribes
           lye,
       Kinghod and knighthhod, for oughth I can aspie,   kingship; anything; see
       Helpeth not to heveneward at one yeres ende,   toward heaven
230   Ne richesse, ne rente, ne rialte of lordes.   wealth; income; aristocratic status
*   "Powel proveth inpossible the riche in hevene,   Paul; declares it's impossible
       Ac pore men in paciense and pacient togederes
       Have here eritage in hevene, and riche men none."   inheritance
       "Contra," quod I, "be Crist! that can I withsay,   On the contrary; by; contradict
235*   And prove hit bi the postel that Peter is ynemled: support; apostle; called
       Qui crediderit et baptizatus fuerit, salvus erit."   "Whoever shall believe and be baptized will be saved" (Mark 16:16)

       "That is in extremis," quod Scripture, "among   "at the moment of death"
           Sarzynes and Jewys;
       Thei mow ben ysaved so, and that is oure byleve,   may; in this way

That oncristene in cas may cristene an hethene,   non-Christian; in case of
                                                       necessity; baptize; pagan
240   And for his leal byleve, whan he his lif tynyth,   faithful; is losing
      Have eritage in hevene as an hey Cristene.   inheritance; the same as; virtuous
          "Ac Cristene men, God wot, com not so to hevene;   knows
      For Cristene have a degre and is oure comoun speche: higher standard; (this is) our
                                                       general opinion
*   *Diliges dominum deum tuum, et proximum tuum sicut*   "You shall love the Lord your God,
          teipsum.   and your neighbor as yourself"
245   Godes word witnesseth that we shul dele oure enmyes   should; distribute alms to
      And alle men that arn nedy, as pore men and suche: in need
      Dum tempus habemus, operemur bonum ad omnes,   "While we have time, let us do
          maxime autem ad domesticos fidei, et cetera.   good to everyone, but especially
                                                       to those in the household of the
                                                       faith, etc." (Gal. 6:10)

      Alle kynde creatoures, that to Crist ben lyche,   living; are; like
      We ben yholde heyliche to herie and honoure,   are required; especially; praise
250   And gif hem of oure good as goud as oureselven,   to them; from; possessions; much
      And soveraynliche to suche that sueth oure beleve: above all; follow
      That is, ech Cristen man be kinde to other,   should be
      And swithe hem to helpe in hope to hem amende.   quickly; aid; improve things for
                                                       them
          "To harme hem or teche hem, God hyghth us nevere;   strike; commanded
255   For he seyth hit himself, and his ten hestes: commandments
*   *Non mecaberis*—'ne sle not' is the kinde Englys—   "You shall not commit adultery"
                                                       [sic]; ordinary
      For, *Michi vindictam, et ego retribuam, et cetera.*   "Mine is the vengeance, and I will
                                                       pay back, etc." (Deut. 32:35; Rom.
                                                       12:19)

      'I shal punishe in Purgatorie, or in the pit of helle,
*   Every man for his mysdede, but mercy hit make.' "   unless; balances it out
260*   "Yit am I never the ner, for nought that I have walked,   nearer
      To wite what is Dowel witterly in herte;   know; assuredly
*   For how so I werche in this worlde, wrong other elles,   however; behave; or otherwise
      I was marked withoute mercy and my name entred   marked out
*   In the legande of lyf, longe er I ded were;   book; before; was
265   And ellys onwryten for wicked, as witnesseth the gospel: otherwise; not written; as
      Nemo ascendit in celum nisi qui de celo descendit, et cetera.   "No one ascended into heaven
                                                       except one who descended from
                                                       heaven, etc." (John 3:13)

          "And I leve on oure Lord, and no lettrure betere;   believe in; Scripture
      For Salamon the sage, that *Sapiens* made,   wise man; book of Wisdom; wrote

God gif him grace and richesse togederes — *gave; good fortune; wealth*
270 For to reule his rewme ryghth at his wille; — *kingdom; exactly according to his desires*

Dede he not wel and wisly, as holy cherche techeth,
Bothe in werk and in word, in worlde in his tyme? — *during*
Aristotle and he, who wroughthe betere? — *did*
And al holy cherche holdeth hem in helle! — *believes*
275 And was ther nevere in this world two wisere of werkis; — *more intelligent; in what they did*
For alle connyng clerkes, syn Crist yede on erthe, — *intelligent; walked*
Taken ensaumple of here sawes and sermownis that — *sayings*
      thei makyn,
And by here werk and here wordes wissen us to Dowel; — *they encourage; toward*
And yif I shal wirke by here werk to wynne me hevene, — *act according to; what they did; gain*

280 And I for here werkes and here wit wende to payne, — *go; punishment*
Than wroughthe I unwittily, with al the wit that I lere! — *I acted foolishly*
      "On Gode Fryday, I fynde, a feloun was ysaved — *criminal; saved*
And hadde ylyved al his lyf with lesynges and thefthe; — *lived; lies; thievery*
And for he kneled to the cros, and to Crist shrof him, — *because; confessed himself*
285 Souner hadde he savacyoun than Seynt Jon the Baptyst, — *Sooner; salvation*
Or Adam or Ysaie, or ony of the prophetes,
That hadden yleye with Lucifer manye longe yeres; — *lain*
A robbere hadde remissioun rather than thei alle, — *pardon; sooner*
Without penans of Purgatorie, to have paradys for evere. — *suffering in purgatory; gain*
290   "Than Marie of Mawdelein, who myghthe don worse? — *Mary Magdalen*
Or dude worse than David, that Urie destroyed? — *killed*
Or Poul the postel, that no pite hadde,
Cristene kinde to kylle to dethe? — *people*
And arn non, for sothe, so fer in hevene, — *are; high*
295 As these that wroughthe wickedly in world whan thei — *behaved; lived*
      were.
      "And yit am I forgote, for sothe, of fyve wittes teching, — *have I forgotten; indeed*
That clergie of Cristes mouth comindeth was hit nevere; — *learning; praised*
For he seyde hit himself to some of his desiples: — *disciples*
Dum steteritis ante presides nolite cogitare, et cetera. — *"When you stand before judges don't think, etc." (Mark 13:9–11)*

300 That is as moche to mene, to men that ben lewyd, — *are uneducated*
'Whan ye ben aposed of princes and prestes of the lawe, — *are questioned by*
For to ansuere hem have ye no dowte; — *fear/hesitation*
For I shal graunte you grace, of God that ye serven, — *from; whom*
The help of the Holy Gost to ansuere hem alle.' — *Spirit*
305   "The douttyest doctour, devinour of the Trinite, — *greatest; theologian*

*   That was Austyn the olde, and hyest of the foure,   Augustine; highest
     Sayde thus for a sermoun, so me God helpe:

*   *Ecce ipsi idioti rapient celum, ubi nos sapientes in infernum*   "Behold, complete idiots will grab
         dimergimur, et cetera.   hold of heaven, while those of us
                                                                          who are wise will be plunged into
                                                                          hell, etc."

     And is to mene in our mowth, more ne lesse,   language
310 'Arn non rather raveshid fro the ryghthe beleve   Sooner; carried away; true faith
     Than are thes grete clerkes, that konne many bokes;   know
     Ne none sounere saved, ne sadder of conciens,   more easily; trustworthy
     Than pore peple, as plowmen and pastourres of bestes.'   like; herders
     Souteres and souestreres, and suche lewed juttes,   shoemakers; seamstresses;
                                                                          uneducated nobodies

315* Perchen with a *pater noster* the paleys of hevene,   Enter; Lord's Prayer; palace
     Withoute penauns, at here partyng, into the hye blysse."   death

Passus Twelve

*   *Passus tercius de Dowel.*   "The third step of Dowel"

"Crist wot," quod Clergie, "knowe hit yif the lyke,   knows; admit it; pleases
I have do my dever the Dowel to teche;   duty
And whoso coveyteth don betere than the boke telleth,   whoever desires to; Bible instructs
He passeth the apostolis lyf, and put him to aungelys.   surpasses; apostles'; raises himself; angels'

5   But I se now as I seye, as me soth thinkyth,   to me; true; it seems
The were lef to lerne, but loth for to stodie.   you would desire; not willing
Thou woldest konne that I can and carpen hit after,   would like; to learn; what; know; chatter about

Presumptuowsly, paraventure, apose so manye,   perhaps; to confront in this way
That myghthe turne men to tene, and Theologie bothe.   so that it might; trouble; also
10 Yif I wiste witterly thou woldest don therafter,   knew clearly; wanted to act
Al that thou askest asoylen I wolde."   answer fully
Skornfully tho Scripture sterte up her browes,   quickly raised
And on Clergie crieth, on Cristes holy name,   at; yelled; in
That he shewe me hit ne sholde, but yif I schriven were   unless; confessed
15* Of the Kynde Cardinal Wit and cristned in a font;   By; baptized; baptismal font
And seyde so loude, that shame me thoughthe,   stated; loudly; to me it seemed
That hit were bothe skathe and sklaundre to holy
     cherche   injury; slander
Sitthe Theologie the trewe to tellen hit defendeth.   Since; faithful; forbids
"David, Godes derling, defendyth hit also: forbids
20* *Vidi prevaricationes et tabescebam.*   "I have seen violations and I wasted away" (Ps. 118:158)

'I saw synful,' he seyde, 'therfore I seyde nothing,'   about which
Til tho wrecches ben in wil here synne to lete.   are; intention; leave
And Poul precheth hit often—prestes hit redyn:
Audivi archana verba que non licet homini loqui .   "I have heard secret words which it is not permitted a man to speak" (2 Cor. 12:4)

25   'I am not hardy,' quod he, 'that I herde with erys,   brave; what
Telle hit with tounge to synful wrecches.'

	And God graunted hit nevere; the gospel hit witnesseth,	allowed
	In the passioun, whan Pilat aposed God almyghthi,	confronted
	And asked Jesu on hy, that herden hit an hundred:	aloud; so that
30	'Quid est veritas,' quod he, 'verilyche, tel us.'	"What is truth?" (John 18:38); truly
	God gaf him non answere, but gan his tounge holde.	did
	Right so I rede," quod she, "red thou no ferther;	just; advise
	Of that he wolde wite, wis him no betere.	what; wants to know; instruct; further
	For he cam not by cause to lerne to do wel,	for the purpose
35*	But as he seyth, such I am, when he with me carpeth."	trades words
	And when Scripture the skolde hadde this wyt ysheued,	nag; revealed
	Clergie into a caban crepte anon after,	immediately
	And drow the dore after him, and bad me go do wel,	shut; told
	Or wycke, yif I wolde—whether me lyked.	evil; wanted; whichever; pleased
40	Than held I up myn handes to Scripture the wise,	
	To be hure man yif I most, for everemore after,	servant; might
	With that she wolde me wisse wher the toun were	as long as; instruct; settlement was
	That Kynde Wit hure confessour, hure cosyn, was inne.	natural knowledge
	That lady than low, and laughthe me in here armes,	laughed; took
45	And sayde, "My cosyn Kynde Wit knowen is wel wide,	very widely
·	And his loggyng is with Lyf, that lord is of erthe.	lodging
	And yif thou desyre with him for to abyde,	live
	I shal the wisse where that he dwelleth."	instruct
	And thanne I kneled on my knes, and kyste her wel sone,	very quickly
50	And thanked hure a thousand sythes with throbbant herte.	times; pounding
	She called me a clerioun	to me; schoolboy
	That hyght Omnia-probate, a pore thing withalle.	was named; "Test all things" (1 Thess. 5:21)
*	"Thou shalt wende with wil," quod she, "whiles that him lykyth,	go; as long as; it pleases
	Til ye come to the burgh, Quod-bonum-est-tenete.	town; "Hold onto what is good" (1 Thess. 5:21)
55	Ken him to my cosenes hous, that Kinde Wit hyghth;	Direct; cousin's; is called
	Sey I sente him this segge, and that he shewe hym Dowel."	to him; fellow; should show
	Thus we laughthe oure leve, lowtyng at onys,	took; bowing together
	And wente forth on my way with Omnia-probate,	
	And ere I cam to the court Quod-bonum-est-tenete,	before

60* Many ferlys me byfel in a fewe yeris.   *wonders; happened to me*
The fyrste ferly I fond afyngrid me made;   *wonder; experienced; very hungry*
As I yede thurgh youthe agen prime dayes,   *went back; toward early morning*
I stode stille in a stodie, and stared abowte;
"Al hayl," quod on tho, and I answered, "Welcome, and   *then; are*
    with whom be ye?"
65   "I am dwelling with Deth, and Hunger I hatte;   *am called*
To Lyf in his lordshepe longyt my weye.   *tends*
I shal felle that freke in a fewe dayes."   *kill off; fellow*
*   "I wolde folwe the fayn, but fentesye me hendeth;   *willingly; delusion; me; troubles*
Me folweth such a feyntise, I may no ferther walke."   *weakness*
70   "Go we forth," quod the gom: "I have a gret boyste   *man; box*
At my bak of broke bred thi bely for to fylle;   *On; pieces of bread*
A bagge ful of a beggere I boughthe hit at onys."   *from*
    Than maunged I with him up to the fulle;   *ate*
For the myssyng of mete no mesour I coude.   *lack of food; I knew no moderation*

75   With that cam a knave with a confessoures face;
He halsed me, and I asked him after   *greeted; then*
Of when that he were, and wheder that he wolde.   *from where; was; to where; wanted to go*

    "With Deth I duelle," quod he, "dayes and nyghtes;
*   Mi name is Fevere-on-the-ferthe-day; I am athrest evere.   *thirsty; always*
80   I am masager of Deth—men have I tweyne: *messenger; attendants; two*
That on is called Cotidian, a courrour of oure hous,   *the one; daily; courier*
Tercian that other: trewe drinkeres bothe.
We han letteres of Lyf, he shal his lyf tyne;   *for; lose*
Fro Deth that is oure duk swyche dedis we brynge." *boss; documents*
85* "Myghth I so, God wot, youre gates wolde I holden."   *If I could; knows; paths; follow*
*   "Nay, Wil," quod that wyghth, "wend thou no ferther,   *fellow; travel*
But lyve as this lyf is ordeyned for the;   *laid out*
Thou tomblest with a trepget, yif thou my tras folwe;   *You will trip yourself; trap; track*
And mannes merthe wroughth no mor than he   *pleasure; achieves*
    deservyth here,
90   Whil his lyf and his lykhame lesten togedere.   *body; survive*
And therfore do after Dowel whil thi dayes duren,   *act in accord with; last*
That thi play be plentevous in paradys with aungelys.   *so that; eternal*
Thou shalt be laughth into lyghth, with loking of an eye,   *taken; light; in the blink*
So that thou werke the word that Holy Wryt techeth,   *As long as; act in accord with*
95   And be prest to preyeres, and profitable werkes."   *prompt; with*

———

Wille thurgh inwit tho wot wel the sothe—   understanding; then; grasped; truth

That this speche was spedelich—and sped him wel faste;   profitable; benefited him; very greatly

And wroughthe that here is wryten, and other werkes bothe—   did; what; deeds; in addition

Of Peres the plowman and mechel puple also.   (those done) By; many other people

100   And whan this werk was wrought, ere Wille myghte aspie,   finished; notice

Deth delt him a dent, and drof him to the erthe,   blow; knocked; ground

And is closed under clour—Crist have his soule!   buried; sod/grassy mound

And so bad Johan But, busily wel ofte,   prayed; very

When he saw thes sawes busyly allegged   opinions; insistently; proclaimed

105   By James and by Jerom, by Jop and by othere;   Jerome; Job

And for he medleth of makyng, he made this ende.   because; he played around with versifying; conclusion

Now alle kenne creatures that Cristene were evere,   kinds of

God for his goudnesse gif hem swyche happes,   May God give; opportunities

To lyve as that lord lykyth that lyf in hem putte.   it pleases

110*   Furst to rekne Richard, kyng of this rewme,   mention; kingdom

And alle lordes that lovyn him lely in herte,   faithfully

God save hem sound, by se and by land;   May God preserve; in good health

Marie, moder and may, for man thou byseke   maiden; may you pray

That barn bryng us to blys that bled upon the rode.   child; cross

Amen.

Explicit Dowel.   The End

Nomen scriptoris Tilot, plenus amoris.   The name of the scribe (is) Tilot, full of love

Textual Notes

This edition departs from the base manuscript (MS. Rawl. poet. 137: hereafter Ra) in a number of regular ways. Modern English graphs are substituted for the Middle English þ (thorn) and ȝ (yogh). The letters *v* and *u*, and *i* and *j*, are used in accord with modern orthography. It regularly capitalizes line initials and a number of other names (personal names and personified abstractions). In addition, the somewhat irregular spacing of letters in the manuscript is brought into conformity with Modern English practice. A few of the scribe's regular (*mis*)spellings have also been changed:

> word] world: e.g., 4.119; 5.197; 8.170; 9.35, 39; 10.71, 90, 136, 147; 11.272;
> wordle] worlde: e.g., Pr.4, 19; 1.8, 37; 7.124, 158; 11.262, 275.

Another regular feature of the scribe's orthography, a final *-tȝ* or *-ȝt*, we have silently emended to the more usual *–th*: e.g., Pr.91 (mowȝt), 3.191 (lytȝ), 3.20 (cravytȝ), 3.230 (grypytȝ), 7.50 (dureȝt) 9.43 (steryȝt), 9.86 (suffretȝ), 10.99 (conceylytȝ), 10.124 (arisetȝ), 10.130 (gynnytȝ), 11.71 (meuyȝt), 11.58 (mowtȝ), 11.240 (tynytȝ), 11.297 (moutȝ), 11.310 (mowtȝ), 12.5 (thinkytȝ).

Finally, we have introduced a number of individual corrections or emendations, into our text, when demanded by sense. Below are the main variants from the base manuscript, listed by line, manuscript reading, and printed text.

Pr.3	von-holy] unholy
Pr.11	anerwelous] a merwelous
Pr.22	Þat] Wonne that wyt] wyth
Pr.50	hernytes] Hermytes
Pr.55	*blank*] Vicars
Pr.99	symple] symble
Pr.105	deusa dam*m*eme] Deusa Damme Eme
1.27	loot] Lot
1.36	ȝut] your; alþer] a lyer
1.40	*This line is missing from Ra (and E).*
1.50	sesaris] Sesari
1.54	trosour] tresour
1.62	falfhede] falshede
1.68	sonered] sonere
1.69	haddy] had Y
1.74	ȝut] your
1.75	brouȝtes] broughtest
1.81	trosour] tresour
1.83	aren] arn
1.86	tel hit] tellith
1.110	wat] was

1.124	trosures] tresures
1.128	cores] cors
1.129	he] sche
1.137	ʒe] the
1.138	whem heny] when eny
1.157	þei] Ye
1.166	Wonkynde] Unkynde
2.40	kyʒthys] knyghthys
2.52	vestyment] feffyment
2.55	haue] have feffed
2.70	douʒter] doctor
2.95	for] for cosyn
2.117	þat] That sche
2.127	sofly] softly
2.137	paulyus] Paulynus
2.138	myn self] myself
2.141	here] Liere
2.183	hem] hym
3.14	hym] hem berthe] berde
3.37	lawed] lewed
3.41	conciensce] Conciense
3.47	vus] us
3.55	lyʒft] lyft
3.59	co coueytes] coveytes
3.95	Won wyttyly] Onwyttyly
3.116	þorþ] thorw
3.126	letyyʒ] letyth
3.147	his] hure
3.156	schuche] Suche
3.162	qwat] qwath
3.166	For] Ne
3.180	knowde] klowde
3.187	haue] have me
3.198	hure] hem
3.206	me] men
3.229	muner] muneribus
3.230	oure] hure
3.235	amn] amen
3.236	Thaþ] That
3.243	and] of
3.255	bylle] Byble
3.260	Thou] The
3.278	schuche] suche; lawe] loue
4.3	hirre] hure
4.11	with] with the

4.17	kanue] knave
4.23	ry3th] ryt
4.28	fchame] schame
4.54	wytes] wyth
4.70	*This line and the first half of the next are missing from Ra.*
4.83–87	*Five lines have been supplied (omitted by eye-skip: final "no more").*
4.100	he] her
4.103	kyghtthes] knyghtthes
4:124	bonum] bonum be
4.131	ac] Ac whan
4.132	was] nas
4.137	he] he be
4.143	here to] hereto hit
4.145	te] to
5.28	to take to take] to take
5.40	and] And ye
5.51	nysseyd] mysseyd
5.78	fore] sore
5.83	durste] I durste
5.89	byhelde] byholde
5.130	he] sche
5.131	almes] aunsel whem] when
5.155	faftyng] fastyng
5.165	vp holders] upholderes an hep
5.172	ho so] whoso
5.182	ho so] whoso raþes] rather
5.194	ho so] whoso
5.207	an] And þherste] therste
5.231	wepd] weped
5.232	synful] the synful
5.234	him] the
6.2	blustre] But blustred
6.14	haie] haue
6.45	wores] worse
6.51	3ou selue] yourselve
6.52	buxum] Be-buxum
6.53	honowred] honowre
6.57	name] the-name
6.75	burased] butrased
6.90	clepe] slepe
6.107	*This line is missing from Ra.*
6.116	quod] quod a
6.118	an] and
7.10	spynnet] Spynneth
7.13	þe] thei

7.18	syke] sylke
7.24	quod] quod the
7.29	wateres] wasteres
7.31	beres] bores
7.51	aparayle] aparayle me
7.76	pylgermage] pylgremage
7.95	wp] up
7.108	dusada*m*meme] Dusa Damme Eme
7.109	I] in
7.124	sWhyche] Swyche
7.144	wanne] whanne
7.201	wonbys] wombys
7.230	wit] wight
7.241	maketh] maketh hem
7.252	alabre] calabre
7.272	lammasse] hervest
7.292	he] be
7.302	thour] thorw
8.5	hodde] holde
8.6	þat ȝe] al that
8.20	marchaunt] Marchauntes
8.25	him] hem
8.26	him . . . him] hem . . . hem
8.32	ofter] .after
8.38	his] your
8.43	choþes] clothes
8.44	copede] copiede
8.54	do] to
8.92	to] two
8.112	scitis] sitis
8.114	*this line is missing from Ra.*
8.125	Ecce] Eice uirga] iurgia
8.127	an] and
8.136	dauid (daniel, *in margin*)] Daniel
8.138	sweue] swevene
8.159	þis] This is
8.163	heue] have
8. 166	now . . . þei] ye ne . . . ye
8.170	for who so] and wise
9.10	And] And I
9.19	he] I
9.39	þow] thorw
9.40	syþen] Syneth
9.56	madene] made
9.57	vnder] under a

9.66	thout3] Thought
9.68	thout] Thought
9.77	he] ac he
9.99	de wel] Dowel
9.107	thou3t] quod Thought
9.109	am] and
10.3	of eyre] and of eyre
10.17	withalles] withalle
10.18	and] and hath
10.27	ceatour] creatour
10.33	thur] thurgh
10.47	He] Sche
10.68	kepn] kepyn
10.71	wit] wight
10.78	to rote] ne to rote
10.110	trist] Trift
10.137	reychest] rychest
10.157	cursed] curses
10.177	and] and of
10.180	þhur3] thurgh
10.195	Thei] Thei thei
10.197	forswon] forsworn
10.217	comeþ] cometh Dobest
10.218	and] And that
11.14	þat] than
11.21	swicham] swich an
11.30	damseld] daunseld
11.58	many] mene
11.69	Thur3t] Thurgh
11.72	me] men
11.92	we] he
11.97	he] I
11.99	al] al laughinge he
11.124	wit] wight hit] his
11.127	gete] grete him] hure
11.138	thologie] theologie
11.148	uel] nec
11.162	alkononye] alkonomye
11.166	hem] Founded hem
11.197	grauteþ] graunteth and techeth
11.209	oþ] other
11.232	and] in
11.239	and] an
11.241	her] hey
11.258	punshe] punlshe

11.262	whom so] how so
11.265	wiled] wicked
11.276	of] For
11.296	vyue] fyve
11.297	what is] was hit
12.12	his] her
12.14	stryf] I schriven
12.54	burgher] burgh
12.62	ȝou · þe] youthe
12.73	wit] with him
12.83	tyme] tyne
12.88	þe] Thou
12.96	þou wost] tho wot

Notes

Prologue

Title   *Prologus*: Rawlinson 137 (Ra) is the only manuscript in which this first *passus* (Latin for "step") is called *prologus*. This is, however, the usual title accorded the opening *passus* in editions of the A and B versions of *Piers*.

1   The late spring opening is a common feature of a number of medieval poems and is particularly common in dream visions, like this one. As the season of new beginnings, it is frequently associated with love and with new discoveries.

    whenne I south wente: This reading (supported by only three *Piers* MSS, all of them A versions: Ra, U, and E) cannot be explained away as derived from the more commonly attested *whanne soft was the sonne* (see Kane, *A Version*, 433 n.1). Because the latter could be explained by contamination from the universal reading in the B/C MSS, and because no other argument would contest the conclusion that *whenne I south wente* may well be the harder reading, this edition has opted to favor the more unusual reading found in these three manuscripts, two of which (Ra and U) have (in Knott-Fowler's "family" and Kane's "well established . . . genetic . . . large group" [39]) a persistent and close relationship to MS T, the base manuscript chosen for all previous critical editions. The third (E) is often aligned with Ra and U in what Kane characterizes as (along with RaUD) one of the "two major discrepant groups" (Kane, *A Version*, 97) among the persistent affiliations of manuscripts. Ra's *whenne* (as compared to *as* in U and E) may offer some further slight testimony to the direction of "contamination" here.

2   In view of the *unholy of werkys* in line 3, possible ambiguities of this line are worth considering. Dressing in woolen clothes (*schroude*) may simply be a realistic detail, indicating what hermits (Pr.3) usually wore. But *schop* (in its more usual meaning) may also suggest that the *schroude* is intended explicitly for concealment or disguise. Dressing as a *schep*, a common image of innocence, and of a faithful Christian, will invite the audience to reflect on the exact meaning of *as*: our judgment of the narrator will vary, depending on whether we take it as a simple statement of similarity ("like") or whether it suggests an intentional, or even innocent, deception or misrepresentation: "as if." In other words, we are quickly put at some yet-to-be-defined critical distance from this Narrator.

3   Because not all hermits are unholy of works (see Pr.28), and presumably one's moral status cannot be unambiguously determined from one's *abyte*, what determines this particular hermit's unholy works may be the fact that he travels around with his ears open for *wondrys* (Pr.29). As a specific category of devout religious, hermits were expected to remain in certain sites and often performed useful services in remote places, for which they would qualify for donations from travelers and be accorded protection by civil and ecclesiastical authorities. In Passus 7.133ff.,

Piers will specifically state that he will work to provide alms for those anchorites and hermits who keep to their *sellys*.

5   *Malverne hyllys*: A string of hills (running nearly ten miles north-south, with its highest point near fourteen hundred feet) in western England (Worcestershire-Herefordshire), near the border with Wales. The reference here as the opening location for the poem *may* indicate the author's familiarity with the area.

12   *wildernysse*: Like *ferly* (Pr.6), this points to something beyond the ordinary. It is possible, of course, that in the poet's day the Malvern Hills themselves were seen as something of a "wild," uncultivated place. In the metaphorical (or allegorical) mode, it defines the Narrator's place as distinct from the *fayr felde* (Pr.17) that represents the earthly world, poised between a heavenly *tour* (Pr.14) and a hellish *doungon* (Pr.15).

13   If the dreamed landscape corresponds to the Malvern Hills of the Narrator's waking scene, then he is apparently on the Hereford side of the hills and looking eastward, up the hillside, on one of the summits (*in a coste*: next line) of which he sees the *tour*.

    tryly: the word's root meaning is "excellent" or "exceptional" and, like other words in these opening lines of the dream, point to a construction that is out of the ordinary.

15   *doungon*: A castle keep: the chief, or most secure, tower in a medieval castle. Modern *dungeon* suggests this tower was often the place to secure prisoners.

17   *fayr felde*: A field, presumably relatively flat and open, on which a fair or market was being held. Perhaps the presence of numerous people would itself suggest the idea of a *fayr*. This everyday *fayr* world only seems to be *fayrye* (Pr.6) to the Narrator at first.

19   *as this worlde askys*: The folk are engaged in the ordinary activities of life. The following lines detail some of those activities and do not immediately suggest that the *worlde* here must be taken as in opposition to some higher realm. The *fayr felde* is placed between the castle and the dungeon; it is not inevitably associated with either of the extremes (heaven and hell) with which those two constructions can be connected.

24   *In countenance of clothing*: "In an outward show of [fine] clothing; ostentatiously dressed." Unlike the Narrator of the opening lines, however, these folk are clearly dressing inappropriately: even if the Middle English word *dysgysed* does not have quite the same meaning as modern *disguised*, *in countenance of* carries some implication of deception. There was considerable concern around the time of this poem's creation about proper dress for various estates, and attempts, even by parliamentary statute (so-called sumptuary laws, e.g., 1363), to regulate dress (and food) were not uncommon.

28   Anchorites and hermits were devout solitaries, participants in a long-standing tradition that sought religious benefits by retreating from the ordinary world to devote themselves to ascetic denial, meditation, and contemplation. Anchorites and anchoresses lived an enclosed life, often in locked, prisonlike cells, sometimes attached to churches or houses in towns. Hermits tended to be less firmly enclosed but often resided in caves or primitive huts more or less removed from inhabited settlements. Some, for example, lived near rivers where they could direct travelers

to fords or to bridges (which they might also maintain), and be supported by the alms or tolls they were offered. Aside from such practical benefits they could offer, many hermits (as did anchorites and anchoresses, such as Julian of Norwich) attracted people to their cells because of their reputation for prayer and holiness.

31   *chosen hem to chaffare*: "Took up buying and selling." The *ys sene to oure syghth* in the next line suggests that the success (*chevyd the betere*) of these people may be, again, more apparent than real to the Narrator's (and perhaps the poet's) way of thinking.

33   *menstralys*: This is the first mention of another group that, like hermits, is associated with the poem's Narrator and whose moral status is not necessarily determined by the choice of vocation: the *synneles, I trowe* in the next line may be a left-handed compliment, but it is strongly contrasted with a firm rejection of *Judacys chyldryn* in the following line.

38   Most, following Skeat, take this as an allusion to 2 Thessalonians 3:10 (*Si quis non vult operari nec manducet*: "If anyone is not willing to work, let him not eat").

39   *Qui loquitur turpiloquium*: "He who speaks evil." The idea, though not the exact phrase apparently, has been found in St. Paul (cf. Coloss. 3:8 and Eph. 5:4). The syntax does not require line 39 to be the essence of Paul's preaching in line 38; it may instead be the Narrator's reason for (or rationalizing of) his own reticence here and indicate that he would consider an effort to *provyn* it as lowering himself to the level of those he is criticizing. The word *turpiloquium* is not limited in meaning to "slander"; the phrase may amount to little more than "say bad things about" or even "use bad language." The Narrator, as himself a kind of "minstrel," may be eager to avoid the appearance of being a pot calling a kettle black: judge not lest you be judged!

44   *robertes knavys*: There seems to be a play on "Robert" and "robber" here, which appears also in Passus 5.230, 238. The association is known in other English works (see Bennett's note to B Pr.44, in his 1972 edition).

46   *palmeres*: In its strictest use, "palmers" are pilgrims to the Holy Land, who took the palm leaf as their symbol. By this point, however, the term seems to have become a more general one. If there is a real distinction between "pilgrim" and "palmer" here, it is probably fairly minor.

47   *Seynt Jame*: The pilgrimage to Santiago (St. James) de Compostela in Galicia (northwest Spain) was (next to Rome) the most popular in Europe in the Middle Ages, with a series of diverse routes threading their way across France and the Pyrenees and west across northern Spain. The scallop shell was the "sign" of this pilgrimage, attesting (perhaps) to the appeal of the seafood in that region.

50ff   It is difficult not to notice, in this criticism of *Hermytes*, the similarities they have to the Narrator/Dreamer of the opening lines, who *schop* himself *In abyte as an ermyte unholy of werkys*.

51   *Walsyngham*: The shrine of "Our Lady of Walsingham" in Norfolk (about one hundred miles north of London and about five miles from the beaches of the North Sea coast) was one of the most popular (and wealthy) pilgrimage sites in England, second only to the shrine of Thomas Becket in Canterbury. An Augustinian monastery there had a chapel representing the home of Mary and Joseph in Nazareth. Often called a Loreto, the Nazareth house was a model for devotional chapels at a number of sites in Europe.

55   *Vicars*: These are deputies employed by canons to perform some of their liturgical, choral, or administrative duties for them. There is a blank in the Rawlinson MS at the beginning of this line, suggesting that Tilot (an ordained priest, and a vicar of Chichester Cathedral from before 1415) might have intended to substitute another word for one so closely associated with himself. He apparently never settled on an appropriate replacement, and this unique blank remains in his manuscript.

57   *freres*: The title "brother" (Lat. *frater*; Fr. *frère*; Engl. *friar*) was given to members of a new type of religious order founded in the early thirteenth century. The four main fraternal orders were the Franciscan (Minorites, or gray friars), Dominicans (Preachers, or black friars), Carmelites (white friars), and Augustinians (Austin friars). In the fourteenth century, the fraternal orders were expanding greatly and were subject to much criticism from secular clergy (i.e., clergy responsible to bishops and looking after geographic parishes) because they felt the friars were trespassing on their prerogatives and income and, by being "easy" in granting absolution in confession, weakening the moral atmosphere and the local social control exerted by resident parish clergy. This poem reflects many features of this anti-fraternal criticism (see Szittya).

59   *Glosede*: The basic meaning is "interpret," "translate," "comment upon." However, because all translations in one way or another alter or "spin" the meaning, the connotations of the original word, "glossing," frequently carry connotations of deceit and self-serving. Cf. *Oxford English Dictionary* (*OED*) *gloss*.

67   *pardoner*: An individual licensed to proclaim an "indulgence" or "pardon." He is not, strictly speaking, a member of the clergy, and therefore there is criticism involved in noting that he preached "as if he were a priest." Most pardoners (*quaestores*) were laymen, who had been granted the right to make known the existence of a grant of indulgence and were authorized to take up collections on behalf of the institution to whom the indulgence had been granted.

So, for example, Chaucer's Pardoner is licensed to go about announcing an indulgence being granted individuals in return for contributions to the activities of the religious house of Roncevals, which ran a hospital near Charing Cross in London and was one of the houses affiliated with the monastery at Roncevals in the Pyrenees. Presumably, these "traveling salesmen" retained portions of these donations for their own expenses, and some of them were no doubt charlatans. However, nothing aside from a complete rejection of the idea of pardons, which was indeed being questioned by some in the period of *Piers Plowman*, could automatically condemn Chaucer's Pardoner as an outright "fraud." While he admits his relics are clearly fraudulent, there is no explicit doubt cast on the authenticity of his "pardoun."

At the root of the late medieval church's practice of issuing indulgences lay the doctrine of the "treasury of merit." The principle behind the "treasury" is that, as the earthly representative of Jesus Christ, the church had access to the inexhaustible merits achieved by Jesus's passion and death. To use a banking metaphor, the church had the power to draw on an endowment, whose funds it could distribute as it saw fit, and these "funds" could be used to pay off debts accumulated on earth and remaining to be paid by souls who would have to undergo punishment for their sins in purgatory, These benefits could, of course, be granted gratis, but the church insisted on some sign of reformed character and good intention in return for which the benefits of the indulgence could be granted (or, actually, assumed by the recipient). So writs of indulgence spelled out terms in return for which the effects of the indulgence would apply: for example, going on a pilgrimage, performing certain devotions, contributing to the care of the sick or to the maintenance of bridges, and making donations in support of sanctioned activities of religious groups.

Because the sacrament of Penance (Confession) would absolve (*asoyle*: Pr.69) the guilt (Lat. *culpa*) but not the "punishment" (Lat. *poena*) due for sins, sinners were directed to make "satisfaction" for their sins through certain penitential acts, which would remove the *poena* remaining after absolution. If all the *poena* was not removed by penitential acts in this life, it would be purged in the next. To avoid fear of the sufferings in purgatory after death, sinners could gain "indulgences" or "pardons," which would reduce (or do away entirely with) those accumulated penalties. For sinners this became an attractive option, and for the church, and confidence men, a lucrative business. Indulgences, to begin with, were partial, releasing souls from certain days (e.g., seven or forty) in purgatory. Eventually, the value of these declined and inflation set in, which resulted in the proliferation of full (or "plenary") indulgences, which would remove *all* the accumulated penalties due for one's sins. These were sometimes (improperly) called pardons *a poena et a culpa* (from penalty and from guilt).

In strict, official terms, no indulgence could remove the *culpa*, but because the efficacy of any pardon depended on the prior grant of sacramental absolution following a full and complete confession, it was common to refer to this cumulative effect by this phrase. There were without doubt many who misunderstood, or misrepresented, these indulgences, and the Roman Church properly reformed the entire practice in response to the Protestant reformers of the sixteenth century, who decried the abuses as beyond reform and attacked the fundamental principle of the "treasury of merit." The Roman Catholic Church still holds to the doctrine of the "treasury of merit" and of "indulgences," but the granting of the latter in return for monetary contributions is no longer permitted, as it was in the later Middle Ages.

The pardoner here is clearly misrepresenting his powers, and it is only the illiterate (*lewde*) who believed him. He is not a *prest*, and therefore does not have the right to absolve anyone's sins. Indeed, even a priest did not have that power, except in cases of necessity. In strict canon law (after the Fourth Lateran Council), it was the sinner's *parish* priest who was authorized to hear his parishioners' confessions and grant absolution, and one of the central points in the controversies surrounding the fraternal orders was that they repeatedly asserted the right (and the support of the pope) to absolve anyone whose confession they heard.

68   *bullys wyth busschopys selys*: *Bullys* were (papal) documents, in this case those identifying the terms of the indulgences being proclaimed; the *selys* would indicate that local bishops authorized the preaching of the "pardon" in their dioceses.

69   *asoyle*: Because it is quite clear from the previous line that the pardoner is not in fact a priest, he has no power to "absolve" anyone of anything in a strict sense, certainly not of the guilt (*culpa*) associated with *falsnesse or avowes brokyn*.

75   *ye . . . yore*: This direct address by the Narrator to his audience/readers here is the
        first striking instance of the immediate social relevance that this poem's Narrator
        (and Poet) repeatedly declares. The critical issues being addressed here are not set
        off in some distant world, unconnected to the lives of those listening to or reading
        the poem. Like the geographic reality of the Malvern Hills, the characters being de-
        scribed, and castigated, in this poem are not limited to the realms of fantasy or
        fayrye (Pr.6) but are inhabitants of the everyday world of fourteenth-century En-
        gland.

77   *worth bothe his erys*: Having one's ears cut off was not unusual as a punishment for
        fraud. There is little likelihood, however, for a bishop's facing such a punishment,
        so this may be a metaphorical reference to the shape of a bishop's miter. That dis-
        tinctive headpiece usually has two separate peaks, which may be likened to ears. Or
        this may be an instance of the poet's linguistic playfulness, with the *erys* here refer-
        ring to a bishop's mit*er* and croz*ier*, two signs of his episcopal office.

79   Although the pardoner displays *busschopys selys* on his writ, the Narrator's opinion
        is that the collusion is not between him and bishop but between him and the parish
        priest. They are in cahoots to squeeze money out of the people, money that might
        otherwise go to support of the poor. The passage as a whole implies that the (Narra-
        tor's) ideals of religious leadership and social responsibility are being betrayed. If
        the bishop allows his seal to be used, even if he does not give a license to preach, he
        is nonetheless implicated in any deception that occurs. The Narrator sees a range of
        unconscious and conscious corruption at various levels of the ecclesiastical institu-
        tion. Some (like the bishop) contribute to the corruption through ignorance and in-
        difference; others (like the pardoner and parish priest) are motivated by greed.

82   *Parsonys and parrys prestes* were the secular clergy assigned to geographic parishes.
        The parson would have been the clergyman responsible for the parish and the recip-
        ient of its tithes and other income; a parish priest would have been paid by the par-
        son to serve as his assistant, or his deputy if the parson did not reside in his parish.

83   Plague (*pestelens*) was recurrent in late fourteenth-century England. The reference
        here is probably to the particularly devastating bubonic (and pneumonic) plague
        that spread across western Europe in the later 1340s and 1350s. The so-called Black
        Death arrived on English shores in 1348, and *tyme* may refer to this particularly
        memorable episode. On the other hand, one of the recurrences of plague closer to
        the time of the poem's composition, such as those of 1361–62 and 1368–69, may
        be the more immediate referent here.

84   *Londoun*: As a major population center, it would provide more occasions for rural
        priests to gain greater income, as chantry priests, for example, whose stipends
        would come from saying masses and prayers for the dead. Because there was a pro-
        portionately large loss in the ranks of the clergy during the Black Death, the laws of
        supply and demand increased the economic benefits for them, as it did for others
        who lived in rural areas. To offset the movement of workers, various government
        regulations (such as the Ordinance and Statute of Laborers, in 1349 and 1351, re-
        spectively, the latter reintroduced in 1361–62) were enacted in an attempt to re-
        strain the mobility of rural laborers, for whom a move to London had distinct
        economic attractions.

85 *symonye*: Simony is the name given to mixing together the things of Caesar with those of God (1.46ff.), specifically the sin of exchanging money for spiritual office or other items of spiritual value (e.g., ecclesiastical appointment, sacramental forgiveness of sins, indulgence). The sin is named for Simon Magus, who in the Acts of the Apostles (8:9ff.) offers the apostle Philip money in exchange for some of the power he displays.

87 *Serjauntis* are members of the select, highest rank of prestigious lawyers, who were distinguished by wearing caps (*howys*) of white silk.

88 *penys*: There were twelve pence (or pennies) in a shilling, twenty shillings in a pound. There is another instance of wordplay here, in *poundyt* (meaning both "expounded" and "pulverized; crushed"), which in a number of manuscripts appears as, more simply, *poundis*, reducing the phrase to the equivalent of "dollars and cents."

92ff As among the few with university education, clergy were often employed in governmental service and administration. The Narrator here, however, clearly wants to maintain a distinction between the pastoral and administrative/judicial responsibilities (whether ecclesiastical or secular) of those in clerical orders. He is insistent that the position (*dignyte*: Pr.94) to which clergymen are preferred ought first and foremost be to "preach to the people and feed the poor." Their seeking to advance in the royal service will destroy (*schynde*: Pr.97) the country.

94 *archedeknys and denys*: Archdeacons are a bishop's second-in-command in his diocese, dividing up with him responsibilities for its administrative and judicial institutions. A dean is the administrative head of one of the smaller subdivisions of a diocese.

97 *kynges bench*: The royal court of justice.

100 While the *-estere* endings are derived from Old English feminine forms, by later Middle English the forms may have generally become nongendered. Nevertheless, in the absence of clear marks of gender here, it *may* be that at least some of these forms here still point to female practitioners of these crafts. For a brief account of the position of women in the crafts and guilds, see Lipson, 359–63.

105 *Deusa Damme Eme* (i.e., "Douce Dame Emme") is presumably a line from a (French) song, or else a common phrase used to make excuses for not doing what one should. It appears again at 7.108. There is a song (a *virelai*) by the famous French poet-musician Guillaume de Machaut (1300–1377) whose chorus begins "Douce Dame jolie."

107 *Go we dyne, go we*: "Let's go eat" was perhaps equivalent to "Come and get it" as a call to meals.

109 Imported wines (from Auxerre [i.e., Chablis, or northern Burgundy; or possibly Alsace], Gascony, the Rhine, and La Rochelle) were plentiful and attractive aids to the digestion (*defye*) of hearty meals.

Passus One

3 *lufly lady*: Lady Holy Church (not identified until 1.73) appears in the role of the Bride of the Lamb (Apoc. 19:8) "dressed in . . . linen." Women appear as guides and interpreters in many important medieval visionary poems (e.g., Lady Philosophy in

Boethius's *Consolation of Philosophy*; Nature in Alan of Lille's *De Planctu Nature*; Raison in the *Roman de la Rose* and in Deguilleville's *Pelerinage de la vie humaine*; the Pearl Maiden in the Middle English *Pearl*).

4   Presumably the *chyf* is to be identified with the *mounteyn* and the *coste* (Pr.14). Her descent from there will be consistent with the positive meaning associated with the *tour* and contrasted with the dark dale and its dungeon.

5   She addresses him as "son," and repeatedly uses the familiar and intimate form of the second-person-singular pronoun ("thou"). Her language establishes the lady as one who is superior to the dreamer (in class, age, authority). He, for his part, addresses her respectfully with more formal modes of address ("ma dame" and "you").

6   *the mase*: A "maze" as a state of confusion, disorder, and perplexity is an apt image for the world. (See Doob, 98–99, 145, 148–58.)

19   The idea that *Mesure is medycyne* (1.33) is first introduced here; the theme of moderation or balance is developed in the following lines.

27   The story of Lot and his daughters is frequently used by medieval preachers as an example of the dangers of drunkenness. Nevertheless, as recounted in Genesis 19:30–38, the story assigns responsibility for the incest and their pregnancies to the daughters who, after the destruction of Sodom, are without hope of husbands (and children) and decide to get their father drunk. The interpretation here clearly attributes the *wyckede dede* (1.31) to Lot's *lykyng of drynke* (1.27) and his *lecherye* (1.30).

36ff   The "three temptations"—the world, the flesh, and the devil—are a medieval commonplace. See Howard.

41ff   The Dreamer's question moves discussion from the three common natural things to consideration of *money*, which is neither a common necessity nor a natural treasure.

44   The story recounted in the gospels (Matt. 22:17–21; Mark 12:14–17; Luke 20:21–25) shows Jesus's opponents attempting to trap him into choosing between the demands imposed by religious and by secular laws. Jesus's response avoids the apparent dilemma the question was intended to raise and does not reject the payment of taxes to Rome. While he posits two distinct realms of responsibility—what have tended to be called *church* and *state* in modern political thought—his answer leaves indefinite the final determination of what *does* belong to Caesar and what to God. The Dreamer's posing his question about money would seem to put him on the side of the Scribes and Pharisees, and Holy Church's response takes the meaning of Jesus's words into a rather different direction and ends by insisting that *welthe* (1.53) is also to be ruled by *resoun* (1.52) and by common sense (or natural understanding—*kende wit* [1.53]), and she places *tresour* (1.54) among those things (like clothing, food, and drink) that can be appropriated in cases of *nede*. This discussion will become even more complicated in the episode involving Lady Mede, which follows.

61–62 If Truth is to be linked with God and Christ, Wrong is described in a manner that explicitly associates him with the Devil, the "father of lies" (John 8:44).

66   Popular accounts of Judas's desperate suicide (filling out details not present in

Matt. 27:3–5—but cf. Acts 1:18) in English (and Anglo-Norman) identify the tree as an elder tree (or shrub). While the tradition is well established, the reason for it is not clear. Perhaps it derives from a false etymology of the *eld* in the name and an association with the *Old* Law superseded by Jesus's redemptive death?

71 The "high name" presumably refers to the name of God, being invoked by the Dreamer to reinforce his request.

74–76 Holy Church identifies three stages in their relationship: first, she received him in Baptism, then educated him in the essentials of religion, and finally received the Dreamer's commitment to live according to her commands. All of these may refer to Baptism, with the *borwys* being the promises made on the infant's part by his godparents. But because she has already mentioned teaching, the pledges are more likely those of a later, more mature "contract" between Dreamer and Holy Church. It perhaps refers to the rite of Confirmation—or even to his being installed in (minor) clerical orders.

81–82 The Dreamer appears now to reject his earlier concern with money and *tresour* and asks the Lady ("you who are considered holy [*seynt*]") to teach him the fundamental lesson: how he can save his soul.

84 *do hit on*: The idiom is quite common in Middle English and means "call as witness; invoke." (See 3.175.)

   The Latin text (*Deus caritas* [God is love]), from the first Epistle of John (4:8, 16), provides the fundamental axiom whose moral corollary is that we should love one another because God has first loved us. Fidelity to love, both of God and of our neighbor, is presented as the highest treasure and equated with *trouthe*.

88 No explicit text in James's epistle (or Luke's gospel, to which other manuscripts refer) has been identified that literally says a person who does these things "is a god." But it may be implied in Luke 6:35 (Dunning) or 8:21 (Skeat). In strict terms, however, it is *eke lyk to oure Lord* (89) that is explicitly paired with *Seynt Jamys wordys*. The epistle of James especially addresses topics associated with being *trewe of his tonge* and *werkes* in the preceding lines. The reference to "a god be the gospel" may be alluding to John's gospel (10:34), where Jesus invokes Psalm 81:6—"you are gods"—to defend himself from the accusation of blasphemy in claiming to be God and the Son of God.

92 The duties of secular authorities, those who rule and fight, are laid out here, and the parallel with the heavenly King of Kings (*kyngene kyng* [103]) and his angelic knights is drawn in what follows.

96 The Old Testament's King David is presented here as a medieval king. The reference to his dubbing knights may be pointing toward passages in 2 Samuel: one that lists David's champions (23:8ff.), or another, where he organizes to attack Absalom (18:1ff.).

103 Traditionally there are nine orders of angels: Angels, Archangels, Cherubim, Seraphim, Thrones, Dominions, Virtues, Powers, and Principalities. The "ten" here conceives of the followers of Lucifer, cast out of heaven, as another distinct order.

114 There are well-established traditions in medieval Europe that not all the fallen angels ended up in hell. Some of the traditional "spirits" (fairies et al.) associated with various elements of nature were associated with the fallen angels. It was not just

human nature that was affected by the two Falls (of Lucifer and of Adam and Eve); all creation is affected.

115 Lucifer's position at the bottom of hell is echoed in Dante (*Inferno*, Canto 34). The eternity of hell (*hath non ende* [116]) is an element of Christian belief, and Lucifer's fall is usually associated with his pride. The origin for many of these details is Isaiah 14:9ff. and commentaries and sermons upon this text.

123 *by sent of these tyxtes*: This invocation of textual authority (the citations from Scripture) is repeated later, 1.180. Holy Church's homily is full of biblical words and associations.

124 Lady Holy Church follows the instructions of preaching handbooks and repeats the earlier statement of the main thesis (1.83) of her homily and then rephrases it here two lines later. The line is repeated again at the end of the next (concluding) section of her homily: l.181.

125 *Leryth thus lewyde men*: Since *leryth* can mean in context either "teach" or "learn," this passage can be translated as an imperative ("teach it to these uneducated men") or a subjunctive ("let the uneducated learn it"). Because this homily is addressed in the first place to the Dreamer, who remains rather ignorant (see *Thou dotede daffe* four lines below), the latter reading may make better sense, by including the Dreamer among the *lewyde*. It is unlikely that she is instructing him here to teach others when his own understanding of fundamental truths is not yet fully informed. And the Dreamer confirms this in the response immediately following, which asserts his lack of *knowynge*.

127 *Knowynge* (see *kynde knowynge* [1.130]) should probably be distinguished from *kende wit* and *resoun* (l.52–53), but the distinctions are not altogether clear. The dullness of the Dreamer's *wittes* suggests that this "knowing" may result from the operation of the senses (including *kende wit*) when they are freed from dullness. The concept of *kynde knowynge* (natural understanding?) is crucial in *Piers*, and as Holy Church argues below (130ff.), it is a power (*crafth*) that inhabits the Dreamer's heart to inspire him to love the Lord more than himself and to commit no mortal sin, even if it cost him his death. Kind Knowing may include some sense of prelapsarian wisdom (of the state of human understanding in its original natural state in Eden), the kind of right thinking that is recovered after the Fall by repentance based on a fully "informed" conscience. (These matters will return later: cf. 9.49ff.)

133 The equation of love and truth is explicitly made here. Because God is both "Love" and "Truth," they must be identical. The two great commandments of the gospels (Love God with your whole heart, and mind, and soul; and love your neighbor as yourself) are at the core of this part of Holy Church's homily. Although the speaker is Holy Church, there is an appearance of humility in her words here (*I trowe* and *who can teche the betere*). These may, however, be only conventional gestures of humility, an "appearance" and not a genuine hesitation about the truth of what she's saying.

137 The *plente of pes* is a striking image that may allude to Isaiah 53:2 and Ezekiel 34:29, though neither explicitly invokes the idea of "peace." See Adams, "*Durior Lectio*," 12–13. The reference to *thyn harpe* is the first suggestion we get that the character of the Dreamer is to be considered an entertainer of some description. This should be

connected with the passage in the Prologue (Pr.33ff.) where particular mention is made of *menstralys* who provide *myrthes . . . synneles, I trowe,* who are in turn distinguished from *japeris and jangeleres.*

139ff   This passage carries important theological weight and returns to the main theme that we should love God and our neighbors more than ourselves. In humans, *kynde knowynge* is linked with the Creator (who formed humans in his image and likeness) and with the patient, redemptive suffering of Jesus, whose meekness and *pyte* (145) for those who caused him mortal pain provide examples particularly to the *riche* (149) and the *myghthy* (150) to show *reuthe* (149) to the poor and to be *meke* (150) in their works. This is the essential measure of truth in this world.

151–52   Cf. Matthew 7:2; Luke 6:38.

155   Lady Holy Church adopts a strong position here about the need for something more than religious or moral formalism and insists on practical virtue in the service of Christian social justice. If you observe only the strict commands to avoid doing evil, going through the motions of your religious duties (going to mass, or participating in the prayers assigned to the various hours of the day) reveals little more than a passive virtue. Such behavior has the appearance of "virtue," but because it lacks any genuinely moral action, it gains you no merit. It is easy to keep your virginity, when no one desires to take it away, but that sort of feeble "virtue" is meaningless: it is virtue in name only and is as dead as a doornail. Sexual chastity or cleanness is not, she says, enough; it is not in itself a sign of love and will get you chained in hell, if it is not accompanied by charitable action. At 1.159–60, she explicitly draws on the Epistle of James (2:26), mentioned earlier (1.89), to insist that faith without good deeds is useless.

158   *Malkyn* (a diminutive of "Matilda") was a fairly conventional name for a lower-class woman, proverbially associated with the alliterating *maydynhede* (cf. Chaucer's "Introduction to the Man of Law's Tale," lines 27–31); while some of the associations make her out to be a wanton, that is not the case: her remaining a virgin here is clearly not the result of any moral choice on her part. See Whiting and Whiting, M 511.

159ff   An explicit reference to the Epistle of James (2:26), mentioned above (1.89), to insist that faith without good deeds does not attain salvation.

180–81   At her conclusion, Holy Church repeats the statement of her theme, already presented at the beginning (83) and in the middle (123 24) of her sermon.

Passus Two

1   The line echoes his earlier response to Holy Church's identifying herself to him (in 1.76). Having learned what Truth is, he now asks to be able to recognize its opposite.

2ff   His invocation of Mary and her *blessede barne* shows that he knows at least the essence of the Christian faith: Jesus, born of Mary, redeemed (*boughthe*) humanity by suffering on the cross (*rode*).

5   Given the usual negative associations of the "left" (i.e., "sinister"), it is appropriate that that is where False is located. If the Dreamer is still facing east, then the north is on his left, and this would reinforce the negative suggestion, because the north is associated with Lucifer (Isa. 14:13).

6   Fals is not alone but is accompanied by, among others, Favel (lying, fraud, deceit).
           Favel, the "hero" of the early fourteenth-century Old French *Roman de Fauvel*, ap-
           pears here in English apparently for the first time. In the French work, Fauvel's
           planned marriage to Fortune is prevented.

8ff   When the Dreamer looks to the left, he sees not the male characters Fals and Favel
           but, instead, another lady, dressed much more finely than Holy Church, with whom
           she is contrasted. Mede's description here also suggests the Whore of Babylon (Rev.
           17:4), and in some details, and by a possible pun (*perreye*), she may also be linked
           with Alice Perrers, the powerful, and in certain quarters notorious, mistress of King
           Edward III. This latter suggestion (if it is indeed at all intended in this earlier ver-
           sion of the poem) gains more weight in the revised B and C versions, written after
           the death of King Edward and the "fall" of Alice Perrers.

13   *quene*: The word (descending from Old English *cwen*, "woman") has by late Middle
           English extended its range of meaning to what is distinguished by spelling, if not
           pronunciation, in Modern English—that is, *queen* and *quean* (prostitute, loose
           woman).

15   The precise meaning of the lady's name, Mede, will become the subject of substan-
           tial disagreement in what follows. Its basic meaning is "reward," but in addition to
           its more positive connotations (pay, salary), it can also carry more negative ones
           (bribe, graft) consistent with the less-than-positive views of "money" in Holy
           Church's eyes in the previous passus. Holy Church represents the competition be-
           tween her and Mede in highly personal terms (e.g., 2.20: *I aughthe be hyere than
           sche, for Y come of betere*). It may be quite difficult, therefore, not to sense a less than
           objective tone in her description of this well-dressed competitor. Of course, as an
           idealized personification of the Catholic Church, she may be correct in criticizing
           the ways in which rewards and gifts and bribes corrupt ecclesiastical institutions of
           education and administration. On the other hand, she shows a rather personal an-
           tagonism to this other woman.

19   Holy Church insists unambiguously "like father, like daughter." The parentage of
           Mede will later be complicated by Theology, who (2.80) insists that Mede is *of
           frendis engendryt* and intended by God as the wife of *Truthe*. He later adds that *Sche
           myghthe kysse the kyng for cosyn* (2.95). Because Theology, who after all should have
           some connection with Holy Church (and Truth), offers an alternative sense of
           Mede's character and status, we should note here the tone of Holy Church's initial
           characterization of her and not accept it as complete and determinative. In addition
           to asking what *is* the (proper) relationship between Holy Church and Theology, we
           should also note that Holy Church seems to distance herself from the pope's palace
           a couple of lines before (2.17). While this might be consistent with critical views of
           the papal court and ecclesiastical institutions more generally, it may also highlight
           the impracticality of an idealized personification like Holy Church.

22   The prospective marriage of Mede and Falce is being urged on by his companions
           Favel, Gile, Lyere. Because these are actual players in the scene that follows Holy
           Church's departure, we cannot accuse her of misrepresenting Mede's current pros-
           pects. It is worth noting, however, that, even in Holy Church's account, Mede ap-

pears to be the object of manipulation and of being led, not an active agent in the proposed marriage. When the power shifts later, she is led in a different direction.

27ff   Lady Holy Church's final words put the burden on the Dreamer himself: you would be able to discover, if you wanted to, the identity of these "false" characters. Once you have identified them, she says, you should keep away from them if you want to dwell with Truth. Having completed her responses to his questions about money, truth, and falsity, with these final words, she commends the Dreamer to the Lord, and advises him to avoid covetousness, here being defined as the desire for Mede, if he is to become a good man.

30ff   Immediately after Holy Church's departure, the announced marriage festivities are described, without any explicit break in narrative time consistent with Holy Church's announcement that it would occur *[t]omorwe* (21). Details of the marriage proceedings that follow correspond fairly closely to contemporary English practices: see Tavormina, chap. 1.

32   Simony: See Pr.85. In the next line, the phrase *by ony fyn holdeth* continues this idea of simony: the clause suggests that the *chartres* for the marriage have been obtained by payment of a "fine," a license fee paid to the issuer of the charter/seals. Because marriage is a sacrament, it is under the jurisdiction of ecclesiastical courts; but it is also a civil contract, and it may be difficult—in the cases of upper-class arranged marriages at least—to avoid the appearance of there being improper exchanges of earthly treasure and spiritual benefits.

40   The exact meaning of *comeres aboute* is probably "visitors (from other places)." The *Middle English Dictionary* (*MED*) reports *comere* as "(a) A visitor or guest; (b) a messenger."

41   *sysores*: These are jurymen who are sworn to give evidence or provide witness in a local court (assize). The implication is that such individuals are subject to bribery. A summoner is the church officer responsible for summoning (arresting) those accused to appear before an ecclesiastical court (e.g., that of a bishop).

47   Like *Falsnesse* below (55), *Falshede* is apparently another name for *Fals/Falce*.

48   Terms like *buxoum . . . At bedde and at bord* are common in the contemporary forms of the marriage ritual: Tavormina, 14–17.

54ff   This charter, conveying property to Mede, parallels in form and phrasing actual legal documents of this kind (see Tavormina, 20ff.). Included in the list of property are representations of the Seven Deadly Sins—that is, Pride, Envy, Lechery (and Lust), Covetousness, Gluttony, Sloth. As in the later Confession of the Seven Deadly Sins (5.43ff.), Anger (or Wrath) is noticeably omitted. The addition of the *vycys of Usures* (usury being the practice of charging extravagant interest) and *Avaryce* attest to this section of the poem's particular interest in money and wealth. Gluttony's connection with *Gret Othis* links two sins of the mouth.

62   The term *lytes* may be a variant (unrecorded in the *MED*) of the plural of the noun *lith*, a form to which the *MED* gives four distinct definitions. The most relevant one, given the other properties being recounted here (e.g., *seygnorye of Scleuthe* in the next line), would be "An estate, landed property, a household, habitation." Slightly less attractive, but still possible, might be "A slope, hill."

65   The territory and property here stretch through the appurtenances (subsidiary
         properties) of purgatory, up to the boundary of hell. Purgatory, though a place of pu-
         rification (primarily conceived as accomplished through punishment), is temporary,
         and (according to Catholic theology) all the souls that are in purgatory eventually
         enter heaven, after completing their time of cleansing. Hell, on the other hand, is
         (like heaven) eternal: *whilys God is in hevene* (2.68).

70   *Paulyns doctor*: Because *Paulynus peple* are later (2.137) explicitly associated with the
         bishops' court (*constorye*), and because someone named Peres is unlikely to be any-
         one's daughter (the reading in Ra), this probably refers to a learned clerk (*doctor*) of
         the consistory court at St. Paul's Cathedral. The earlier suggestion that Paulines re-
         fers to Crutched Friars is now judged as very unlikely: see Alford, *Glossary*, 109–10.

72   *reve*: A reeve, like a beadle (*bydul*) in the previous line, is a title applied to a number
         of different minor officials. Chaucer's Reeve is, for example, a manager of a man-
         orial estate. The pairing with *sokne* suggests it may be here the title for a judicial of-
         ficer who oversees the land and legal procedures conducted under the jurisdiction
         of a local lord's court.

74   The parodic nature of the charter is underlined by substituting "In the date of the
         devil" for the usual "In the year of our Lord."

75   Notaries were clerks trained to draw up and witness legal documents.

76ff   A new stage of the action is introduced by Theology's objections to the marriage.
         While by this time academic theology *may* have become such a rarefied study that it
         was no longer in touch with practical realities (or, alternatively, that it had become
         corrupted by the money economy), there is little in the following scene—aside, that
         is, from the disagreement with Holy Church—that marks this as a wrongheaded or
         corrupt argument in favor of Mede's more positive character.
              The seriousness, and complexity, of Theology's position is attested by the sub-
         stantial revisions it underwent in the B and C versions. His argument, directed
         against Civil Law, argues that reward (i.e., Mede) also plays a significant role in the
         spiritual order, and he distinguishes his more idealized view of Mede from that of
         Simony also. It is not clear, however, whether his view is purely conceptual; his
         identifying Mede as the daughter of *frendis*, and intended by God as a spouse for
         Truth, may indicate that he is arguing that there are proper ways (distinct from si-
         mony) that earthly treasure may be used in ecclesiastical or religious spheres. The
         marginal grant of (partial) pardon to the merchants in Truth's pardon (8.20ff.) at-
         tests to a similar attitude.

80   Theology insists here (and again at 2.94) that Mede is *muliere*, that is, "a woman of
         legitimate birth" (from Anglo-Norman *mulier* [derived from Lat. *mulier*], "freeborn
         lady, woman").

84   The quotation from the gospels is translated in the following line. Jesus's words are
         his justification for evangelical poverty: he tells his disciples that they do not need to
         provide themselves with gold or silver, spare clothes, or sandals and a staff as they
         go to the lost sheep of Israel proclaiming that the kingdom of heaven is close at
         hand.

93   Beelzebub is associated with Satan and with the "prince of devils" in Mark 3:22–24.

97   While it is the archbishop of Canterbury's court that sits in London (and this may

be Theology's intention), the proceedings detailed later actually involve the king's court, which sits at Westminster, at that time a separate town upriver from London. The journey is repeated as being to London (2.118), but by line 123 it is said to be to Westminster. Insisting on the distinction may be pedantry, but it is worth asking whether the journey is being subtly redirected by False and Co. from the archiepiscopal court to the royal one. See lines 2.131ff.

106   A florin was a gold coin (introduced by Edward III in 1344 and bearing his image) worth six shillings and eight pence (= one-third of a pound). The name goes back either to the Latin word *flores* (flowers) or the French *fleures* because the coin was stamped with a fleur-de-lys. It is distinct (in form and value) from the earlier florin associated with the Italian city of Florence. The Edwardian coin is also called a "noble."

109   That Favel needs to bribe False Witness and others to "master" Mede, and that they claim to have accomplished this through *merye speche* (116), reinforce the conclusion that Mede is without agency and has to be led to London as Theology said (97). Her passive nature throughout should be noted: she is powerless to direct her own life and how she is used. This *could* be an indication of the essential neutrality of money: the people who get and use money are the responsible agents.

125   *folys*: "Foals" and "fools" (see 2.142). Both meanings are appropriate to the context, and the pun reinforces the extended metaphor about proceeding on horseback.

126   A sheriff is a "shire reeve," the secular administrative official in charge of a shire, a considerable geographical region.

131   "By the Rood" or "By the Cross" is a common oath.

133   Provisors are clergymen who have been "provided" to an ecclesiastical position directly by the pope. This papal prerogative was a matter of continuing dispute between secular and religious leaders and led to a number of specific statutes in England during the period of this poem. The 1351 Statute of Provisors is probably the most relevant of these. Such "provisions" were often made as a result of monetary contributions to the pope and his court, and that seems to be the point of their inclusion here.

135   Deans and subdeans are diocesan clergy who serve in official positions under a bishop, responsible for administrative matters in portions of a diocese.

137   Paulines are here explicitly associated with proceedings in bishops' consistory courts (for trials conducted under canon law). See above, 2.70.

138   Civil Law claims precedence here over ecclesiastical officers, asserting that they should serve him. Cf. note to 2.97.

139   *comysarye*: A diocesan official, a deputy of the bishop, often the one who oversees the consistory court.

140   Under Civil Law's revision of the legal arrangements, the bribes (or fines) paid by fornicators will supply him and his companions with their food and drink. In practice, this sort of arrangement was common as the way of covering the costs and salaries for various royal and parliamentary commissioners, tax collectors, and other officers.

144   *tayl*: This "tail" refers to the "retinue" or "staff" that attends these important people and would include various hangers-on or camp followers.

157ff   The king, immediately responding to Conscience (who was informed by *Sothnesse*,

2.147ff.), orders a constable (a royal peace-officer) to proceed against these *tyrauntes* and warns him, repeatedly, against accepting any bribes: *tresour* or *gyftys*.

169ff The dispersal of the "tyrants" shows the corruption of religious and secular "businesses" and the continuing competition for the services of Liar especially, even after he is hunted and shunned by others: among pardoners, physicians, sellers of spices, minstrels, messengers, and friars (who already have Falseness living with them). Only Mede, trembling with fear, is left behind in the general rout caused by *Drede*. Her almost catatonic situation at being abandoned by her erstwhile supporters should be noted in the closing lines of the passus.

181ff Medical doctors (*lechys*) are included among those who give Liar accommodations. Clearly, not all doctors were considered trustworthy. Examining a patient's *wateres* (urine) was an important diagnostic practice, but one that could be misused for personal gain (e.g., by extended treatment or from expensive medicine). Chaucer's Physician is shown in the Ellesmere MS portrait carrying a glass container of urine (presumably) as an exemplary tool of his trade.

186 In his note to the equivalent line in the B version (2.228), J. A. W. Bennett points out, "Six months and eleven days was exactly the length of Edward III's French campaign, 1359–60: he landed on 28 October, and the Treaty of Bretigny was signed on 8 May (for details, see Bennett, "Date of the A-Text")." If the number is not simply meant to be an indefinite one, then it clearly would support an argument that this version of *Piers Plowman* cannot be dated earlier than the end of this campaign.

188 In order to prevent his recognition by visitors (perhaps investigators), they disguised him as a friar.

Passus Three

1ff The proceedings combine both judicial and social activities: for example, having the clerk put Mede *at ese*. These may point to the operations of the king's council, or to the court, but a strong case has been made in favor of seeing the bulk of these scenes as set in the Parliament, with the king and the lords, as well as the commons, involved in a legislative undertaking. See Giancarlo.

12ff While at first the king and his attendants seem above suspicion, what follows makes it clearer that *worschepyn* may not be only a convenient alliterating word but that it reveals the extremity of affection that those in Westminster have for Mede.

21 These are hardly insignificant gifts. Her "thanks" for their offers of help are substantial, and inappropriate, if not in fact unusual, for one whose case is being considered in the king's court.

23 A *motoun* was a gold coin worth one-third of a pound (6 shillings 8 pence). This is the same value as a florin or a noble.

41 *felle*: The friar's final goal—to destroy Conscience—makes explicit his purposes, and those of others who before him comforted Mede. The criticism of friars for providing easy absolution is common during the fourteenth century—and later: see Szittya.

43–44 The friar offered to hear Mede's confession and give her absolution (*asoyle*: 39). Her confession, however, is flawed, and in fact perverts the three requirements of the sacrament: she is *schameles* and so does not show true contrition; she gives what may be characterized as a false appearance of contrition, a plausible fiction (*tokne*; a *tale* in other manuscripts), and so does not confess a true account of her sins; and she offers a payment of money instead of making satisfaction in a more personal, active fashion. See Dolan.

45   *bedman*: This is either an offer to be her beadsman, one who offers *bedes* (prayers) for another, often in return for some gift or donation. Or it is an offer to be her go-between; the word may also refer to a messenger or servant: one subject to another's "bidding."

47ff   This is a blatant invitation to simony by the friar: making a donation to build or restore a church is not guarantee of salvation. This practice (which the Narrator explicitly rejects below, 53ff.) is, however, one frequently attributed to friars by their critics. The rationale is that, in return for the donation, the friars (and others who look at the window) will pray regularly for the soul of the one whose name is inscribed there and that this will shorten her time in Purgatory.

    The phrase *wil stonde us hyghe* in this context is probably best translated as "will cost us a lot."

52   Fraternal orders (and other religious communities) offered lay supporters enrollment as official affiliates of their orders (a "sister," or "brother": i.e., a member of a lay confraternity, what later comes to be referred to as a "third order"). This ensured them certain benefits, such as remembrance in prayers and masses, the right to be buried in the convent grounds, memorial services, and indulgences.

53ff   The Narrator speaks directly against the practice of making such overt donations, because the motive behind them may not be truly pious.

62   Calling attention to their giving alms and praying is the mark of hypocritical behavior, according to Jesus: see Matthew 6:1–6 (v.3 of which has already been quoted in l.54; v.2 is invoked to similar effect by Conscience at 3.235)

63   *An auntere* (and 261: *En aunter*) [Fr. *en aunture*], "by chance."

65ff   The transition to mayors and masters is rather abrupt in other manuscripts and editions, and this has led some (e.g., Bennett, *Piers Plowman*) to identify this passage as a scribal addition. Taken as another narratorial direct address (as in Ra), however, it becomes more consistent with his address to *you lordes* (60) and calls on these officials to fulfill their responsibilities in enforcing the law, which Mede's request below (76ff.) will pervert.

68ff   The criticism of food retailers is not simply that they provide impure goods (*poysone*) but that they mark up prices disproportionately on small quantities (*parcelmele*). Because the poor cannot afford to purchase in bulk or wholesale, they are at the mercy of unscrupulous suppliers, who compound their profits by engaging in price-fixing and other monopolistic practices. With these profits they can purchase income-producing properties (*rentes*) and display their wealth by building timber-framed, multistoried houses. These are not, of course, criticisms of marketplace practices limited to fourteenth-century England.

78   By accepting *presentes* that are not in the form of cash (*withoute pens*), they may avoid the appearance of blatant bribery. The complementariness of "presents" and "pennies" is reinforced below (151). The term *regrateres* (cf. *regratyng* [72]) in the following line means people engaged in retail trade, but it clearly is thought of as a

negative term, and practice, perhaps even with the connotation of "bloodsuckers," or "capitalist scum."

82ff   The reference to *Salomon the sage* is generic, Solomon being thought of as the author of many of the "Writings" (or Wisdom books) of the Old Testament. The text in 85 is from Job 15:34, translated in 87–89.

92   *to boure*: The king's (apparently private) interview with Mede fulfills his promise above (5ff.).

101   Mede's quick agreement to the king's proposal is consistent with her usual pattern of agreeing readily to those who have her in hand.

104ff The king addresses Conscience in public, before the council and others. The change of scene is significant, given the distinctive character of Mede and of Conscience: she is more at home in private dealings, he with more public ones.

109ff Unlike the always agreeable Mede, Conscience rejects the king's request, refusing to marry her because she is disloyal and fickle. His rejection of Mede is based on principles different from those voiced by Holy Church earlier. Mede's weak faith and fickleness are failings particularly offensive to Conscience, who judges issues in stark absolutes.

116   Edward II (1307–27), father of the long-reigning Edward III (1327–77), was indeed murdered, at Berkeley Castle, after he was deposed in 1327. The *falce behestes* more probably refer to those which Edward II made to his friends, not any that were made to him. This is one of the accusations that Mede specifically rebuts (173ff.).

117   If, again, a literal historical reference is intended here, it appears to be to the alleged death by poisoning of Pope Benedict XI (1306). If the poisoning is metaphorical, however, it may be referring to the so-called Donation of Constantine: in the B version, Passus 15, *venym* (559) and *poison* (564, 566; and cf. 560) are the words used with regard to the imperial grant of secular possessions to the church, which many considered a particularly damaging event in European church history.

121   A well-attested proverb (Whiting, C 64), it characterizes Mede as a prostitute, available to all and used by many.

129   Ra (along with MSS T and H²) reads *He* here, which would attribute these actions (and those which follow in the next three lines) to *Falce* rather than to Mede; the majority of manuscripts, and all modern editors, however, present a feminine pronoun.

135   The king's secret, or signet, seal was the most personal of the three seals used to effect royal actions, such as make appointments. The Great Seal and the Privy Seal had by the reign of Edward III become established as official institutions, branches of the administrative bureaucracy; the signet remained much more immediately with the king, retained by his personal secretary: see Waugh, 172. The accusation here is that bribery effects things even more quickly than the royal will.

136   On this point, Conscience and Holy Church (2.17) agree: Mede is a power in papal court.

140ff The church's rule of clerical celibacy was well established by this period, as were breaches of the rule.

148   *lovedayes* are days set aside for reconciling local differences (in the manorial court or elsewhere); the implication is that they provide occasions for bribery. See Bennett, "Medieval Loveday."

162ff   Mede's complaint to the king is marked by courteous deference and politeness. As Skeat noted, Mede uses the polite and respectful *ye* to the king (163) but the more familiar and contemptuous *thou, thy* to Conscience (165ff.). Mede's account of Conscience's activities draws (apparently) on events in recent history. However, few of these have been convincingly identified from the surviving records.

168   *ellevene*: This odd number may be an exaggeration, or simply an effectively concrete way of saying "many." The idiom "hang on my half" seems to mean "clung to my side"—that is, "sought my support and assistance."

176ff   This passage has proved crucial in arguments for assigning a date to the composition of the A version. Various scholars (e.g., Skeat, *Parallel Texts*; Bennett, *Piers Plowman*; Huppé, "A-Text") have identified historical referents for the (admittedly rather vague or general) accusations that Mede makes against Conscience. Some identify Mede with Alice Perrers and Conscience with John of Gaunt (whose military exploits never rose to the level of his oldest brother Edward's), and events of 1359, 1369, and even as late as 1373 have been claimed as the referents for the allusions here.

    The events in Normandy have been associated with the campaign of 1359–60 (perhaps earlier alluded to in the "half year and eleven days" mentioned in 2.186). The *colde* and the *dym klowde* may allude to the frightening hailstorm (on "Black Monday," 14 April 1360), which allegedly inspired Edward to make peace. The Treaty of Bretigny (1360) marked the high point of English power during the Hundred Years' War. In the treaty, the English (in the person of John of Gaunt) promised to have King Edward renounce his claim to the French throne (which he in fact never explicitly did) and in return the French ceded to England great portions of southern and western France. To ransom King John, who had been a prisoner in England for more than three years, the French promised to pay three million gold crowns, only a portion of which was in fact paid. If this is the *lytel sylver* mentioned by Mede (194), it suggests that she was aware of the emptiness of the promised ransom or was expecting greater wealth to accrue if Edward had successfully effected his claim to the French throne.

    According to Bennett (*"Date of the A-Text"*), if Mede is to be associated with Alice Perrers, then the *bras* she accuses Conscience of carrying to Calais (183) may allude to John of Gaunt's plunder during the 1369 campaign; his argument counters Huppé's, who had argued that the events alluded to are those of John's disastrous winter campaign in 1373.

188ff   Mede claims that if she had been commander in chief of the king's army, the outcome would have been the conquest of France. Her criticism of Conscience (who may stand in for the princes who actually led the English army, Edward the Black Prince, Lionel [Duke of Clarence], and John of Gaunt [Duke of Lancaster]) implies that he was cowardly and shortsighted, settling for personal comfort and plunder, when greater public rewards could have been achieved. This would not have been a unique criticism of the conduct of the English forces, and the use of English taxes, during these stages of the French wars.

196ff   The next portion of Mede's speech defends the giving and receiving of *mede* as essential to the working of society and its institutions, secular and religious. She equates *mede* with wages and taxes, with tithes and donations. Her defense comes close to convincing the king (215–16).

217ff   As earlier (105), Conscience kneels to address the king, and his speech is directed entirely toward his monarch. His response to Mede's self-defense (and attack on him) distinguishes two separate meanings of *mede*, one good and the other bad. He equates Mede only with the negative meaning, *mede mesureles* (226), in a pointedly *ad feminam* attack. The distinction he makes is clearly important, and there will be repeated efforts in the B and C versions to clarify the distinction and its precise terms.

In the C revision, Conscience concludes by denying that the positive uses Mede has just argued in favor of are not in fact properly called *mede* at all, but should be called *mercede*. But this resolution of the debate is clearly a later attempt to deal with some critical ambiguities in the debate being conducted here: just because it makes sense of the issue in the C version does not negate A's less decisive resolution of the matter, and the fact that *God of his grace* (219) does in fact give one kind of *mede* leaves open the question whether Mede can be properly identified *only* with Conscience's *mede mesureles*.

236ff   Although Conscience said at the beginning of this speech that there were *two maner of medes* (218), he now is intent to deny the term *mede* to Mede's positive versions. The negative species of *mede* he called *mesureles* (immoderate) above (225) has now become *no maner of mede* contrasted with *mesurable hyre* (reasonable salary) or simple *permutacioun* (equal exchange).

240ff   *Regum*: The story of Saul's war with the Amalekites is told in 1 Samuel 15. The Bible of the medieval church titled the two books of Samuel as 1, 2 Kings, and the two books of Kings, as 3 and 4 Kings.

253   The idea that *Crist* is the one who delivered the command to Saul indicates the conventions of Christian interpretation of the Old Testament as the Word of God, specifically of a Triune God. Because all three persons of the Trinity are equally God, the poet has the option (here driven by alliteration) of identifying the Second Person of the Trinity (Christ) as the source of the command. Three lines later, it is *God* who speaks.

260   *culorum*: These are the concluding syllables found in the common form of closure to Latin prayers: *in secula seculorum* (for ever and ever) and is used here in the sense of conclusion or end.

262ff   Conscience's *ende* (taught him by Reason) is that the story of Samuel and Saul provides an exemplary instance of what the ideal Christian society should be. In this millennial image, bad kings (Saul) will be punished, and the clergy (Samuel) will establish the true king (David), who will defeat all evildoers and inaugurate a period dominated by love, humility, and loyal faith. The only thing preventing the realization of this golden era is Mede, who perverts servants (272) and fosters unnatural behavior.

Some manuscripts read *kynde wit me taughte*, and this reading is adopted by modern editors, even though their base manuscript (T) reads *kynde it*. I have retained the reading in Ra (and U and E)—despite its breaking alliteration, and the repetition of *resoun* in the following line. His image of a good society is achievable through the alliance of reason and conscience, and Conscience is asserting that this is not a far-fetched or fantastic idea, but rather something that we can all agree with.

271   *don hym lawe*: Has the meaning "inflict the rigors of the law on him; impose justice."

Passus Four

1   The king orders the two of them to stop arguing: the *you* is more likely a plural than a polite singular pronoun addressed to Conscience, a point reinforced by *bothe* at the end of the second line. He addressed Conscience as *thou* earlier (3.107). While the king earlier explicitly said he thought Mede was winning the argument (3.215–16), his reaction here suggests that he remains unpersuaded by Conscience's counterargument about the two kinds of reward and the equation of Lady Mede only with the negative version. The kiss of reconciliation (equivalent to the modern deal-sealing handshake) ordered by the king is rejected by Conscience. The king is, as a result, made to appear somewhat weaker by what follows.

5   As Conscience indicates here, the choice between right and wrong depends on one's understanding of what is right and true. His appeal to Reason offers, therefore, an external (even transcendent) authority that may allow the king (and us) to resolve the he-said she-said debate between himself and Mede. Because he must be sent to find Reason by the king, the preceding argument can be ruled a draw, as the king's frustrated command that the two of them be reconciled and kiss indicates. Conscience's invoking the authority of Reason, however, initiates a new, and final, stage to this debate. Until he is perceived as being aligned with Reason, in other words, Conscience is helpless to persuade the king of the rightness of his case. Absent Reason's authority, Conscience will be either dismissed from the king's court or die. Like Mede, then, Conscience requires another to direct and validate him. While Catholic theology asserts the primacy of the individual conscience as determining whether one's action is to be judged sinful, it insists that it be a *properly formed* conscience, one that takes full account of the dictates of both human reason and divine revelation.

       On Reason (= Latin *ratio*) as a "moral absolute" identifiable with "eternal law," "supreme truth," and "divine order," see Alford, "Idea of Reason." As he says, "the eternal law of Truth consists *in* reason (order) and reveals itself *to* reason (the faculty)" (206). The human faculty is not an independent, autonomous power, but rather one that is naturally capable of probing to the underlying truth that should guide, and determine, proper action.

6   The king is inspired by Conscience's ultimatum to consult Reason. The wording of his decision is noteworthy: the king wants Reason first *my counseyle to here*, and only then to *give* him his advice (*rede* [9]). Further, there is a likely double meaning to *counseyle* (8) because it may mean both the king's own personal thinking *and* the body of his advisers (his council). Both of these are essential to ruling the kingdom. Reason will be specifically asked to give the king advice about Mede's marriage (and others').

17   Dionysius Cato was the (putative) author of the late classical (fourth century A.D.) *Distichs of Cato* (*Disticha Catonis de Moribus*), a widely known and important gram-

mar school text in the Middle Ages, full of proverbial sayings of practical wisdom. Its collection of versified moral maxims provided an early grounding in moral education. It was one of the very first texts children came across in schools, once they had begun to master their Donatus, the basic Latin grammar. The maxims were frequently translated, and there are a number of Middle English manuscripts.

The association of Reason with this sort of practical wisdom is reinforced by the names of those who follow him, Wary Wisdom and Witty (24).

18   Reason's horse evidences forceful energy (21) and needs to be well restrained (19–20), while waiting for the proper moment to act.

24   *Were Wisdoum* and *Witty* are aspects of worldly, practical wisdom, and it is not surprising that they might have business before the Exchequer and Chancery. The Exchequer was directed by the treasurer and handled all matters having to do with royal revenues, taxes, fees, and the like. Chancery, overseen by the lord chancellor, was responsible for issuing official government documents, such as writs and charters, that bore the Great Seal; it often functioned as a sort of court of appeals. These branches of the government were of great bureaucratic importance but of lesser political influence (usually) than the king's council.

32   The mention of the king's son alludes to the important status of Edward of Woodstock (1330–76), Prince of Wales and Duke of Aquitaine, in his father's court. Much later dubbed the Black Prince, Prince Edward fought as a teenager at Crécy in 1346 and had become a significant leader by at least 1355, when he led one of the two major military expeditions against the French, ranging victoriously across southern France from Bordeaux and Gascony to the Mediterranean and back. One of the reasons for dating this version of *Piers* to sometime around 1369 is that it gives no indication the prince's incapacitating illness (contracted in Spain in campaigns during 1367–69) that would erase his force as a military leader and progressively weaken his political power as his father aged and weakened as an engaged and effective leader. Prince Edward died the year before his father, and his place as heir to the throne was taken by his eldest son, Richard, then ten years old.

34ff   Although the king has summoned Reason to advise him regarding Mede, the matter is not taken up immediately—or rather it is not taken up in quite the way one might have expected from the debate between Conscience and Mede. The bill brought in by Peace initiates what appears to be a new case, one that involves not only Wrong, Mede's father, but also Mede herself. In the course of dealing with this case, Reason renders his advice to the king regarding Mede.

The enumerated crimes of Wrong are all obvious challenges to the public law and order, breaches of the peace, and as such are not really subject to new statutes as much as the enforcement of existing laws. The substitution of money payment for injury and injustice is not, however, any sort of abhorrent practice. It is at the root of much English (and other) law and custom. Individual complainants, like Peace here, were able to petition the king through the "commons," and to receive justice through money payment where other forms of restitution were impossible, for example, in a case of rape, injury, or death.

The reign of Edward III was particularly important in the development of Parliament's powers, especially of the "lower" house. (See Jolliffe, chap. 4, part 2, Parliamentary Monarchy.)

42   Interfering with free trade (at fairs and markets) by forestalling (i.e., buying up supplies and then reselling them at marked-up prices) is placed on the same level, apparently, as murder, destruction of property, theft, and nonpayment for goods.

72   He will not see his feet because he is (or they are) enclosed in the stocks (cf. 93). "Seven years" is commonly used for an extended and indefinite period of time, here corresponding to king's *As longe as I lyve* (94).

73ff   The argument between those who insist on imprisonment and those who argue for fines (or other compensation) has a long history. The king, however, does not see it simply as an either-or option.

83–87 These lines, not found in our base manuscript (Ra), regularly appear in other manuscripts of *Piers*. Without them, the change of voice between lines 82 and 88 would be, unusually, unmarked.

98   Reason rejects the advice to allow Mede to go bail for Wrong and insists that such *ruthe* has no place in a world like the real one in which he and his audience live. The idealized world he invokes here provides a standard for satirizing the actual society imagined in the poem. This provides the basis for the rejection of Mede: in the fallen world of human self-interest and greed, Mede is inevitably going to be led astray by those who use her.

100   Peronel is used here (and later: see 5.26, 45) as the name for a proud woman. Her expensive clothes are the mark of her vanity.

101   The "cherishing" here is seen as negative, resulting in spoiled and unmanageable children: those who indulge their children in this way should themselves be punished.

102   A *hyne* is the term for a "servant" or "peasant." It is used figuratively here to mean "something of little or no worth" (Schmidt, *Parallel-Text*, 2.514).

107   Consistent with the critique of those who seem outwardly religious but are not truly so, Reason criticizes the pilgrimage trade. The pilgrimage to Santiago de Compostela (St. James's shrine in Galicia, northwest Spain) is perhaps the most famous in Europe (next to Rome). Reason rejects these as an indefensible drain on the English economy and, presumably, on the kinds of benefits that distributing such alms closer to home could accomplish. Lines 113–14, however, clearly exclude important economic and ecclesiastical activities from this condemnation of foreign expenditures.

109   Rome-runners are those who journey to the papal court to obtain deeds, pardons, and the like. Reason appears to distinguish *Rome-renneres* from those (113–14) who have more defensible reasons for journeying to Rome. "Rome" may be used generically here for the papal court, which during much of the fourteenth century was in Avignon. If, however, we take the city name literally, it would signal that the date of this version of *Piers* could be assigned to the period 1367–70, when the pope was in fact resident in Rome: see Bennett, "Date of the B-Text," 60.

110   While there had been statutes issued since at least 1299 making it illegal to send abroad English coins bearing the king's *sygne*, other laws during the reign of Ed-

ward III (e.g., 1355) attempted to control the flow of money out of and into England: see Waugh, 78–84.

123–24 The Latin phrases, derived from a treatise of Pope Innocent III (*De contemptu mundi*, III.15) became proverbial. Innocent used them to describe the essential qualities of the just judge.

129ff Reason's speech ends triumphantly, and its principles are accepted by the king's *confessoures*. Mede is rejected and made fun of (134ff.), and Wary Wisdom and Witty are renamed with negative prefixes (*Onwarned* and *Onwittes*: 138) and reduced to the condition of dumb beasts (140ff.). The king assents to Reason's views, even though he acknowledges the difficulty of ruling according to Reason's dictates. Reason affirms that he will stay with the king forever as long as Conscience is also made part of his council.

With the king's agreement to this (148ff.), the first dream concludes, although this event is not formally noted until the beginning of the next passus.

Passus Five

1 The unanimity achieved in the royal entourage at the end of the preceding passus is marked by the communal participation in religious services (matins and mass) and in sharing a meal together. The Dreamer awakes, but it is clear that the second dream, which follows shortly, is meant to be fairly continuous with the first. The poet could have ended the first dream at the conclusion of the previous passus, but chose to postpone it till the beginning of this one.

3ff The waking of the Dreamer here marks him as separated from the community in the preceding lines. His *wo*, then, may be at his waking to a world in which this dreamed ideal is missing.

It is not "realistic" to attribute, as he does here, his inability to walk more than a furlong (a few hundred yards) to a literal lack of sleep (6): he has only been awake a few minutes, after all. Hence, the alternative attribution of his tiredness to *fantasye* (i.e., "a deluded notion or false supposition": *MED*, 2b). But if it is his separation from the sleeping world of his dream that is being emphasized, then this may reflect on his own moral and spiritual condition, his unworthiness, perhaps, to participate in the community united in the liturgy and at the dinner table. (A similar situation occurs at the beginning of B Passus 19, where the Dreamer wakes in the middle of the Easter Mass: see Vaughan "Liturgical Perspectives," 143–55, and "Til I gan Awake," 178–83.) His saying his creed here, though clearly positive, is not really an adequate substitute for matins and mass, and babbling his prayers probably has sufficiently negative connotations to make us suspect his status as something of an "outsider" (or as unregenerate) at this transitional moment between the two dreams. In any event, his journey is not complete, and he is able to proceed only a short distance on his own.

7 *byleve* refers to the Creed (from the first word of the Latin prayer, *Credo* ["I believe"]), which articulates the traditional body of fundamental beliefs held by Christians. The fourth-century Nicene (or Niceno-Constantinopolitan) Creed was (and is) regularly recited in the mass; other forms of the creed (e.g., the Apostles' and Athanasian) were also widely known in the Middle Ages.

8   The basic meaning of *bedes* here is "prayers." It is conceivable that the word refers to a rosary, or prayer beads, which are frequently used to keep count of (repetitive) prayers (see Bennett, *Piers Plowman*, 151n).

9ff   The dream is presented as a continuation, or a later episode, of the preceding dream. In the B version's revision, Conscience is replaced by Reason. The *cros* Conscience brings is a bishop's staff of office, his crozier. A number of the elements in his sermon echo those in Reason's speech in the previous passus: Peronel and her *purfyl*; chastising children; requiring priests practice what they preach; seeking St. Truth instead of going on pilgrimage to St. James or Rome. This would confirm that Conscience is now properly aligned with Reason.

13   There were recurrent epidemics or plagues in the middle of the fourteenth century, the most memorable of which was the Black Death, which struck England in 1348–49 after ravaging much of the Continent. There were notable pestilences also in 1361–62 and 1368–69 and in 1374–75. The specific reference, if one was intended or is necessary, must depend on what date we assign the creation of the poem.

14   There was a famous storm with a southwest wind on Saturday, 15 January 1362. The pairing with the pestilence in the previous line may therefore point to 1362 as the date after which (*terminus a quo*) the poem was written. A number of the detailed effects of the storm here correspond to those mentioned in the chronicles. (See Bennett, "Date of the A-Text.")

18–20   The mention of Doomsday (20) suggests that the image of trees with their roots turned upward can be associated with the familiar tradition of the Fifteen Signs of Doomsday: depictions of the earthquake of the eighth day include upturned trees. See Heist.

24–25   The linking of "winning" and "wasting," while a conventional alliterative pair, recalls the Middle English poem *Wynnere and Wastoure*, one of the earliest poems of the so-called alliterative revival of the fourteenth century in England, which has an opening very similar to that in *Piers*. *Wynnere* was probably composed shortly after 1352 (the date of the *Statute of Treasons* to which it alludes) and refers to social and political upheavals following the Black Death. Much of its social and economic criticism finds echoes in *Piers*.

29   The *pyne* probably refers to the *pynnyng-stolys* mentioned earlier (3.67). Wives were often subject to public punishment for shrewishness or gossiping. Tom is being told that it is his duty to correct his wife, with beatings if required, to prevent her having to be punished by ducking or sitting in the stocks. Compare the comments on correcting children in the previous passus (4.101).

31   The point is that Watte's wife (or perhaps Watte himself *for* her) has spent an unconscionable amount on an ostentatious headdress: a mark (13 shillings 4 pence) would be approximately a month's salary for a good worker, and forty times the cost of Watte's hood.

42   This is the common ending of Latin liturgical prayers (to the Holy Spirit): "who with the Father and the Son [live and reign, One God, forever and ever]." The words also appear, in a less "conclusive" form, in the Nicene Creed said at mass, where they also characterize the Holy Spirit. The phrase here identifies *Seynt Truthe*, therefore, with the Third Person of the Trinity, rather than with the Father or Son (Jesus)

43ff   With the appearance of *Repentauns*, we begin the episode usually referred to as the Confession of the Deadly Sins. These sins are traditionally seven in number: Pride, Covetousness, Envy, Sloth, Anger, Gluttony, and Lust. However, the number (and the identity) of the sins varies from time to time: see Bloomfield, *The Seven Deadly Sins*.

In this episode of *Piers*, Anger (Wrath) is omitted from the usual seven. Some have attributed substantial significance to this: that it shows, for instance, that there has been significant corruption in the transmission of the text. Alternatively, the omission might have been intentional and points to the poet's belief that anger is not a vice but rather a righteous emotion (even one particularly favored, indeed, by his critical stance toward the social and ecclesiastical misbehavior of his time). Or perhaps he has simply subsumed anger into his characterization of Envy.

44   The character *Wille* here stands for the personified human will (*voluntas*), which is moved by Repentance's sermon to show its contrition by means of tears. The theology of the sacrament of Confession (Penance) in the Middle Ages articulates the necessity of three elements: contrition of heart, confession of mouth, and satisfaction in deed. In other words, in order to benefit from the priest's absolution of their sins, penitents must feel genuine sorrow, recount their sins in words to the priest, and carry out the penitential actions the priest assigns. The specifically detailed sins that follow require voluntary and genuine acknowledgment of sin within—in the heart, in the consciousness, in the will. Some critics have chosen to identify *Wille* here with the Poet/Narrator/Dreamer, although its unqualified introduction, and lack of first-person identification makes this appear unlikely.

48   Peronel's *serk* would be the equivalent of a modern undershirt. Unlike the modern item, however, these were infrequently removed (or washed), and to replace it would require the wearer to *unsewe* it since it would ordinarily have been sewn to keep it tight to the body. It would not, then, be frequently replaced.

Vices are corrected by penitential discipline (like the hair shirt here) and by actively practicing the virtues that counter them. Here Peronel promises humility or meekness as a corrective to pride. Her identifying envy also as one of her sins indicates that these vices are not conceived as fully distinct and that we are dealing with human personifications of sinful behavior rather than with absolutely distinct abstract allegorizations.

54ff   Invoking *oure lady* (Mary, the Virgin Mother of Jesus) is an appropriate countermeasure for a repentant lecher. His promise to be abstemious of drink and food suggests (properly, one might say) that lechery and gluttony are connected. His promise to honor Saturdays (56) specifically reflects the common devotional practice of celebrating votive masses of the Virgin on that day of the week.

61   *caury-maury* is a word unique to the poem whose meaning is a scholarly guess. If Envy's foresleeves and frock are meant to associate him with friars, then the word may refer to the kind of rough cloth used for the friar's habit. But it may have other associations altogether, because the jacket, coat, and knife (in the following line) would be inappropriate for a friar, and the point may be to reinforce the idea that although Envy is a mark of the friars, it is *not* in any sense limited to them. The (apparently) lower-class *caury-maury* may not quite fit with the more genteel *kyrtel* and *curtepy*.

66ff   These lines, with their prominent mention of *wroth* (66, and cf. 79) and *wrothlyche*

(67), may indicate that *Envye* combines elements of both *Invidia* and (the "missing") *Ira*. (The connection is made explicit at the beginning of this confession in the Z version: "Envye ant Yre ayther wep faste" [5.91]. And Wrath's confession follows Envye's in both B and C.) As noted earlier, however, many of these characters are not limited to features of the particular vices whose name they bear. This is perhaps intended to indicate that such vices come (like Hamlet's "sorrows") "not single spies / But in battalions."

101   Envy's expression of doubt about the power of the sacrament of Penance to cure sin prompts *Repentauns*'s intervention to explain the power of contrition.

104–5   This play on the idea of "sorrow" is a pointed irony: unlike the previous sins (and those that follow), Envy does not evidence any serious sign of contrition, the essential sorrow necessary for forgiveness of his sin.

107   *Sire Hervy*: The *Sire* here suggests that this Harvey (identity unknown) was of some importance, a conventional type of the miser, perhaps. *Sire* was also the title for an ordained priest, although nothing in what follows would support this as an attractive alternative.

115   *noke*: The phrase "at the [sign of the] oak" would identify where Simon conducts his business.

117   He is studying the pages of his textbook of avarice. There are recurrent terms running through this passage associated with school: *lessoun* (118, 125) and *my Donet to lere* below (123). His education in the ways of greed starts with basics (those practiced, at least in the first instance here, in the wool and cloth trades). Many of the specific acts of fraud here were legislated against in contemporary ordinances: see Lipson, 274, 329, 461–65.

119   The cathedral towns of Winchester and Weyhill (both in Hampshire, southwest of London) were sites of important fairs. Winchester was particularly important in the wool trade with France.

123   The Latin grammar of Donatus was a standard school text for beginning students.

132ff   Fraudulent practices in the production and sale of ale are commonplace: see Lipson, 294–97, 329–30. *Penyale* (costing a penny a gallon) is apparently the cheapest. It is not clear what *pigwhey* is (or, for that matter, the *pile-whey* of other A MSS), but it is unlikely that the mixture is intended to improve the drink but to dilute the already thin penny ale. Bringing out the choice ale from back room, for four times the price of penny ale, could also permit deceptions in quality and measure. The alewife's "private reserve" might not have anything more than the appearance of high quality. It is highly unlikely that anyone would willingly pay *a grote* (137) for even the choicest ale if the ordinary was one-quarter that. The point may be that by selling it only in (perhaps "short") cups or pints, she was able to increase the real cost of a gallon.

143   On Walsingham, see the note to Pr.51.

144   The priory at Bromholm, near Walsingham, had a relic of the cross (*rode*) on which Jesus was crucified. The *dette* here probably refers to the spiritual debts occasioned by sins, or the more general ones referred to in the Lord's Prayer: "forgive us our debts." But the word may also (given the commercial features of *Covetyse*'s confession) include monetary or other debts.

152–53   The passage suggests that chewing spices may not break one's fast (since they are not real food). We may infer from line 200 that this scene is occurring on a Friday, which was regularly a day of abstinence from eating meat. In modern Ireland, it is still common to refer to Friday as a "fast day" (cf. 155: *fastyng dayes*). Fennel might be mentioned because of its reputed ability to lessen flatulence, and similar benefits may have been imputed to the others. Alternatively, chewing garlic, pepper, or other *hote spyces* could simply be intended to mask signs of drinking.

161   Cock's Lane was a site of brothels in medieval London.

168ff   *newe feyre*: The "new fair" is apparently a game involving an exchange of goods, with the "profits" used to buy drinks for the judges and participants. There was, presumably, a general interest in how the exchange goods were valued and who "won" (i.e., who had to fill the cup). In this instance, Clement's cloak was judged to be worth less than Hikke's hood, so to balance the value of the exchanged clothes Clement had to pay the difference in drinks for the company.

188   *in a pater noster whyle*: In the time it takes to say the Lord's Prayer. *Pater noster* are the opening words of the Latin prayer.

195–96   Because his eyes were long accustomed to the dark of the tavern and his senses affected by drink, when he got close to the door, he was blinded by the daylight (even though it was past evensong!).

202   A nice realistic touch: when he first wakes, he thinks he is still in the tavern and is feeling "dry."

208   His proposed penance here goes beyond what is required (to abstain from eating meat) and excludes (or at least postpones) even eating fish (which could be eaten on Fridays).

212   *Vigilate*: Latin "watch; wake up; stay awake." It may be intended as a specific allusion to Jesus's eschatological warnings to his disciples (Mark 13:33–37)—or to another passage in the New Testament: e.g., Matthew 26:41; 1 Corinthians 16:13; or 1 Peter 5:8.

222ff   Like some of the previous confessions, Sloth's includes other sins, specifically those associated with Gluttony and Covetousness. His proposed pilgrimage to Truth (rather than Rome: at line 229) recalls Conscience's sermon at the beginning of the passus (40–41).

225   *syn I wit hadde*: This likely alludes to the idea that one reached a state of moral responsibility ("age of reason") sometime late in the first decade of life. Only from that point on, moral theologians held, could the individual be said to be capable of committing personal sin. The modern Catholic tradition suggests this occurs around the age of seven, at which point children are introduced to the sacrament of Penance and allowed to receive Holy Communion.

228   A legendary cross stood on Rood Eye (i.e., Cross Island) in the River Dee, near the walls of Chester, in northwest England.

230ff   Moved by Sloth's repentance (or by the entire series), an individual sinner (*Roberd the robbere*) breaks in and associates himself with *Dismas my brother*, the so-called Good Thief of Luke's Gospel (23:39–43; the Crucifixion account in Matthew identifies the two who are crucified beside Jesus as "robbers" [*latrones*: 27:38, 44]). He despairs of forgiveness because he cannot see himself being able to pay back (*Reddite*)

what he has stolen. The term alludes to Romans 13:7 (about the Christian's responsibility to pay taxes) or to Matthew 22: 21 (or Mark 12: 17; Luke 20:25): about paying
Caesar what is Caesar's and paying God what is God's. While despair is regularly associated with Sloth, robbery is not; but as we have seen elsewhere in this series of
confessions, the various sins are not kept sealed off from one another.

234   Dismas is traditionally the name given the penitent thief crucified beside Jesus, the
name appearing originally in the *Gospel of Nicodemus*. Only in Luke's account of the
Crucifixion are the two crucified with Jesus distinguished one from the other. The
Memento ("Remember") in line 235 is taken from this passage of Luke (23:42).

242   The Narrator's uncertainty about the fate of Robert stresses his individual humanity, a nicely realistic touch after the confessions of the abstracted deadly sins. The
doubt seems to derive from the fact that however repentant Robert is and however
genuine and lasting his cries for forgiveness, he does not avail himself of the ordinary sacramental means to ensure forgiveness for sins contritely confessed to a
priest. His contrite speech is only *to himselve* (232) and *to Crist* (244). Catholic theology would hold that his sincere contrition, outside of the sacrament, might indeed
gain forgiveness in a case where access to a priest is not possible, as long as the sinner has the intention to avail himself of the sacrament when and if the opportunity
arises. While the sacrament can effectively absolve a penitent of sin, God's power is
of course absolute and not bound to absolve *only* by means of the sacrament.

246   *lep . . . over lond* refers to pilgrimage as a penitential act (with *Penitencia* as the walking stick the pilgrim uses), and perhaps as a metaphor for earthly human life as a
whole (*al his lif tyme*).

247   *Latro* is the common legal (Latin) term for a robber or thief. Why he is identified as
Lucifer's aunt is not clear, beyond providing an alliterating crime to link *leye* and
Latro.

Passus Six

1   The penitents' expressed desire to "seek Truth" at the end of the preceding passus
marks an important response; but without a sure guide, they cannot discover the
way on their own.

4   The outlandish dress of this pilgrim would be consistent with attempts by such
travelers in foreign lands to blend in with the local inhabitants. Clearly, this pilgrim
is calling attention to himself by maintaining the *paynym* dress at home.

5   *burdoun ybounde*: The pilgrim's staff has a cloth strip wound around it. This may allude to its being some "sign" from a particular shrine or region, like the shells and
keys below.

6   Pilgrims were expected to travel light (as the apostles sent out by Jesus in Matt.
10:1ff.), and to depend on alms and local hospitality.

7   Although the *hundred* is clearly an exaggeration, miniature flasks (usually made of
pewter or lead) were common souvenirs; they were frequently stamped with distinctive shapes or marks from their shrines, and often contained (holy) water or oil
from the site. A number of these survive, including many from the shrine of St.
Thomas Becket at Canterbury, which (presumably) contained water from the site of
his murder.

8ff   The scallop shells of Galicia were the pilgrim sign from the shrine of St. James at
        Compostela (Santiago de Compostela). Presumably, the pilgrims enjoyed the sea-
        food of the region as well as the spiritual benefits of the shrine. The convent of St.
        Catherine in the Sinai Peninsula was a popular pilgrim site and would have offered
        its own distinctive souvenirs for pilgrims.

        A cross (9) was a sign of having journeyed to the Holy Land and visited sites such
        as Bethlehem and the Holy Sepulcher (13–14), the sites, respectively, of the birth
        and burial of Jesus. The crossed keys (9) of St. Peter (the keys of the kingdom, to
        bind and to loose) were souvenirs of Rome.

        The *vernicle* (10) is another sign from Rome. The "veil" of Veronica with the im-
        age of Jesus is preserved in St. Peter's. Veronica is the name traditionally given the
        woman who wiped Jesus's face as he carried the cross to Calvary. In return for this
        kindness, the image of his face was imprinted on the cloth. Unnamed in the Gos-
        pels, her name may be derived from the claim that this was the true image (Latin
        vera icon) of Jesus.

14–15   As the birthplace of Jesus, Bethlehem was (and is) an important site for pilgrims.
        Babylon (the Less: near Cairo) had a shrine to the early virgin-martyr Barbara, and a
        church at the site where Mary and Joseph purportedly lived with the Child Jesus af-
        ter they fled Herod's persecution. Armenia was the site of Mount Ararat, where
        Noah's ark came to rest. Alexandria had shrines to Sts. Mark and Catherine.

22   A palmer was, strictly speaking, a pilgrim to the Holy Land: a palm leaf was another
        pilgrim "sign." The term, however, often had the more general sense of "pilgrim."
        The failure of this widely traveled pilgrim to identify the home (or even the exis-
        tence) of Truth recalls the criticisms leveled by Reason and Conscience earlier
        against traveling abroad on pilgrimage.

24   At his first appearance, Piers the Plowman invokes St. Peter, his name-saint (*Piers* is
        an English form of *Peter*) and the "rock" on which Jesus erected his church. Piers
        (whom the pilgrims address by name at line 42) is presumably sticking his head
        through a hedge or above a wall that borders the road and his half acre.

29   Forty years may signify "a long time" or "all my life," but he does later say he is *olde
        and hore* (7.75). Whether the forty years are literal or symbolic, Piers can rightly
        claim to be as knowledgeable about Truth as a scholar is of his books.

38   While it may have been common practice to pay workers for each day's work at the
        end of the day, the line also recalls the parable of the vineyard (Matt. 20:1–16) in
        which even those who worked only an hour got the same daily wage as those who
        worked from early morning. There are verbal similarities in this passage with the
        account of the parable in *Pearl* (497ff.), perhaps indicating a common source in ver-
        nacular translations of the Gospel.

43–44   Piers's response to the offer of *hire* recalls the discussions of *mede* in the previous
        dream. He is rejecting any hint of simony in the exchange of something of spiritual
        value (e.g., his instructions about the "right way" to Truth) for earthly reward. His
        mention of Thomas Becket's popular (and wealthy) shrine at Canterbury (the goal
        of Chaucer's pilgrims) may in the context imply a criticism of local pilgrimages
        along with the earlier criticism of the wastefulness and inanity of foreign travel to
        other shrines.

47ff   The pilgrimage to Truth is a virtual, moral journey, one that travels through a landscape of virtues (Meekness, Mercy), Jesus's summary of the Law (Love God and your neighbor: Matt. 22:37–40; Mark 12:29–33; Luke 10:25–28), the Golden Rule (51: Do unto others . . .), the Sinai commandments (Honor your fathers, Swear not, Covet not), various moral faculties (Conscience, Wit), and the institution of the Christian Church.

52–70   The journey goes through the Ten Commandments (Exod. 20 and Deut. 5), most of which are easily identified. The first, however, *Be-buxum-of-speche*, does not correspond directly to any of the commands, as the others do, but the emphasis on telling the truth and speaking properly is also emphasized at the end of the series. The commandments alluded to are, in order: the fourth (honor your parents), second (do not take the name of God in vain), ninth and tenth (covet not others' property or wives and servants), seventh (do not steal), fifth (do not kill), third (observe the Sabbath), eighth (bear no false witness; tell the truth, do not lie). Most of these are quite explicit, but the command against adultery (if it is indeed included) is referred to only obliquely and metaphorically—*if* "breaking the bough (or bow)" (61) is an instance of sexual euphemism.

66ff   The command against bearing false witness provides yet another occasion for condemnation of bribery, improper *mede*.

71   The castle (*court*) with the tower where Truth is (78) recalls the tower on the hill in the opening dream of the Prologue.

73   *Wil* has the meaning of "willfulness" or "uncontrolled desire" here, the enemy of "good sense" (*Wit*).

79   *daysterre*: This is a reference to the wisdom and power of God, as revealed in his speech to Job from the whirlwind (38:32) and in the defeat of Babylon (Isa. 14:12). The latter is also interpreted as referring to the fall of the Angels, led by Lucifer (= Daystar).

103ff   The Seven Virtues are the antidotes to the Seven Deadly Sins, whose confession inaugurated this journey to Truth, a journey that now has turned inward to find Truth within the penitent's own heart. Abstinence overcomes Gluttony; Humility, Pride; Charity, Envy; Chastity, Lechery; Patience, Sloth; Peace, Wrath; and Largesse, Covetousness.

119   Mercy's *mayden* is identified with the Virgin Mary, the Mother of Jesus (*hure sone* [120]). The association of Mary with mercy is traditional: one of her titles is *mater misericordiae* (mother of mercy).

Passus Seven

4   *half akre*: Individual strips in the open-field system were this size. It would take less than a day for a single worker to plow and plant that much, hardly a *long letting* (6). As will be clear from what follows, however, the half acre is a metaphor for all the ordinary, necessary activities of life, which correspond to the duties assigned by Piers to the prospective pilgrims.

6   The veil she wears designates her as well-to-do, probably a member of the gentry or aristocratic class.

8ff   The production of cloth and of cloth goods Piers assigns to women, a practical reality as well as one that corresponds to the picture of the ideal of the perfect wife that closes the Old Testament book of Proverbs (31:10–31).

18   The use of expensive fabrics, such as silk and cendal (a fine silk), was frequently controlled by statute in what are referred to as sumptuary laws. There were contemporary attempts (e.g., 1363) to limit the wearing of silk to knights and ladies whose income was more than forty pounds a year (*Statutes of the Realm*, 1.380).

22–24   The knight's ready acceptance of Piers's guidance and his expressed willingness to learn how to plow is taken by Piers as a sign of genuine humility (even if it would be a breach of the conventional duties of the knight's estate). The *teme* (23) may have a double meaning: the "team" that pulls the plow, but also the "theme" (as a subject of teaching).

26ff   Piers reasserts the conservative view of the roles of the various estates: it is the duty of laborers to work and sweat; knights are to protect religion and to hunt down and control wasters and evildoers, whether human and animal.

34–36   The social and legal relations between laborer (Piers) and landholder (knight) are defined in explicitly contractual terms: in response to Piers's *covenaunt* (28), the knight plights his *trouthe* (35) to keep his *forward* (36). The agreement is, furthermore, one to which the knight responds *[c]urtesly* (34).

37ff   Perkyn (a diminutive of Piers) is clearly in a position of power here and insists on additional components of the knight's agreement: namely, that he commit himself not to mistreat his tenants and bondsmen, not to accept gifts, and to keep his word and not to listen to *talis* (44). As the various statutes regarding laborers (e.g., 1349, 1351, 1361, 1368) during the period following the Black Death attest, the value of labor in these years was clearly increasing as a result of supply and demand.

53ff   Piers dresses appropriately for working in the field and not in any way in pilgrim's fashion (51). This, reinforced by his substituting his *hopur* for a pilgrim's *skrippe* (55), suggests that what he is undertaking is, metaphorically at least, his form of pilgrimage. This is consistent with the virtual pilgrimage to Truth that he previously substituted for actual pilgrimages to distant shrines.

56   A bushel of wheat would be about the ordinary amount to sow a half acre.

63ff   Such low-life "entertainers" are not included among those whose lives are faithful. Their categorical exclusion from accepted society is reinforced by firmly citing (66, 68) biblical authority: Psalm 68:28. (See also Exod. 32:32–33; Rev. 3:5.) The ideal that the church would not accept offerings from such people, of course, may not have been rigorously followed in practice.

69   Their "escape" and "good luck" are obviously meant ironically, as the prayer for their amendment makes clear.

70–73   The listing of Piers's allegorical family here anticipates their being mentioned in his *bequestes* (77ff.). Their names articulate the kind of straightforward practical and proverbial wisdom that Piers himself instructs others to follow. His wife's name may allude to Galatians 6:9–10 (Schmidt, *Parallel-Text*, 2.553, note to C. VIII.80) or to the command to observe the Sabbath (Pearsall, *C-text*, 149, note to VIII.80ff.): Exod. 20:8ff. and Deut. 5:12ff.

74   The sense is, Leave everything to God. Because this is an appropriate position for a mature and wise Christian to take, one that Piers indeed forcefully adopts (in frus-

tration, admittedly) when he tears the Pardon (8.100ff.), I follow Knott-Fowler in not including this line as part of the son's name. (Most other editors of A and B favor that latter assignment. In C, however, the line is revised to appear a few lines later and is clearly intended to be in the voice of Piers.)

75   *have of myn owe*: The idiom means "I have enough to meet my needs"—that is, "I do not have to answer to or look after anyone else; I can be my own boss."

77ff   It was usual (if not indeed a duty) for prospective pilgrims to make a will before setting off, and the form of Piers's will here corresponds closely to contemporary examples (which by this date can be written in English, with some Latin [or French] phrases).

     The idiom *do wryte* (i.e., "cause to have written") indicates that such documents were frequently inscribed by someone more qualified to do so than an illiterate plowman. Despite his frequent Latin quotations, that is what Piers seems to be: he has to have the priest read Truth's pardon at 8.88ff.

83ff   These lines state that the parish (in the person of the pastor: "he") has the responsibility for the burial of Piers's body, in return for his faithful tithes to support it/him. In addition, the pastor is bound to remember Piers's soul in his masses.

92   The line literally repeats the promise of Sloth: 5.228.

94–96   The substitution of plowing for pilgrimage is continued here. As the *hopur* replaces the *skrippe* (55), his plow replaces his pikestaff.

104   The plowing of the half acre is completed by about 9 A.M. (*hey prime*: prime runs approximately from 6 A.M. to 9 A.M.), at which point the work that remains involves the use of hand implements, like shovels and spades. Piers is concerned to identify the good workers at this more demanding labor, with an eye to his hiring when the harvest comes in.

108   A refrain from a popular song already mentioned earlier (Pr.105), where other *dykeres and delveres* (Pr.104; like those mentioned here at 7.99) prefer to devote themselves to singing instead of doing the field work.

109   Piers expresses righteous anger here, as he will later (8.100) when he tears the pardon. Such anger may be the poet's justification for omitting Wrath from his cast of Deadly Sins in the previous parade of Vices.

     Bennett (*Piers Plowman*, 205, note to B 6.119) notes that "his words here are precisely in the spirit of the Commons' petition in 1376 that vagrant beggars should be imprisoned unless they promised to return home to work and that it should be forbidden to give alms to persons able to labour." The principle is, of course, neither original nor unique to the 1376 petition.

114   *alery*: The exact nature of the deception here is not clear. Either the leg is tied up so that it appears to have been cut off (Pearsall, *C-text*, 161, note to C VIII.129), or the pretense is that the leg is unable to bear weight: a "trick knee" or the like.

139   This personification of parasitic members of society (mentioned already in Pr.22) recalls the alliterative Middle English poem *Wynnere and Wastoure* (early 1350s: ed. Trigg).

140   Offering one's glove is a variant on throwing down the gauntlet, a way of issuing a challenge to a fight; if the opponent takes the glove, he accepts the challenge.

145   *maugre thy chekys*: This idiom ('in spite of your cheeks'), like *Wille thou, nelle thou*

	(above, 7.143) would be the medieval equivalent of 'Try and stop me!' or "What you gonna do about it?"
149ff	The courtesy of the knight is emulated in the "polite" language of these lines: the knight is politely restrained in warning and advising. The courteous approach, however, does not achieve much, and Piers is forced to invoke stronger measures.
157	Piers steps out of his human, social role here in invoking Hunger to punish the wasters, and he becomes an almost divine force in league with nature to effect punishment for injustice.

The fact that Hunger hears (and responds) immediately (*at the fyrste*) indicates that this may not indicate an extraordinary condition of famine, but something a bit more ordinary, the result, say, of the reduced availability of food in the early summer period, between spring plowing (and planting) and the beginning of harvest: when the previous year's supplies are running out and the new crops are not yet ready to eat.

164 Loaves of bread made from dried peas were a staple food for the poor even long after the Middle Ages and were probably on a par with the *barly bred* (129, 169) and the *houndys bred and horse bred* (200) mentioned elsewhere in this episode. They all certainly rated much lower than the *coket and cleremyn*, the fine white loaves favored later, in the plenty of harvest time (7.286).

169 It is not clear what the medicinal advice here is. It *may* mean that overindulging in barley bread and beans could cause discomfort (even death) if they expand in the stomach as a result of drinking water.

189ff The proper response to beggars is a recurrent concern in *Piers*: Pr.40ff., 8.66ff. Bennett's notes (*Piers Plowman*, pp. 208–9, on lines B 6.216 and 220ff.) are particularly useful; and see also Tierney.

210–11 The alliterating *Mathew* is regular in the A manuscripts, but the Latin text that follows is from Luke. This is not the only instance of misattribution in the poem: the same mistake occurs ten lines later, 221–22.

215 If it is not merely a handy and striking alliteration, the *geaunt* may refer to the size of the book of Genesis: it is the longest book of the Pentateuch and one of the longest books in the entire Bible. It is also, of course, the book that provides the account of human origins (the *engendrour of us alle*).

218 *Sapiens* refers to the author (sometimes identified as "Solomon") of Proverbs, and other Old Testament books of "wisdom" literature, otherwise called "Writings," to distinguish them from the "Law" (Torah or Pentateuch) and the "Prophets."

221–22 The four gospel writers are traditionally associated with the four beasts of Revelation 4:6–8, derived from the four-headed beasts drawing Yahweh's chariot in Ezekiel 1:4–12. In medieval iconography, Matthew is associated with the man, Mark with the lion, Luke with the bull, and John with the eagle.

The *servus nequam* is wording from Luke 19:22, from his version of the parable of the talents. In Matthew, the equivalent passage (25:26), in which the master condemns the fearful recipient of the one talent, he addresses him as *serve male et piger*. Similarly, the unusual word *mnam* (here given as *name* and *namme* [224]) is the term used in Luke; the term is *talentum* in Matthew's account.

227–29 This translation of the moral of the parable, closest perhaps to that in Luke (cf.

19:26), gives particular point to using one's talents *to helpe* where there is need. On the other hand, the punishment of one who *ne wolde worche* (224) is the denial of equivalent *helpe*. This unusual application of the parable is not unprecedented, as Bennett noted (*Piers Plowman*, p.210, note to B 6.241).

236ff   Piers now seeks a solution to the problem of sickness, which also prevents some from working.

240ff   Hunger focuses on overindulgence in food and drink (i.e., Gluttony) as the primary cause of illness. It may be a little surprising to modern readers that Hunger refers to *hunger* in the third person (244); the reference clearly was not problematic to the scribes of this poem.

As earlier, in the confession of the Deadly Sins (5.57), excess in food and drink is here (248) associated here with lechery.

255–56   In addition to focusing on their love of fine clothes, the long tradition of satiric criticism of doctors repeatedly castigates them for an inability to tell the truth and for a tendency to kill their patients with their "cures."

260–61   Hunger's response to Piers's second invitation (cf. 186–87) that he leave makes clear that he is not altogether in Piers's control, as seemed to be the case *at the fyrste* (157) when he called for his assistance.

274ff   The foodstuffs offered Hunger are those available in early summer. The baked apples are probably those stored from the previous autumn, because few would be ripe enough to eat (even after baking) before August.

280   As Kane notes (*A Version*, p. 449, note to 7.282) in rejecting the widely attested *poyson* here, the root meaning of the word is "medicinal draught"; even in the absence (from the *MED*) of any earlier use of the form as a verb—to administer a potion—that seems a quite acceptable sense here.

294ff   The Black Death of 1348–49 and other outbreaks of plague (e.g., 1361–62, 1368–69) during the middle of the fourteenth century had marked effect on the availability and stability of laborers, in rural agriculture particularly. Following an Ordinance of 1349, the king's council issued a Statute of Laborers (1351) to control the wages and movement of workers. This and similar statutes were enforced (somewhat intermittently) during subsequent decades (virtually for the next century). These rules were the cause of much unrest in this period and accounted for at least some of the dissatisfaction that led to the Rising of 1381 (the so-called Peasants' Revolt).

302–5   The prophecy of flood and famine is associated with the influence of Saturn (305), the most inauspicious of the planets and prone to cause floods, especially when it is in the constellation Aquarius.

Passus Eight

1   The antecedent of *therof* is presumably all the action of the previous episode. Its most immediate referent is, of course, the warning of Saturn, but it must include also the activity of Piers in overseeing the plowing of the half acre, as a prelude to his guiding the others on their pilgrimage. Clearly, the significance of Truth's pardon will be different, depending on which of these is taken as the immediate cause of his action.

Lines 2 and 5–6 instruct Piers to stick with tilling the half acre and not undertake any literal pilgrimage away from it. This would be consistent with earlier views about the essential interiority of the pilgrimage to Truth. The pardon is granted for this virtual pilgrimage, in other words.

3   A pardon *a pena et a culpa* is the ordinary title for a plenary or full indulgence, which frees its recipient from all the accumulated debts of sins that would need to be paid off in purgatory. An indulgence does not, however, of itself remit guilt (*culpa*), which can only be effected through the sacrament of Penance, which requires the penitent's contrite sorrow, confession to a priest, and performance of an assigned penance (to offer some satisfaction). When those three requirements are met, the absolution offered by the priest is effective in removing the guilt of sin. But there remain penalties (*poenae*) which need to be paid off, by good works in this life or by purgation in the next. The efficacy of an indulgence, whether plenary or partial, depends on the recipient's being in the state of grace—that is, having removed the burden of guilt of sin by making a good confession.

Of course, the proper theological, canonical understanding of indulgences was not fully appreciated by everyone, and sometimes the benefits of obtaining a pardon were misrepresented by those who publicized them. Chaucer's Pardoner offers a good example of the kinds of criticism leveled against pardoners. In his case, while there is no specific indication that the pardon he offers is anything but a true indulgence, authorized by the pope, his representation of its requirements and its effects play on popular misunderstandings of the power of such papal indulgences.

The word *purchas* (here an infinitive, with *Peres* as its agent) in Middle English has not yet narrowed its meaning to the modern one, "obtain in exchange for a cash payment." That is a *possible* meaning but would be highly unlikely to have been the primary meaning in the context of this poem.

4   *For him and his eyres* is a common legal term but not one employed in papal indulgences or an idea consistent with the standard theology of indulgences. This may, therefore, suggest that the *pardoun* here is more symbolic than literal. (See Bennett, *Piers Plowman*, 216–17, note to B VII.4.)

13ff   *bothe lawes*: Given their religious office, the easier assumption is perhaps that the two laws are those of Old Testament and New Testament. But the phrase may indeed be referring to civil (secular) and canon (ecclesiastical) laws, because bishops very often functioned as civil as well as religious authorities, many being employed in government service or serving the nation as spiritual "lords" with responsibilities and power similar to those of secular "lords." And even if not in secular offices, they would have considerable properties and dealings with civil processes. There was no full "separation of church and state" in England at this time (and, indeed, until recent reforms, bishops in England were included among those who had seats in the House of Lords).

Line 14 may pose some difficulty for this interpretation, but if *Loke on* means "keep an eye on, watch over, or oversee," then the proper relation of bishops (and their primary responsibility to teach and apply canon law) to civil law would seem to be what is at issue here.

15   Probably alludes to bishops who function in both the secular and ecclesiastical

realms. Many of the high administrators in Edward's court were bishops: for example, his chancellor, William Wykeham, bishop of Winchester.

16ff   Bishops are responsible for instructing and guiding the priests who serve as their deputies among the people of their diocese. As pastors (i.e., shepherds), they look after the sheep that have been entrusted to their care. The sheep-shepherd figure goes back to the New Testament (e.g., the good shepherd of John 10) and earlier (e.g., Ps. 22) for the relation of priest and people. Cf. Chaucer's portrait of the Parson in the "General Prologue" to the *Canterbury Tales* (I.501ff.).

    Scabies or mange, caused by parasitic mites, causes intense itching and loss of wool, and this would have severely affected the quality of a major product (and export) in medieval England in the fourteenth century.

20ff   A codicil is appended in the margin of the pardon that grants merchants a less-than-plenary indulgence, *manye yeres* remission of purgatorial suffering, because they do not strictly observe all the commandments. While its marginal location may cast some doubt on the authority of this the grant, the *lettre* (25) from Truth itemizes additional benefits for a variety of good works. Issued under the equivalent of the English King's secret, or signet, seal (cf. note to 3.135), this would be a species of nonpublic "pardon," a private understanding between Truth and the merchants. On the relations between the king and merchants, see Smith.

22   The Catholic Church held (and still holds) that the requirement to "keep the Sabbath" extended beyond going to mass on Sundays. The observance also included obligatory "holy days" (which varied from place to place and from time to time), on which the faithful were expected to attend mass *and* to avoid labor.

28   *Meysoun deu* is the common term for a "hospital" (or "hospice"), which would probably be equivalent not to a modern hospital but rather to a "long-term-care facility" or "old folks' home."

29–30   Repairing roads and bridges was (apparently) not usually considered a government activity, and was seen (as here) as an act of charity, a "corporal work of mercy."

31   *Maryen maydenys*: That is, to provide the dowries that would make it possible for young women to marry and set up their own homes. Dowries, similarly, were required to underwrite the cost of supporting young women who wished to become nuns.

32   This calls attention to the reality that support for widows was not guaranteed simply by their outliving their husbands. In many cases, of course, the death of the husband would have ended the widow's income, and she would need to marry again for economic reasons. Even well-off women might not have full legal control of their spouses' property and wealth.

36ff   While the earlier lines (of indirect speech) permit merchants to profit from their enterprises, this quoted conclusion to the marginal codicil offers angelic assistance but also makes clear that there are lines over which merchants are not allowed to go, whatever use they might make of the profit gained by means of usury and deceit.

43–44   The identity of this scribe Will is by no means clear. There are a number of characters with that name in the poem, and it is not certain what their relations to each other are. It is unlikely, for example, that this scribe is identical with the Will mentioned at 6.73. In other cases, however, it is less clear. Likewise, the character of that

name who appears weeping at 5.44 is not identified by occupation, but his close-
ness to the action of the dream is similar.

The use of the third person, in these cases, offers some obstacle to any easy identification of Will with the Dreamer/Narrator (and Poet), although this has become,
nevertheless, the general assumption of most critics. The Dreamer/Narrator regularly uses the first person about himself, as, for example, fifty lines later in this
passus, when the priest demands to read Piers's pardon: *And I, byhynde hem bothe,
behelde al the bulle* (8.91). See the introduction.

44   Kane has noted the difficulties with this line. This line and the foregoing are omitted in the B and C versions, where thanks are given to Piers for obtaining the pardon for them.

The use of *mede* here may be quite loaded, given the prominence of the idea in the
first dream. We might choose a relatively neutral translation (e.g., "thanks") but it
could, arguably, carry connotations of "payoff" or "bribe." This would of course put
a much less positive spin on the relations between merchants and Will. Could there
be a hint that the "clause" that is being copied here may not be altogether what the
pope put in the *margyn* (if indeed anything was put there by papal authority)?

47   The two Latin verses are (loosely) translated, in reverse order, in the following two
lines. The first verse is Psalm14:5. The exact source of the second is not clear: it is
variously completed in A manuscripts with *erit merces eorum* (or *eius*) ("will be their
[his] reward"—i.e., *pencioun* in line 48), or *erunt merces super innocentem &c.* ("will be
their rewards over the innocent"). Skeat noted that the line resembles Ecclesiasticus
38:2, but the resemblance is not close. Alford (*Guide*, 53–54) suggests it comes from
a commentary on this verse and notes the proximity to a quotation from Ecclesiasticus 38:1 in the Z manuscript (7.267–71).

50ff   Like the merchants, lawyers are encouraged to do works of charity, in their case to
provide free legal representation and advice, and they are promised similar protec-
tions at the day of death. Their *wit* (54) is a gift of God, like wind and water, and
should be made available to others in the same fashion. Lawyers who charge fees
(*mede* [59]) of the poor are not doing anything to benefit the spiritual state of their
own souls. The view of lawyers here is similar to that voiced in Pr.86ff.

67   On the legal concept of *suggestio* (i.e., "an allegation or information not upon oath"),
see Alford's *Glossary*, 149. The condition that they be *soth* implies that many were
indeed false: see Schmidt, *Parallel-Text*, 2.563 (note to this line: = C9.62).

73   *whehe*: Chaucer uses a similar form in the "Reeve's Tale" (*Canterbury Tales*, I.4064–
66) for the whinnying of the clerks' horse after its been set loose and runs off to the
fen in search of *wilde mares*.

87   Those who accept with resignation their sufferings in this life as the will of God
were thought to merit grace as do those who voluntarily perform penitential actions
or undergo penitential deprivation on the instruction of their confessors. Both are
ways of paying off the *poena* of personal sin, which if left unpaid in this life will be
paid off in purgatory.

88–89   The priest implies either that Piers cannot read (Latin) at all or that he simply lacks
the skills to *construy* it properly. We have had many indications of Piers's ability to
quote Latin, and his lengthy interpretation of the pardon he has received from

Truth suggests some facility at reading between the lines. The priest may either be genuinely puzzled at the unusual breadth of the pardon Piers has received or be revealing his clerical condescension toward a *lewde* plowman.

91 This is the first time that the Dreamer has explicitly entered this second dream as a first-person participant. A *bulle* (Lat. *bulla*) is an official document issued by the pope: see Pr.68.

94–95 The lines are from the Athanasian Creed (verse 41), one of the three great early articulations of Christian belief, frequently included in various hours of the Divine Office.

96ff The priest is technically correct: this is not the language of a bill of indulgence. But the priest's literal-mindedness, or legalistic pedantry, prevents him from recognizing that there is an implied "pardon" for those who do well (since all are sinners), just as there is an explicit punishment promised here for those who do evil. *Peter* may be an oath—By St. Peter!—as it apparently was when Piers himself used it earlier (6.24). It may as easily, however, be a form of direct address to Piers himself, parallel with his *Peres*, at lines 88 and 121.

100 The tearing of the pardon has been widely discussed: as a sign of Piers's (or the poet's) accepting the spirit (over the letter), or of his rejecting entirely the idea of indulgences. The episode resounds with echoes of Moses's breaking of the tablets of the law in Exodus 32, with the priest's role here being analogous to that of Moses's brother, the priest Aaron, who was responsible for the Golden Calf that was the cause of Moses's anger. (Note, again, that anger in these cases is not treated as a sin, as vice: another reason, perhaps, for Wrath's being omitted from the parade of Deadly Sins.) For earlier interpretations, see Frank; more recent readings of the scene by, for example, Woolf, Adams, Schroeder, Simpson, and others, offer useful refinements of our understanding of the complexity of the episode. The result is a virtual standoff among critics on the *meaning* of this powerful, and crucial, scene.

101 Psalm 22:4: This is the psalm which begins "The Lord is my shepherd." The *mala* here establishes a nice correspondence with the terms of the pardon above (95).

102–5 This is a crucial moment in the poem and marks a dramatic change in the direction of Piers's life: he earlier approached his *sowyng* as a valid form of the Christian life, and the text repeatedly presents it as an acceptable form of virtual pilgrimage, providing access to the same sorts of spiritual benefits. Now, because of the priest's impugning the pardon, Piers is abandoning his field for a more literally religious life of prayers and penance. If this new way of life marks a proper redirection of Piers's views, then it suggests that the priest's reaction to Truth's pardon may be indeed a proper, if conservative, ecclesiastical response to the sort of utopian hope for being able to live a fully Christian life while engaged in the activities of the "real world." On the other hand, however, it may simply mark the triumph of literalism over more symbolic modes of understanding in the spiritual realm.

106 David is frequently included among the prophets by medieval preachers and writers, and Psalm verses are often used to point to Jesus (as the Gospel writers themselves had often done).

Ra's reading *peyne hath* is unique among the manuscripts. (There is a similar sense found in H²'s *hadde his peynes*.) Other editors prefer the striking *payn eet* (i.e., ate his bread) supported by a number of manuscripts. But the Ra reading ("received his punishment") makes very good sense, especially in light of 87 above—even if it loses the connection to one allusive term (*panes*) in Psalm 41:3, quoted three lines below.

110–16   The Latin in 112 comes from the beginning of a passage (6:25–34) in the Gospel of Matthew, encouraging trust in God's Providence, a variant of which appears in Luke (12:22–32).

122   The Latin verse is from the Vulgate version of Psalm 70:15. The *teme* is changed in B to *Dixit insipiens*, the opening of Psalm 13: "The fool says in his heart 'There is no God!' "

126   This opposition of the priest and plowman (as representatives of the *lerned* and *lewed*) also appears (as Bennett notes, *Piers Plowman*, 224, l. 138n) in *The Scale of Perfection*, i. 61. Chaucer, on the other hand, presents his Parson and Plowman as brothers (clergy and laity) in the "General Prologue" to his *Canterbury Tales*.

127ff   The sun, standing high in the south, indicates it is midday. The Narrator fell asleep one May morning *on Malverne hyllys* (Pr.5), and his first dream also begins with the morning sun in the east (Pr.13); he now wakes at midday *upon Malverne hullys* again (129) at the end of the *Visio*'s second dream. Given the important roles played by Mede and Hunger in his two dreams, it cannot be entirely coincidental that he wakes without food or money.

   This epilogue is the longest waking scene in the A version and shows the Narrator wrestling with two substantial, and finally unresolved, questions: the value of dreams and the validity of pardons.

130–32   The sense of the lines is, These dreams caused me many times to reflect and thoughtfully meditate—recalling Piers the plowman and what I saw while I was asleep—whether these things might be true. The problem of the meaning of dreams sets the views of the educated (Cato and canon lawyers) against the witness of the Bible.

133–34   The Latin quotation cited against the value of dreams here comes from the *Distichs* (see note to 4.17), book II, distich 31, which reads in full:

> Somnia ne cures, nam mens humana quod optans
> Dum vigilat sperat, per somnum cernit ad ipsum.
> (Pay no attention to dreams, for the very thing that the human mind, spurred by its desires, hopes for while it lies awake, it will perceive while asleep.)

136–42   The story of Daniel here conflates elements of two dreams of Nabugodonosor (see Dan. 2:31–45; 4:1–25) and perhaps one of his son Beshazzar (5:17–31).

143–48   The account of Joseph's dream is from Genesis 37:9–10. The speech of his father (Judah/Israel) is a very loose translation. The story of Joseph in Egypt is told in the succeeding chapters of Genesis.

153   The line is (perhaps unintentionally) ambiguous: we must either supply "I" as the subject of *demed* or, if we continue *prest* as the subject, treat Dowel as the object of *passyth*—that is, "indulgence surpassed Dowel"—because the priest nowhere (unlike the Dreamer/Narrator) holds that simply doing well surpasses papal indulgences. Because neither word order nor spelling unambiguously makes clear which

is the subject and which is the object of *passyth*—*Dowel* or *indulgence*—readers must depend on their interpretations of the positions established in the preceding dispute between Piers and the priest.

154   Memorial masses were regularly offered for the dead over periods as long as two, three, or more years, to gain their release from the *poena* of purgatory. Bishops' letters were the authorizing documents licensing (among other things) preachers and pardoners to publicize an indulgence within a given diocese. See Pr.77ff.

155ff Insisting on the primacy of doing well, the Narrator is still conservative, or circumspect, enough to acknowledge the efficacy of papal indulgences. The supporting biblical verse is from Matthew 16:19, the concluding commission to Peter as the "rock" upon which the Christian church is erected, as the first among the apostles and first pope. The prominent *Now* at the beginning of 157 may imply that this is a temporary (or temporal) concession. Any potential hesitation it expresses is underlined by the forceful conclusion (164–68), which warns, and warns again, against trusting one's salvation to memorial masses (and, by implication, indulgences).

176–77 A provincial was the regional head of a religious order, and he would be responsible for authorizing the induction of a layperson into its *fraternite*. In more recent times, these have been termed a "third order" community of laypersons who undertake to participate in some way in the prayer and work of the order and receive the benefits of the prayers and works of the members of all three communities of the order. The "first order" would be the order made up of, say, professed Dominican friars; the "second order" would be that of professed Dominican nuns. As noted above (Pr.57), the four orders (of friars) are Dominicans, Franciscans, Carmelites and Augustinians.

Passus Nine

Title The prologue to an independently titled work begins here: *The Life of Do-well, Do-better, and Do-best according to Wit and Reason.* The following passus (numbered 10 in the conventional consecutive numbering of *Piers Plowman*) is called "Passus One." While a few surviving manuscripts of the A version may offer some evidence that the first nine passūs (Prologue through Passus Eight) of the *Visio* might have circulated independently at an earlier stage in the development of *Piers*, nearly all the manuscripts regularly distinguish, by the separate titles and numbering, the *Vita* from the *Visio*. Many of the B and C manuscripts maintain this distinction, frequently presenting a double-tiered numbering system.

8–9   Members of the fraternal orders regularly circulated in pairs rather than singly. *Maysteres* were holders of Masters degrees (in Theology). *Menoures* were Franciscans (members of the Order of Friars Minor). Franciscan theologians were particularly prominent in fourteenth-century English universities: see Courtenay.

16   Like the *Ergo* below (21), *Contra* is part of the vocabulary of formal disputation, and a regular element of university education. The speaker marks himself as being a part of this world: *as a clerk*.

25   *forebysne*: Exemplary stories were a common feature of vernacular sermons of the Middle Ages. They remain an effective way of presenting complex, abstract topics in a digestible, memorable fashion.

49   *Kinde knowyng* sounds like a technical term, and it will appear in various forms and

situations in the dream that follows (as it has earlier: see 1.130ff.). Because *kinde* can be best translated as "natural," the knowledge it defines is not the product of learning or of revelation. This may suggest that the Narrator is being particularly obtuse here, in suggesting that he can in time and after searching *lere ferther* (50) something that ought by nature to be known to him already. But the Dreamer repeats this desire to *lerne* more *kynde knowing* in response to Thought (105), and this may indicate that the search is one that turns not to external sources but, more properly, to his own inner mental processes.

The Friar's lively *exemplum* makes a quite clear, almost commonsensical, and fairly orthodox point: one can sin, even repeatedly, without committing deadly sin. The *forebysne* (25) is not so subtle that it needs highly developed literary or theological skill to understand it. So it is also striking that the Narrator, who knows the verbal machinery (*Contra* and *Ergo*) of academic debate, is at a loss to understand. Granted, the *application* of the exemplary narrative to actual living situations may require knowledge, to distinguish *synnes* from *dedly synne* (41).

67   *sevene yere*: This may mean a literal "seven years" or be a more general "long time." If we take the traditional computation of when a person reaches the "age of reason" (i.e., when one is capable of responsible thinking and choosing) as the age of seven or thereabouts, then we might compute these *sevene yere* of Thought's service, whether literal or general, as beginning then. This would put the Dreamer in his mid-teens, an age at which he could have been beginning his university education (i.e., *as a clerk*, 9.16). The waking search for knowledge about Dowel is now turned inward, from simple instruction to more reflective consideration.

70   It may not be surprising that Thought, like the Dreamer who debated with the friars, shows some grammatical sophistication: the positive form of any adverb (or adjective) logically admits of a comparative and superlative form. There is an air of the classroom at many points in this dream. Whether such academic distinctions are crucial to solving the essentially moral riddle of finding Dowel remains to be seen—and argued about.

82   This alludes to the lesson drawn by Jesus from the parable of the crafty steward at Luke 16:9.

105   See 9.49–50. If the inward journey into the realm of Thought constitutes the Dreamer's investigation of his *kynde knowing*, then he is now indicating that thinking alone is not the answer; there must be standards that can lead to informed choice among competing ideas. This is where Wit (Intelligence or Understanding) must be sought, as Thought suggests (107–8).

109–11   This may recall the episode in Luke's Gospel (24:13ff.) when the resurrected Jesus appears to the two disciples on the road to Emmaus.

Passus Ten

1ff   Wit's answer describes Dowel's home as the human person, described as a *castel* (i.e., the physical body) made by Nature (*Kynde*, who also is God the Creator: 10.27ff.) from the four elements (with *eyre* meaning "fire," derived from Latin *aer* [the upper air, ether], heavenly fire: see Wittig, 217). The *castel* (a common medieval metaphor for the body), later named *Caro* (flesh: 10.39), is the protective enclosure for *Anima* (soul: 10.7)—also called *Lyf* (10.44)—the beloved (*lemman*) of *Kynde*. The allegory of the body as a castle is quite common in medieval sermons and literature.

The enemy is called *Princeps huius mundi* ("Prince of this world" = the devil: the *pouke* in 10.63) and is identified as a French knight, a not unusual association in this period of the Hundred Years' War (ca. 1339–1453) between England and France.

18ff   Inwit's five sons correspond to five physical faculties (a variant of the modern five senses): eyes, ears, mouth, arms, and legs.

32   Cf. Genesis 1:26, and *ymage to himselven*, 4 lines below. The creation as presented here invokes Genesis 1, where it comes about as a result of God's speech: "God said . . . And so it was." The point is reinforced in the Fourth Gospel, which opens (John 1:1–4), with the assertion that "all things came to be through [the Word]," who "was God" and "was with God in the beginning."

52   *reccheles*: Recklessness, along with *hot blod* below (56), are presented as the main sources of injury or damage to *reule* and *resoun* as the natural condition of humans (body and soul). When *blod* overcomes Inwit it makes humans *wantoun and wilde, withouten ony resoun* (58), like *bestes* (62).

91   For this canon law maxim, see Alford, *Guide*, 61. The meaning of *iudicat* here is something like "assigns moral status to the actions of" a person.

96   Because the source of this passage has not been identified, and previous interpretations of how to expand the abbreviations are not convincing, I have left them unresolved here.

Kane's *edificat* may be reasonable enough; but even he puts a question mark after his *ad condemnationem* (*A Version*, 384). If the line should be read *Qui agit contra conscienciam, edificat ad iehennam*, as other editors interpret it, then this would appear to be a quotation going back to Gratian's *Decretum*: see Alford, *Guide*, 61.

100   From the *Distichs of Cato*, book III, distich 2: cf. notes to 4.17 and 8.133–34.

111   The source of this Latin has not been identified. Alford (*Guide*, 61) suggests a grammatical context.

157ff   Medieval interpretations of the "sons of God" and the "daughters of men" (Gen. 6:1–4) as the descendants of Seth and Cain go back, ultimately, to Augustine's *City of God* (15.23).

167ff   The account of Noah and the Flood is found in Genesis 6:9–9:29.

192   The *pestilens* presumably refers to the years of plague called the Black Death (1348–49): see, above, Pr.83.

195   *Donmowe*: Little Dunmow in Essex, traditionally offered a flitch of bacon to any couple who (after a year and a day of marriage) could swear that they had never quarreled. Chaucer's Wife of Bath also refers to it in her Prologue: *Canterbury Tales* III.318.

Passus Eleven

18   *carded with conciens*: The process of preparing wool for spinning involves "carding," using stiff wire brushes to straighten, disentangle, and clean the strands of wool. Our base MS Ra is unique in turning a sarcastic comment involving carding with *coveitise* (avarice) into one that appears to give *conscience* an ironic meaning, putting

it in quotation marks as it were: that is, what passes for "conscience." Study's voice is full of such complex tones.

75   No exact source for this text (from Rom. 12:3) has been identified in Augustine's works, though (as Skeat noted, *Parallel Texts*) similar phrasing can be found in his *On Baptism*, 2.5.

148–49 From book I, distich 26 of the *Distichs of Cato*.

161   It is not quite clear what sort of con game is being alluded to here, some trickery associated with multiple boxes, like a shell game, perhaps.

162   *Albertes*: The thirteenth-century Dominican scientist and theologian Albert the Great (Albertus Magnus; died 1280), teacher of Thomas Aquinas, was (falsely) reputed to have dabbled in the black arts.

176ff   While it is Scripture who makes the Dreamer welcome (*she*: 176), the Dreamer addresses his comments to Clergy (*him*: 178). Whether this is the proper thing to do, or a sign of his sensitivity when faced with another strong woman after his interchange with Dame Study earlier, it is Scripture again (181) who provides him with the long description of Dowel, Dobet, and Dobest (181ff.). While it may be arguable that the scribe has slipped up on the pronouns here, Scripture's response to the Dreamer at 227ff. reinforces the likelihood that the earlier discourse is properly hers also.

187–90 These constitute a number of what are traditionally called the "corporal works of mercy," based on Jesus's account of what will occur at the Last Judgment: Matthew 25:34–37

195   This line is quite irregular in all manuscripts, suggesting perhaps the loss of some text at an early stage of the transmission of its text.

206ff   Gregory I (the Great) was pope from 590 to 604. One of his many influential works was *Moralia in Job* (*Morals on the Book of Job*), called *Morales* in the next line.

209ff   The comparison is a commonplace: Chaucer uses it in the "General Prologue" portrait of his Monk (*Canterbury Tales* I.180). Its exact source has not been located, in Gregory's *Moralia* or elsewhere. Skeat noted (*Parallel Texts*) that it is attributed to Pope Eugenius in Gratian's *Decretals*, and that attribution is repeated in the *Legenda Aurea* (21.4).

217   As the following line implies, these are the terms of curses or oaths (e.g., "Zounds!" [i.e., "God's wounds!"]), rather than theological or devotional matters.

231   The attribution to Paul perhaps points, as Knott-Fowler suggests, to 1 Timothy 6:9 (and cf. verses 10–12, 17–19). But a more memorable passage on this topic in the New Testament is Jesus's assertion that it is easier for a camel to pass through the eye of a needle than it is for a rich man to enter heaven (Matt. 19:23–26, Mark 10:23–27, and Luke 18:24–27: "impossible" appears in the last verses of all three passages). The insistence on patience in the next line joins the long-suffering poor (*in paciense*) with those who endure other sufferings or injuries (*pacient*).

235   The misattribution to Peter of the Latin in the following line (Mark 16:16) may result from similar ideas in 1 Peter 3:21.

244   The Latin passage here is found in a number of places in the Bible: Matthew 22:37–39; Mark 12:30–31; Luke 10:27; James 2:8; and cf. Deuteronomy 6:5; Leviticus 19:18.

256   The surprising mistranslation of *Non mecaberis* (Exodus 20:14; Deuteronomy 5:18;
       Luke 18:20) is present in nearly all A and B manuscripts that have these lines, and
       this suggests an error going back (perhaps) to the original of the passage. If this
       were the Dreamer speaking, one might plausibly argue that the error was inten-
       tional; it is, however, unlikely that the poet would have intended to have Scripture
       make such a mistake. The various attempts to explain away this error are uncon-
       vincing.

259   Knott-Fowler, while admitting that there is no specific announcement that the
       dream ends at this point, introduces two blank lines after this line in their edition
       (146); Kane (*A Version*, 421) similarly marks a shift, and begins the following line
       with a long dash. Schmidt (*Parallel-Text*, 1.435–36) has a page break (preceded per-
       haps by a blank line) following this line.
           There is no break in the text between 259 and 260 in Ra, and this is also true of
       most other manuscripts. For a fuller discussion of manuscripts' treatment of these
       lines, and the implications of later editorial interventions, see my article "The End-
       ing(s) of *Piers Plowman* A."

260   I follow Schmidt (*Parallel-Text*) in placing the remaining lines of the passus in the
       voice of the still-sleeping Dreamer, a speech concluding at the end of the passus.
       Knott-Fowler and Kane (*A Version*) put them, at least inferentially, in the voice of the
       awakened Narrator, and thereby providing a closural frame for the poem. This is, in
       part at least, required by their decision to place Passus 12 in an appendix rather than
       as the succeeding passus of the poem. (In the B version, the equivalent of A's 260
       [= B's X.371 in Schmidt] contains a "quod I" in the first half-line.)

262ff The Dreamer seeks release from the moral quandary raised by Scripture's dis-
       course by resorting to the view that he has in fact been predestined for salvation or
       damnation. In what follows, he questions the ultimate value of learning in the
       scheme of salvation, while at the same quoting back an impressive number of scrip-
       tural texts and commentaries *at* Scripture herself!

264   *the legande of lyf*: A reference to the *liber vitae* in Apocalypse 20:12 (Schmidt, *Parallel-
       Text*, note to C XI.205). He follows Pearsall (*C-text*, 211) in taking *onwryten* in A's
       next line (= C XI.208) as referring to those whose names are not found written in
       the book of life (*non . . . scriptus*: Apoc. 20:15).

306   The *foure* refers to the (Latin) doctors of the church, early and influential theolo-
       gians who determined the direction of orthodox doctrine in the early days of Chris-
       tianity: Ambrose (c. 340–97), Jerome (345–420), Augustine (354–430), and Pope
       Gregory the Great (540–604).

308   The passage is from Augustine's *Confessions*, book 8, chapter 8.

315   *pater noster*: The Lord's Prayer, which begins (in Latin) with these two words (i.e.,
       Our Father).

Passus Twelve

Title Both Knott-Fowler and Kane (*A Version*) place this entire passus in an appendix.
       The view is expressed in the introduction to Knott-Fowler that "There are strong ar-
       guments for believing that John But wrote the whole of passus twelve" (11). While
       Kane affirms that "the possibility of its authenticity has not yet been confirmed or

dismissed," his locating it in an appendix attests to its "dubious character" (52). The strongest case for excising the entire passus as the work of John But is Middleton's. Schmidt's is the most extended argument (*Parallel-Text*, 2.119–21) for its being (aside from the last 19 lines) "authentic" and "the beginning of a formal continuation" (121).

15 Kynde Wit, Scripture's confessor (43, below), is here identified as a cardinal. The word order, with title inserted between forename and surname, is the preferred format in the naming of cardinals.

The reference to the Dreamer's need for shriving (14) is not unusual: Confession is required at least annually. However, the requirement that he be baptized (*cristned*) is highly unusual, because, unlike Confession, it is a sacrament that is conferred only once and presumably was received by the Dreamer as a child. In any case, Baptism is a necessary prerequisite for sacramental forgiveness in Confession. All of this may indicate Scripture's doubts about the Dreamer's even being, formally, a Christian, on the basis of his comments at the end of the preceding passus.

20 The Vulgate Latin more often reads *prevaricatores*, "sinners," instead of *prevaricationes*; the poet's translation of the verse (mis)reads *tabescebam* as *tacebam*, "I said nothing."

35 Schmidt's translation makes reasonable syntactic sense of this difficult line: "But when he talks to me, I am what he says I am—[a scold]" (*Parallel-Text*, 2.599: note to XII.33). But the Narrator only calls her a *skolde* in the *next* line, so she may instead be referring us back to the sense of the Dreamer's critical remarks at the end of the previous passus; and his sense of the difficult complexities, and even apparent (to him) contradictions, of written authorities, biblical and otherwise (i.e., in Scripture).

53 This may be (as most editors and commentators read it) one quite explicit occasion when the Dreamer is named *Wil* in the poem (as also *Wille* in line 96 below); but *with wil* (there is, of course, no capital in the manuscript) could also simply be an adverbial phrase, meaning "willingly" or "with unwavering attention"—or simply "in spirit": cf. *pore with wil* as translation for Latin *pauperes spiritu* is noted in the *MED* from John of Grimestone's *Preaching Book*.

60 This is an almost-literal repetition of a line in the opening scene of the poem (Pr.64) and suggests that we are in some sense returning to the original wandering Dreamer / Narrator, whose first dream was also a *ferly* (Pr.6). It is striking, however, that the *fyrste ferly* in this journey, which occurs *before* the hungry Dreamer arrives at the destination (*Quod-bonum-est-tenete*) identified by Scripture, is to meet with a confessor who is quite distinctly *not* Scripture's cousin Kind Wit (who lives with Life) but rather Fever (who is a messenger of Death).

68 These lines recall those at the beginning of the second dream: 5.5–6.

79 Fevers were characterized by their frequency of recurrence, defined in days: quartan (every fourth day), quotidian (every day), and tertian (every third day). Their main feature, here, is thirst, and hence they are humorously called *trewe drinkeres* (82).

85 Because the Dreamer knows that Kind Wit lives with Life, he desires to travel with Fever to where Life lives. This implies, apparently, that he is no longer being guided

by *Omnia probate* or is choosing another guide than the one recommended to him by Scripture.

86–95   The concluding advice of Fever appears remarkably positive, indicating that the Dreamer should not follow him but, instead, get on with doing well while his life lasts. While this is a significantly different map for his journey than the one described by Scripture, it does bear some resemblance to the underlying principle of the pardon sent by Truth (passus 8).

96–114 This appendix, attributed to Johan But (103), is clearly a later addition to the poem: the mention of the king as Richard means that it can be no earlier than 1377.

While I follow Schmidt (see note to title above) in limiting the work of John But to these concluding lines, an interesting and quite plausible (if not completely persuasive) case has been advanced for extending his involvement to this entire last passus: see Middleton.

The interpretation of these first four lines is highly contested, and the punctuation and glossing here should be treated with as much skepticism as those proposed by others.

98   The terms *wroughthe* and *werkes* are ambiguous, and what is referred to as being *wryten* is not necessarily a literary *work*, but rather the actions (*werkes*) Wille performed (*wroughthe*). Readers of the lines, however, have been nearly unanimous in seeing them as referring to the poem *Piers Plowman*, and the *other werkes* as referring to the longer versions of the poem. That may be a plausible interpretation but not an entirely necessary one (Warner). The reference to *Peres the plowman and mechel puple also* may, after all, simply be a translation of the colophon at the end of passus 8: *visio . . . de petro . & cetera* and suggest that the *other werkes* may simply be referring to the other two dreams that constitute *Piers A*.

103   *Johan But*: His identity has not been securely determined. A king's messenger by that name died in 1387, which would fit the reference to King Richard II (110), but there are a number of others named John But from the end of the fourteenth century. see Hanna, 28–31.

110   *Richard*: King Richard II reigned from 1377 to 1399, following the death of his grandfather Edward III (21 June 1377). After a troublesome and very unsettled reign, Richard was deposed by his cousin Henry of Lancaster (King Henry IV) at the end of September 1399.

"Signature." Simon Horobin has convincingly identified the scribe (of the Rawlinson MS of *Piers* A and of a manuscript of the *Prick of Conscience* [University College, Oxford, MS 142]) as Thomas Tolyte (or, as he signs it here, Tilot), an early fifteenth-century Augustinian canon and vicar at Chichester Cathedral.

Select Bibliography

Editions (arranged chronologically)

Skeat, W. W., ed. *The Vision of William Concerning Piers Plowman, Together with Vita de Dowel, Dobet, et Dobest secundum Wit and Resoun, by William Langland. . . . The "Vernon" Text; or Text A.* EETS OS 28. London: Kegan Paul, Trench, Trübner & Co., 1867.

———, ed. *The Vision of William Concerning Piers the Plowman, in Three Parallel Texts Together with Richard the Redeless by William Langland (about 1362–1399 A.D.).* 2 vols. Oxford: Clarendon Press, 1886.

Knott, Thomas A., and David C. Fowler, eds. *Piers the Plowman: A Critical Edition of the A-Version.* Baltimore: Johns Hopkins Press, 1952.

Kane, George, ed. *Piers Plowman: The A Version: Will's Visions of Piers Plowman and Do-Well, an Edition in the Form of Trinity College Cambridge MS R.3.14 Corrected from Other Manuscripts, with Variant Readings.* London: Athlone Press, 1960; rev. ed., 1988.

Bennett, J. A. W., ed. *Piers Plowman: The Prologue and Passus I–VII of the B text as Found in Bodleian MS. Laud 581.* Clarendon Medieval and Tudor Series. Oxford: Clarendon Press, 1972.

Kane, George, and E. Talbot Donaldson, eds. *Piers Plowman: The B Version; Will's Vision of Piers Plowman, Do-Well, Do-Better and Do-Best.* London: Athlone Press, 1975.

Rigg, A. G., and Charlotte Brewer, eds. *Piers Plowman: The Z Version.* Studies and Texts 59. Toronto: Pontifical Institute of Mediaeval Studies, 1983.

Schmidt, A. V. C., ed. *The Vision of Piers Plowman: A Critical Edition of the B-Text Based on Trinity College Cambridge MS B.15.17.* 2nd ed. London: J. M. Dent; Rutland, Vt.: Charles E. Tuttle, 1995.

———, ed. *Piers Plowman: A Parallel-Text Edition of the A, B, C and Z Versions.* 2 vols. London: Longman, 1995; Kalamazoo: Medieval Institute Publications, 2008.

Russell, George, and George Kane, eds. *Piers Plowman: The C Version; Will's Vision of Piers Plowman, Do-Well, Do-Better and Do-Best.* London: Athlone Press, 1997.

Robertson, Elizabeth, and Stephen H. A. Shepherd, eds. *Piers Plowman.* Norton Critical Edition. New York: Norton, 2006.

Pearsall, Derek, ed. *Piers Plowman: A New Annotated Edition of the C-text.* Exeter Medieval English Texts and Studies. Exeter: University of Exeter Press, 2008.

Duggan, Hoyt N., director. *Piers Plowman* Electronic Archive, 219 Bryan Hall, University of Virginia, P.O. Box 400121, Charlottesville, VA 22904–4121. http://www3 .iath.virginia.edu/seenet/piers/. (The Society for Early English and Norse Electronic Texts [SEENET], in cooperation with a varying number of co-publishers, has produced on CD-ROM the PPEA's documentary editions of a number of B version manuscripts of *Piers Plowman* and will in the near future be issuing editions of A and C version manuscripts.)

Translations

Covella, Francis Dolores, S.C. *Piers Plowman: The A-Text; An Alliterative Verse Transla-tion*. Introduction and notes by David C. Fowler. Medieval and Renaissance Texts & Studies. Binghamton, N.Y.: CEMERS, 1992.

Donaldson, E. Talbot. *Will's Vision of Piers Plowman: An Alliterative Verse Translation*. Edited, introduced, and annotated by Elizabeth D. Kirk and Judith H. Anderson. New York: Norton, 1990.

———. *Piers Plowman*. Edited by Elizabeth Robertson and Stephen H. A. Shepherd. Norton Critical Edition. New York: Norton, 2006.

Economou, George. *Piers Plowman: The C Version: A Verse Translation*. Philadelphia: University of Pennsylvania Press, 1996.

Goodridge, J. F. *Piers the Plowman*. Rev. ed. Baltimore: Penguin, 1966.

Bibliographies

Colaianne, A. J. *Piers Plowman: An Annotated Bibliography of Editions and Criticism, 1550–1977*. New York: Garland, 1978.

DiMarco, Vincent. *Piers Plowman, a Reference Guide*. Boston: G. K. Hall, 1982.

Pearsall, Derek. *An Annotated Critical Bibliography of Langland*. Ann Arbor: University of Michigan Press, 1990.

Yearbook of Langland Studies. Annual Bibliographies have been published in the journal beginning with 1985. They are available online at the site of the International *Piers Plowman* Society: www.piersplowman.org/yearbook/biblio.asp.

Criticism

Adams, Robert. "Mede and Mercede: The Evolution of the Economics of Grace in the *Piers Plowman* B and C Versions." In Kennedy, 217–32.

Alford, John A., ed. *A Companion to Piers Plowman*. Berkeley and Los Angeles: University of California Press, 1988.

———. "The Idea of Reason in *Piers Plowman*." In Kennedy, 199–215.

———. *Piers Plowman: A Glossary of Legal Diction*. Cambridge: Brewer, 1988.

———. *Piers Plowman: A Guide to the Quotations*. Medieval and Renaissance Texts & Studies 77. Binghamton, N.Y.: CEMERS, 1992.

Barnett, Gerald. "The Representation of Medieval English Texts." Ph.D. diss., University of Washington, Seattle, 1988.

Bennett, J. A. W. "The Date of the A-Text of *Piers Plowman*." *PMLA* 58 (1943): 566–72.

———. "The Date of the B-Text of *Piers Plowman*." *Medium Ævum* 12 (1943): 55–64.

Benson, C. David. *Public Piers Plowman: Modern Scholarship and Late Medieval English Culture*. University Park: Pennsylvania State University Press, 2004.

Bowers, John M. "*Piers Plowman's* William Langland: Editing the Text, Writing the Author's Life." *Yearbook of Langland Studies* 9 (1995): 65–90.

Brewer, Charlotte. *Editing Piers Plowman: The Evolution of the Text*. Cambridge Studies in Medieval Literature 28. Cambridge: Cambridge University Press, 1996.

Burrow, J. A. "The Action of Langland's Second Vision." *Essays in Criticism* 15 (1965): 247–68.

———. *Langland's Fictions*. Oxford: Clarendon Press, 1993.

Cable, Thomas. *The English Alliterative Tradition*. Philadelphia: University of Pennsylvania Press, 1999.

———. "Progress in Middle English Alliterative Metrics." *Yearbook of Langland Studies* 23 (2009): 243–64.

Cargill, Oscar. "The Langland Myth." *PMLA* 50 (1935): 36–56.

Dahl, Eric. "*Diuerse Copies Haue it Diuerselye*: An Unorthodox Survey of *Piers Plowman* Textual Scholarship from Crowley to Skeat." In Vaughan, *Suche Werkis*, 53–80.

Dolan, T. P. "Shame on Meed." In Vaughan, *Suche Werkis*, 81–88.

Duggan, Hoyt N. "Notes on the Metre of *Piers Plowman*: Twenty Years On." In *Approaches to the Metres of Alliterative Verse*, edited by Judith Jefferson and Ad Putter, 159–86. Leeds Texts and Monographs, n.s., 17. Leeds: University of Leeds, School of English, 2009.

Dunning, T. P. *Piers Plowman: An Interpretation of the A Text*. Dublin: Talbot, 1937.

———. *Piers Plowman: An Interpretation of the A Text*. 2nd ed. Revised and edited by T. P. Dolan. Oxford: Clarendon Press, 1980.

Fowler, David C. "*Piers the Plowman* as History." In *The Bible in Middle English Literature*, 226–96. Seattle: University of Washington Press, 1984.

———. *Piers the Plowman: Literary Relations of the A and B Texts*. University of Washington Publications in Language and Literature 16. Seattle: University of Washington Press, 1961.

Frank, Robert Worth. *Piers Plowman and the Scheme of Salvation: An Interpretation of Dowel, Dobet, and Dobest*. New Haven: Yale University Press, 1957.

Galloway, Andrew. *The Penn Commentary on Piers Plowman*. Vol. 1. Philadelphia: University of Pennsylvania Press, 2006.

Giancarlo, Matthew. "*Piers Plowman*, Parliament, and the Public Voice." *Yearbook of Langland Studies* 17 (2004): 135–74.

Hanna, Ralph, III. *William Langland*. Authors of the Middle Ages: English Writers of the Late Middle Ages 3. Aldershot: Variorum, 1993.

Horobin, Simon. "The Scribe of Rawlinson Poetry 137 and the Copying and Circulation of *Piers Plowman*." *Yearbook of Langland Studies* 19 (2005): 3–26.

Hudson, Anne. "The Variable Text." In *Crux and Controversy in Middle English Textual Criticism*, edited by A. J. Minnis and Charlotte Brewer, 49–60. Cambridge: Brewer, 1992.

Huppé, Bernard F. "The A-Text of *Piers Plowman* and the Norman Wars." *PMLA* 54 (1939): 37–64.

———. "The Date of the B Text of *Piers Plowman*." *Studies in Philology* 38 (1941): 34–44.

Kane, George. "An Open Letter to Jill Mann about the Sequence of the Versions of *Piers Plowman*." *Yearbook of Langland Studies* 13 (1999): 7–34.

———. *Piers Plowman: The Evidence for Authorship*. London: Athlone Press, 1965.

———. "The Text." In Alford, *Companion*, 175–200.

Kelen, Sarah A. *Langland's Early Modern Identities*. The New Middle Ages. New York: Palgrave Macmillan, 2007.

Kennedy, Edward Donald, Ronald A. Waldron, and Joseph S. Wittig, eds. *Medieval English Studies Presented to George Kane*. Wolfeboro, N.H.: Brewer, 1988.

Kirk, Elizabeth. *The Dream Thought of Piers Plowman*. New Haven: Yale University Press, 1972.

Lawler, Traugott. "A Reply to Jill Mann, Reaffirming the Traditional Relation between the A and B Versions of *Piers Plowman*." *Yearbook of Langland Studies* 10 (1996): 145–80.

Lawton, David A., ed. *Middle English Alliterative Poetry and Its Literary Background: Seven Essays*. Cambridge: Brewer, 1982.

Manly, J. M. "The Lost Leaf of 'Piers the Plowman.'" *Modern Philology* 3 (1906): 359–66.

Mann, Jill. "The Power of the Alphabet: A Reassessment of the Relation between the A and B Versions of *Piers Plowman*." *Yearbook of Langland Studies* 8 (1994): 21–50.

Middleton, Anne. "Making a Good End: John But as a Reader of *Piers Plowman*." In Kennedy, 243–66.

Norton-Smith, John. *William Langland*. Medieval and Renaissance Authors, 6. Leiden: Brill, 1983.

Samuels, M. L. "Dialect and Grammar." In Alford, *Companion*, 201–21.

Scase, Wendy. " 'First to reckon Richard': John But's *Piers Plowman* and the Politics of Allegiance." *Yearbook of Langland Studies* 11 (1997): 49–66.

Schmidt, A. V. C. *The Clerkly Maker: Langland's Poetic Art*. Cambridge: Brewer, 1987.

Schroeder, Mary C. "*Piers Plowman*: The Tearing of the Pardon." *Philological Quarterly* 49 (1970): 8–18.

Simpson, James. *Piers Plowman: An Introduction*. 2nd rev. ed. Exeter Medieval Texts and Studies. Exeter: University of Exeter Press, 2007.

Smith, D. Vance. "Negative Langland." *Yearbook of Langland Studies* 23 (2009): 33–59.

——. "*Piers Plowman* and the National Noetic of Edward III." In *Imagining a Medieval English Nation*, edited by Kathy Lavezzo, 234–57. Medieval Cultures, 37. Minneapolis: University of Minnesota Press, 2004.

Smith, Macklin. "Langland's Alliterative Line(s)." *Yearbook of Langland Studies* 23 (2009): 163–216.

Tavormina, M. Teresa. *Kindly Similitude: Marriage and Family in* Piers Plowman. Piers Plowman Studies, 11. Cambridge: Brewer, 1995.

Vaughan, Míċeál F. "The Ending(s) of *Piers Plowman A*." In Vaughan, *Suche Werkis*, 211–41.

——. "Filling the Gap in *Piers Plowman* A: Trinity College, Dublin, MS 213." In *Baw for Bookes* (Festschrift for Hoyt N. Duggan), edited by Stephen Shepherd and Michael Calabrese. Los Angeles: Loyola Marymount University Press (forthcoming).

——. "The Liturgical Perspectives of *Piers Plowman B*, XVI–XX." *Studies in Medieval and Renaissance History*, n.s., 3 (1980): 87–155.

——. " 'Til I gan Awake': The Conversion of Dreamer into Narrator in *Piers Plowman* B." *Yearbook of Langland Studies* 5 (1991): 175–92.

——. "Where *Is* Wille Buried (*Piers* A, Passus 12, line 105)?" *Yearbook of Langland Studies* 25 (forthcoming).

——, ed. *Suche Werkis to Werche: Essays on Piers Plowman In Honor of David C. Fowler*. East Lansing: Colleagues Press, 1993.

Warner, Lawrence. "John But and the Other Works That Will Wrought (*Piers Plowman* A XII 101–2)." *Notes and Queries*, n.s., 52 (2005): 13–18.

Wittig, Joseph S. "*Piers Plowman* B, Passus IX–XII: Elements in the Design of the Inward Journey." *Traditio* 28 (1972): 211–80.

Woolf, Rosemary. "The Tearing of the Pardon." In *Piers Plowman: Critical Approaches*, edited by S. S. Hussey, 131–56. London: Methuen, 1969.

Zeeman, Nicolette. *"Piers Plowman" and the Medieval Discourse of Desire*. Cambridge: Cambridge University Press, 2006.

Backgrounds

Adams, Robert. "Editing and the Limitations of *Durior Lectio*." *Yearbook of Langland Studies* 5 (1991): 7–15.

Augustine. *On Christian Doctrine*. Translated by D. W. Robertson Jr. Library of the Liberal Arts. Indianapolis: Bobbs-Merrill, 1958.

Baldwin, Anna P. "The Historical Context." In Alford, *Companion*, 67–86.

Barney, Stephen A. "Allegorical Visions." In Alford, *Companion*, 117–33.

Bennett, Josephine Waters. "The Mediaeval Loveday." *Speculum* 33 (1958): 351–70.

Bloomfield, Morton W. *The Seven Deadly Sins*. East Lansing: Michigan State University Press, 1952; rpt., 1967.

Courtenay, William J. *Schools and Scholars in 14th Century England*. Princeton: Princeton University Press, 1987.

Doob, Penelope Reed. *The Idea of the Labyrinth from Classical Antiquity through the Middle Ages*. Ithaca: Cornell University Press, 1990.

Heist, William Watts. *The Fifteen Signs before Doomsday*. [East Lansing]: Michigan State College Press, 1952.

Howard, Donald Roy. *The Three Temptations: Medieval Man in Search of the World*. Princeton: Princeton University Press, 1966.

Hudson, Anne. *The Premature Reformation: Wycliffite Texts and Lollard History*. Oxford: Clarendon Press, 1988.

Jolliffe, J. E. A. *The Constitutional History of Medieval England*. 1937. London: Black, 1961.

Lipson, E. *The Economic History of England*. Vol. 1: *The Middle Ages*. 12th ed. London: A and C. Black, 1959.

Mann, Jill. *Chaucer and Medieval Estates Satire: The Literature of Social Classes and the General Prologue to the Canterbury Tales*. Cambridge: Cambridge University Press, 1973.

McIntosh, Angus, M. L. Samuels, and Michael Benskin, eds. *A Linguistic Atlas of Late Medieval English*. Aberdeen: Aberdeen University Press, 1986.

McKisack, May. *The Fourteenth Century, 1307–1399*. Oxford History of England, 5. Oxford: Clarendon Press, 1959.

Middle English Dictionary. http://quod.lib.umich.edu/m/med/.

Ormrod, W. M. *The Reign of Edward III: Crown and Political Society in England, 1327–1377*. New Haven: Yale University Press, 1990.

———. "Who Was Alice Perrers?" *Chaucer Review* 40 (2006): 219–29.

Pearsall, Derek. "Langland's London." In *Written Work: Langland, Labor, and Authorship*, edited by Steven Justice and Kathryn Kerby-Fulton, 185–207. Philadelphia: University of Pennsylvania Press, 1997.

Scase, Wendy. *Literature and Complaint in England, 1272–1553*. Oxford: Oxford University Press, 2007.

——. *"Piers Plowman" and the New Anti-Clericalism.* Cambridge Studies in Medieval Literature 4. Cambridge: Cambridge University Press, 1989.

The Statutes of the Realm. Vols. 1 and 2. London: Eyre and Strahan, 1810 and 1816.

Szittya, Penn R. *The Antifraternal Tradition in Medieval Literature.* Princeton: Princeton University Press, 1986.

Tierney, Brian. *Medieval Poor Law: A Sketch of Canonical Theory and Its Application in England.* Berkeley: University of California Press, 1959.

Turville-Petre, Thorlac. *The Alliterative Revival.* Cambridge: Brewer, 1977.

——. *England the Nation: Language, Literature, and National Identity, 1290–1340.* Oxford: Clarendon Press, 1996.

Waugh, Scott L. *England in the Reign of Edward III.* Cambridge Medieval Textbooks. Cambridge: Cambridge University Press, 1991.

Whiting, Bartlett Jere, and Helen Wescott Whiting. *Proverbs, Sentences, and Proverbial Phrases: From English Writings Mainly before 1500.* Cambridge, Mass.: Harvard University Press, 1968.

Trigg, Stephanie, ed. *Wynnere and Wastoure.* Early English Text Society, O.S. 297. Oxford: Oxford University Press, 1990.

Yunck, John A. *The Lineage of Lady Meed: The Development of Mediaeval Venality Satire.* Publications in Mediaeval Studies, XVII. Notre Dame: Notre Dame University Press, 1963.

——. "Satire." In Alford, *Companion,* 135–54.